T0164570

UNCAGED

MY LIFE AS A **CHAMPION** MMA FIGHTER

FRANK SHAMROCK

AND **CHARLES FLEMING**

FOREWORD BY **MICKEY ROURKE**

CHICAGO
REVIEW
PRESS

Copyright © 2012 by Frank Shamrock and Charles Fleming
Foreword copyright © 2012 by Mickey Rourke
All rights reserved
First edition
Published by Chicago Review Press, Incorporated
814 North Franklin Street
Chicago, Illinois 60610
ISBN 978-1-61374-465-9

Library of Congress Cataloging-in-Publication Data
Shamrock, Frank.
 Uncaged : my life as a champion mma fighter / Frank Shamrock and Charles
Fleming ; foreword by Mickey Rourke.
    p. cm.
 ISBN 978-1-61374-465-9 (hardcover)
1. Shamrock, Frank. 2. Martial artists—United States—Biography. 3. Mixed martial
arts—United States. I. Fleming, Charles. II. Title.

GV1113.S52A3 2012
796.8092—dc23
[B]
                                                                2012021340

Interior design: Jonathan Hahn
All photographs courtesy of Frank Shamrock, Inc. unless otherwise noted.

Printed in the United States of America
5 4 3 2 1

This book is dedicated to my loving wife, Amy, who stole my heart the day we met and has never once offered to return it.

And to my amazing children, Frankie and Nicolette: you have taught me so much about living.

CONTENTS

FOREWORD

Frank Shamrock started out life in a very hard and unfortunate way. He was more interested in reading books and expanding his mind than in hanging out with the other toughs and fighting in the streets. Perhaps those lonely early years molded him into the unique fighting champion he became, understanding that only through hard work, dedication, and a disciplined work ethic could one compete at such a high level. Developing, exploring, and studying the scientific aspects as well as the physical demands of fighting gave him an edge over the others. His brains; his unconditional competitive nature; his outstanding physical attributes, which he honed and developed; his conditioning; and his technique all added up to an arsenal that armed him for his struggle to succeed. I'm speaking of everything from learning how to relax to turning up the gas and finishing off his opponents.

Watching Frank fight over the years, I've noticed that he was so confident and relaxed, you could see him enjoying the moment. His charisma and bravado, although it angered others at times, garnered him millions of fans. To me, Frank is foremost an early legend of the UFC. It's unfortunate that we weren't able to see many of his early Pancrase bouts against all of the Japanese legends. Since Frank was a pioneer of the sport, we didn't get to see him as much as we get to see the fighters we enjoy so much today, now that the sport has expanded so much. But later in his career, his exhilarating fight against the bigger and stronger Tito Ortiz once again put Shamrock on the map, cementing his hall-of-fame status in the UFC. His mesmerizing and overwhelming pummeling of Phil Baroni let us see Shamrock's offbeat character once again as he mimed to Baroni, "I'm putting you to sleep now."

I was at Frank's last fight in Sacramento, sitting in the dressing room as he was smiling after the rising UFC star Nick Diaz had badly beaten him up. It was very obvious in that fight that age and all the past battles had caught up with him, and Father Time was giving him his walking papers. The reflexes and timing were just not there, and no matter how hard one trains, they don't come back. It took me back to my boxing career, when my old trainer Bill Slayton said, "We're all going to fight one last time—we just don't know when that night is going to be."

Frank Shamrock is definitely one of my favorite MMA fighters of all time and will continue to be. Of course, I would rather see him inside the ring than out, with his career and battle scars plastered across that handsome face. Shamrock has definitely given his all to the growth and popularity of the UFC or MMA, however you want to categorize it. I also love the fact that Frank ain't shy about how to have a good time outside of the ring—sometimes a bit too much of a good time.

If I ever needed Frank, day or night, wherever he was, he would be there for me in a heartbeat. I love that man like a brother.

—MICKEY ROURKE

INTRODUCTION

Do not pray for an easy life, pray for the strength to endure a difficult one.
—Bruce Lee

I grew up in rural California, raised by a single mom with four kids. My dad had left us when I was three, which was OK with me. I didn't remember him anyway. Truthfully, I could never remember all that much about my early childhood. I do remember being hungry. I was always hungry. Our family survived on state welfare and I was a very active child. I felt like I was starving all the time.

I also remember being locked in the closet for hours. This was a common punishment administered by my stepdad, Joe. The punishments got more severe as I got older, but as a little boy nothing was scarier than that linen closet. I was a timid child, soft-spoken and shy. I was afraid of the dark. Joe knew this and used it to his advantage, making an example out of me so the rest of the kids would stay in line. I spent countless evenings sobbing quietly in the dark, staring at the tiny light around the door hinges, listening to my family having dinner or watching a movie or sharing a laugh without me. It was a stabbing reminder of all that was wrong with me.

I was lucky. According to the state shrink, I was really smart and just unchallenged in academics. Yeah, that was my problem—I wasn't challenged at school. I never told anyone about the punishments; not my shrink, not anyone. We didn't talk about what happened in our family.

School was my only escape. I loved learning and reading. Even though I was bullied and teased for being an emotional and intellectual freak, I just could not get enough of school. I would read every schoolbook for every class attended as soon as I got them. Books became my life; the characters in the stories became my only friends. My life sucked. My family sucked. I would have done anything to get away from them.

When I was twelve, I broke the law and found a way out. Armed with a junior high school education and parented by the state of California, I left home and never returned.

This is the story of what happened to that little boy, a story that I have always wanted to tell the world but didn't have the courage to. This is the truth about what a person can endure and still blossom.

I wrote this book to give strength to the human spirit. My hopes are that it gives a voice to a child who is afraid to speak, inspiration to those who are challenged, and motivation to help yourself and fellow human beings. I also hope that these words show you that nothing is impossible if you never give up your dreams.

I believe that there is a champion in all of us. No matter the circumstances, each and every human being should be encouraged to achieve excellence in life. You should live your own dreams.

Words and love hold powers unimaginable. I share them both with you now.

1

CHILDHOOD

My earliest memories are of living under a train trestle. Our apartment in Redding, California, was in a big building, and the trestle was the most enormous thing you can imagine—huge and loud, and right over our heads. The trains would go by and the whole world would fill up with a mechanical, quaking sound.

Redding is the star of Shasta County, sitting in the Central Valley of California, the rich agricultural flatland that is scooped out of the middle of the state. Located exactly halfway between the Mexican and Canadian borders, and wrapped around the Sacramento River, it was a kind of dumping ground and very diverse. It was all poor people, mostly whites and blacks and some Latinos, and everybody was living on welfare. My family must have stood out—my white, redheaded mother and her gang of Mexican-looking kids. My real dad was long gone.

My mom, Lydia, was a hippie chick, a flower child from Los Angeles. She had grown up in a strict family of Jehovah's Witnesses. Her father was an engineer, a straight-arrow sort of guy, but her mother was a little wild. She liked to drink and party. So she left her husband and ran off with an alcoholic named Nelson. My mom went from being a rich, private-school girl from a stable and normal home to living in a trailer park with two addicts. Her family and father were not Jehovah's Witnesses at all, but her mother, Jackie, got obsessed with the religion and ran off with a church elder. He, in turn, was especially mean to her. They were fanatical about the religion, or what they called the "truth." After that, Lydia and her brother, Mike, spent their youth in the back of a station wagon while their mother went door to door preaching the word. Their new home was a single-wide trailer with a built-on addition for her brother.

She met my dad at a Jehovah's Witnesses church assembly. He was Mexican. His name was Frank Alicio Juarez II. His family were all Jehovah's Witnesses, too, and they lived in Lancaster, out in the desert north of Los Angeles. Frank was good-looking, very dark with Mexican-Indian features, and he worked with his hands. Lydia had already had my older brother, Perry, and I am pretty sure was pregnant with my sister Robynn when she got together with Frank. I never knew anything about their father; he was gone before Frank came along.

Soon Lydia was pregnant with me. I was born on December 18, 1972. Nine months later, my mom and Frank had another child, my little sister, Suzy. But soon after that, Frank left, too. My mom was a young single mother, without any job skills and without any higher education. She had started having kids when she was sixteen, before she even finished high school, mainly so she could leave her mom. So now she was living on welfare with four children under six years old in a crummy apartment building under a train trestle in Redding, California.

For a while she had a relationship with another man, whom I think she married. But pretty soon he was gone, too, and it was just us again.

My memories are cloudy, very scattered but happy. We were always together—me, my mom, and my brother and sisters. We didn't mix much with outsiders, but we had each other. We liked being together and we always had fun. I remember going to a pre-school surrounded with manzanita trees. I remember playing under the train trestle with Perry. There was a creek there, and a kind of wild area on the other side. After a while we found out there was a golf course past the overgrowth. We started sneaking onto the golf course to find lost golf balls and turn them in for money.

My mother had always been a pretty happy person, and even in our meager circumstances we were a pretty happy family. She always had food on the table, and we were always doing things together.

I was a happy kid, very energetic and physical. I was also smart. One day I was going to kindergarten, then the next day I wasn't. I don't know exactly what happened, but my mom had come to school to talk to the teachers, the next day I was in first grade. Somehow I had already learned all the stuff you were supposed to learn in kindergarten. I don't remember learning it. I just remember *knowing* it.

I liked learning, and I liked being in school. But I wasn't a popular kid. I had no social skills. Maybe because my family was close, I had no training in being with unfamiliar people. I was awkward. I had bowl-cut hair, and I wore goofy, used pants. I was kind of chubby, too, until I was seven or eight. I came from the poor family with the hippie mom. I wasn't ashamed of any of it. But I felt different, and I was aware that I was outside the circle. I just felt a little *off*.

Then my mom met Joe.

I think they met at a bar, some local dive in Anderson. Joe was personable and energetic—very energetic. He was popping and snapping and moving a mile a minute, and my mom said, "This is the man for me."

For a kid like me, with no father and no man around and no male role models, Joe was supercool. He was always moving, always talking. He got things done. He was good with his hands and with machines. He had been in the military, gone to Vietnam, and he had learned to work on engines. He had an appliance-repair business and a utility truck with tons of boxes and drawers built in the sides. It said JOE'S APPLIANCE SERVICE on it.

So when we found out we were moving in with him in Anderson, I was happy. We left the apartment building under the trestle and moved into a nice house on a nice street, just like a regular family. Joe had money, and he had a job. He had a daughter, Michelle, and she seemed nice. We were all going to live together in this four-bedroom house with a big backyard, on a street with mature trees, near a school and a park. It was a huge step up for my family. It seemed like we were going to be OK.

But pretty soon it seemed like maybe we weren't.

Being around Joe was exciting at first. He was cool. He smoked Camel nonfiltered cigarettes. But we soon learned he was a very controlling guy. He liked things his way, and his way was strict. There was no cussing allowed. You couldn't watch TV without permission. You couldn't watch TV during the day. Even my mom couldn't watch soap operas—he hated them. No eating between meals. No taking food that wasn't yours.

He and my mom never entertained, and we never had people over to the house. I wasn't allowed to bring friends home. I wasn't allowed to invite someone to spend the night. I wasn't allowed to have a sleepover at someone else's house, either. We didn't do that. The family was the family, and you stayed inside the family, and you never let anyone inside the family.

If you weren't doing what he wanted, he'd let you know. If you were hanging around and bugging him, he'd push you across the room and tell you to get out. Even when he was being affectionate, it was kind of violent. He never hugged anyone, or touched anyone with kindness. But he'd hit you in the side of the head and say, "Go on—get out of here." That was his way of showing affection.

If you did something wrong, he was the one who'd punish you—with a belt. The punishment was very controlled, too. It was event-based. You did something wrong, you were going to get swats with the belt.

There was other abuse, too. He had learned to hate certain kinds of people in Vietnam. So when he wanted to demean you, he'd call you names. You were a "fucking idiot," or a "fucking jerk." If he was really mad, you were a "fucking nigger" or a "zipperhead." That was about the worst thing you could be. With me, he was often angry because I was dirty, or I had lost something, or I had gotten into trouble at school. He'd call me those names and spank me.

I was scared of him, all the time. He made me feel small and weak. He'd sit across from me at the table, with his hands under the table, and ask me questions. If he didn't like the answer, he'd whip his hand out and slap me upside the head. It was like some sort of interrogation torture. You never knew what was the right answer, or the wrong answer, or when you were going to get smacked next. But you had to stay at the table and answer his questions.

If I had done something really bad, he had other punishments. Sometimes he'd make me kneel in the hall with my nose against the wall. I'd stay there for hours. How long depended on what I'd done—like eaten a piece of fruit from the kitchen that wasn't mine, or left some dirty clothes on the floor. He would also check on me periodically to see if my nose was on the wall. I would always listen closely to see if I could hear him walking on the carpet. If I thought the coast was clear, I would rest on my heels, a big no-no that would bring more time in the hallway or a trip to the closet.

Sometimes the punishment was worse. There was a linen closet down the hall. Joe would make me go down there and take all the towels and sheets out of it and put them on the floor. Then he'd make me climb up on the shelf and squeeze in there, and he'd lock it from the outside. Then he and the others would do something fun, like watch a movie on TV or something, and leave me locked in the closet for two or three hours. Sometimes I fell asleep. When I woke up I didn't know where I was, and I felt scared.

Sometimes the torment was just psychological, and you didn't even know what it was for. One Christmas, I wanted a foot scooter. I *really* wanted it. I bugged my mom, and bugged Joe—*please, please, can I have it? Will you buy it for me?* Joe finally lost his temper and told me to shut up about it or I wouldn't get anything.

When Christmas came, I could see that he'd bought it for me. It was all wrapped up, but I knew from the shape what it was. I was dying to open it, but Joe told me I had to go last. So I waited while my brother and sisters opened all their presents. I was dying with excitement.

Finally it was my turn. I grabbed the present and ripped the paper off. Inside was an old vacuum cleaner. Joe had wrapped it up and made it look like the scooter I wanted, just to trick me. He saw the look on my face and started screaming with laughter. I'd never seen him laugh so hard. Everyone else started laughing, too. So I started screaming, too, and crying. I tried to run away. Joe grabbed me. He told me to calm down. He said my real present was in the garage. He actually *had* bought me the scooter I'd been dreaming about. But now I didn't want it. I didn't want anything, especially anything from him. I was so mad and so hurt that I didn't want any Christmas presents at all.

Joe fought with my mom, too. I didn't realize it at the time, because I didn't know anything about the world, but he was an alcoholic. He'd get tanked up and come home to fight. I never saw him drinking, because he did it outside the house, but I saw the effects. He'd come home and start needling my mom and yelling at her. She was a very mellow person by nature. But after a while, he'd get under her skin and she'd lose it. She was always a very meek, mousy person. But she had a low emotional threshold when it came to communicating her feelings. She'd be really quiet, and then she'd explode. They'd start yelling and screaming, and then they'd start throwing things—plates and glasses and furniture. They'd smash the place all up, screaming the whole time. It was scary. It freaked me out to see my mom like that.

But all this punishment and controlling didn't work the way Joe expected. I started getting into trouble. I was restless and energetic, and I had no idea how to behave. If I saw something I wanted, I took it. I started stealing stuff from people. I'd take something from a kid's desk, or a kid's coat. This wasn't just a habit. It was a more like a tactic. I had grown up poor. All the kids I knew stole stuff. You had to—it was the only way you were going to *get* stuff. Nobody had any money to buy anything. If you wanted something, you had to steal it. So I stole. I took what I wanted. I stole things from my mom and from Joe. I stole things from my brothers and sisters and from other kids in the neighborhood. I'd just see something I wanted, and I'd put it in my pocket.

But I wasn't a very smart thief. I'd forget I had stolen something, and I'd leave it in my pocket where my mom could find it, or I'd give it to somebody as a present. I'd steal one of my mom's rings and give it to a girl at school, or I'd steal a knife from Joe and give it to some boy in my class. Sooner or later, someone would wonder what a five-year-old kid was doing with a ring or a knife. They'd ask me, "Hey, where did you get that?" and I never had an answer. So as soon as I'd steal something, I'd get into trouble for stealing it. I'd get punished—spanked or whipped with a belt, or made to kneel in the hall for an hour, or locked in the closet for a whole night while the family had pizza and watched a movie on TV.

Race affected my life too. When we lived in Redding, we were surrounded by a racially mixed, lower-income group of people. There were black people and brown people and white people, all living together. Everyone was on welfare. No one had any money. Lots of families had only one parent. So we all fit right in.

But Anderson was a little hick town primarily composed of white farmers and agricultural people. My brother and sisters and I were the only brown kids anywhere—on the street, in the park, at school. I was really aware of being different, of being the wrong color, of being the wrong social class. I had always felt like I didn't quite fit in anywhere outside my family. Now I felt even more off.

Maybe that's why I started getting into more trouble.

It was the only thing exciting, that I was in control of, the only thing that provided that kick of electricity and feeling of freedom. When I was nine or ten, I started stealing things from stores. I'd shoplift a piece of candy or a little toy. Sometimes I'd get caught, and I'd get yelled at. My mom and Joe would have to come to the store, and then they'd yell at me, too. I'd get punished in one of Joe's usual awful, creative ways. But after a while Joe got frustrated because the punishments didn't make me behave, so the punishments got worse. I got caught shoplifting something, and he sent me to live in the garage for the night. Not in a room in the garage, just *in* the garage, sleeping on the concrete floor with a blanket and a pillow. It was cold, and the floor was hard, and it smelled bad. I hated it. But I kept getting into trouble. So I kept getting sent to the garage. I stole something, the police were called, and I got sent to live in the garage again.

I didn't keep getting into trouble because I was stupid. Sometime in grade school someone noticed that I was a smart kid—probably because I got in trouble again, and someone was trying to figure out what was wrong with me and had me tested. I tested really high. They may have thought I was getting into trouble because I wasn't being challenged in school, so they put me into the GATE program for gifted and talented kids and started teaching me more challenging material.

That didn't stop me from getting into trouble.

Around that time, I found out about sex. It started with my sister Robynn and my stepsister, Michelle. We just started fooling around. It was kind of innocent. We didn't know what we were doing, or why. We were just curious and experimenting. No one had explained anything to me about sex. I had no information. I knew about the Bible, and Adam and Eve, and the Jehovah's Witnesses stories. I knew there was some weird overtone about that. Somehow sex and religion were connected, but I didn't know how. I only knew sex was dirty and bad and you weren't supposed to do it—but I didn't know what it *was*.

We didn't get caught. We didn't get in trouble. I don't remember feeling too weird about it. But I knew it was something you didn't talk about. One afternoon, when I'd already been punished for something and sent to stay in the garage, Joe came in. I'd gotten into trouble again at school. Joe came in with a belt to give me a whipping and caught me jacking off.

Now he was *really* mad. He called me a fucking nigger and threw me out of the house. I had to go sleep under a tarp in the backyard. I wasn't allowed to come into the house except for breakfast. I wasn't allowed to use the bathroom. My new "room" was on the ground, under a tarp hung on a clothesline in the backyard.

I don't remember the first time I drank alcohol. But I learned that I liked it—a lot. Alcohol made me feel different, kind of numb. I had drunk a few times in the park with the Redding boys. By the time we were living at Joe's, I was really into it. I started stealing alcohol from my parents or from other kids' houses. I'd steal a bottle of something and get drunk in the backyard, under my tarp. I started getting neighborhood kids drunk too, especially the girls. I'd get them drunk and we'd fool around, like I'd fooled around with Robynn and Michelle.

Soon the trouble I was getting in escalated. I got caught stealing a bottle of schnapps from a supermarket. I got caught bringing alcohol to school. I got caught getting another kid drunk. I started getting sent to the school counselors. I started running into the police. My mom and Joe would have to come to the school for a meeting, or the police would come to the house. And then I'd get punished some more. The backyard, under the tarp, must have been too good for me. I was told to go sleep in the shed, where Joe kept his lawn mower and garden tools and stuff. That became my new home.

It was pretty bad. I hated being separated from my brother and sisters. I still wasn't very social. I didn't make friends easily. I was a loner. If I couldn't play with my brother and sisters, I'd go to the park by myself and play alone all day. I'd explore, or climb trees, or find hideouts. It was lonely, but I found things to do. Living in the shed, though, there wasn't anything to do. I felt really alone. I missed my brother and sisters. I missed my mom.

But there was gasoline in the shed for the lawn mower. I discovered I could get high—way more buzzed than from alcohol—by huffing the gas from the gas can. So I started huffing gas—at first just to pass the time and then because it was better than not huffing gas. I'd take these huge hits in the morning before school, and I'd pass out. Then I'd wake up again and walk to school having insane hallucinations.

While I was living in the garage, my next-door neighbor turned me on to pot. His dad kept a stash in their garage, in a little tool pouch on his bicycle. I started making nightly trips to his garage. We'd go in, steal his weed, and get high.

Pretty soon I was getting high all the time. I was either drinking or smoking or huffing every day. My grades and attendance fell apart. Within a few weeks, I got arrested for being drunk in public. It seemed like I was in trouble all the time. Usually it was because I had done something wrong and had gotten caught. Sometimes it was just because I was the go-to guy when something had happened. If something went missing, I got punished for stealing it, even if I hadn't. If something got broken, I got blamed, even if I had nothing to do with it. I was always assumed to be the culprit, or the ringleader—which, admittedly, usually was the case. But it meant that I was in trouble, and being punished for something, all the time.

The right teacher or after-school sports or some extracurricular activity might have helped. But I couldn't stay involved with sports because I was always screwing up. I was on the Little League team, but I cut my knee and they said I couldn't play anymore. When that got better, I fell down and broke my collarbone and couldn't play anymore.

I was only ten or eleven, but I see now that my life was already very messed up. One day a neighbor kid and I were playing in the park, near a train trestle, but not the one I grew up next to. There was some water down below the trestle, and we'd go down there sometimes to catch snakes. This day a train was going by, maybe twenty or thirty feet above us. I wondered whether we could throw a rock hard enough to hit the train. So I started throwing rocks. The neighbor kid started throwing with me. We hit the train a few times. We felt good about that.

After the train passed, we went back to trying to catch the water snakes. But suddenly there were cops everywhere. They drove into the park and jumped out and grabbed us. They put me in handcuffs and threw me in the back of the police car. They told me I was under arrest on felony charges of throwing rocks at a train. I wasn't old enough to understand what a felony was, but I knew the situation was serious. But I was more scared of what Joe was going to do than what the police were going to do. I was really afraid he was going to hurt me.

There weren't any big consequences. The police called my mom and Joe, and they came to get me. I got punished some more. I had to keep sleeping in the shed.

Around the time that I broke my collarbone, I got thrown out of regular school. I was falling apart mentally from everything that was happening and still trying to play sports. One day I was running for a fly ball in left field when I tripped and rolled across my shoulder. I was really embarrassed about missing the ball and didn't tell anyone that my shoulder hurt until I got home. Mom and Joe were mad and we spent the night in the emergency room. I had to wear that collarbone brace thing you have to wear, the one that pulls your shoulders back like a straitjacket, and some older kids said that they were going to kick my ass. I was afraid that I would not be able to defend myself—but I had a knife, so I pulled it and told them to leave me alone. That didn't go over too well. Somebody must have told on me. The next day I got placed in a lockdown program where you had to check in every morning and check out every afternoon. It was just one big room where they put all the kids who cause trouble.

Because it was just me and a couple other kids on our own in this little room, I had nothing to do except my schoolwork. So I did my work; I did it fast and I did a lot of it. It was easy for me, and I got a whole school year's worth of work done in a couple of weeks.

I had already tested high enough to qualify for the GATE program. Now the administrators kicked me up a grade. They gave me some kind of test, and the next thing I knew I was in the ninth grade. I didn't do eighth grade at all. It wasn't the first time I had been tested. When I was seven or eight and just starting to get into all kinds of trouble, my mom started taking me to therapy. We were on welfare, so they must have been some sort of state or county doctors. I remember meeting many times, over a six- or eight-month period, with a really nice guy who taught me how to play chess. He had me take an IQ test, and he told me I was really smart. I liked the guy, and trusted him, and I liked playing chess. When I came home from one of those meetings, I sat down to play chess with Joe. I beat him. He got mad and never played chess with me again.

But even skipping a grade and the GATE program couldn't keep me out of trouble. I took alcohol to school and got some kids drunk, and I got caught. I stole something from a store, and I got caught. I might have been gifted and talented, but I had zero skills as a criminal. Every time I did something, I got caught. After a while my mom and Joe got sick of it. They had tried punishing me all the ways they knew. They beat me and made me sleep in the garage and made me move into the shed, and I was still acting like a jerk and getting into trouble. So my mom decided to send me to live with my dad.

I had not had any contact with him, ever. I didn't even know my mom knew where he was. But all of a sudden I was put on a bus and sent all the way down to Lancaster, near Los Angeles. Frank Alicio Juarez II lived in a dusty tract home on a street in the desert. He seemed nice, not scary like Joe. But he was gone a lot, working. He had a wife, maybe his third or fourth wife after my mom, and some other kids. The whole area was flat and sandy. You'd have dust and grit in your teeth when you ate. And it was hot and dry and the wind was always blowing. There were jackrabbits in the desert, which went on for a hundred miles in every direction, and the kids rode dirt bikes. They took me out and I crashed right away. I fell down and messed up my knee and got dirty. My dad's father—the original Frank Alicio Juarez—lived nearby, in an old house in the old section of Lancaster, with his wife. They were Jehovah's Witnesses, and they had been married fifty years.

I stayed for a few weeks over the summer and got to meet more of my dad's family. My great-grandmother stayed with us for a few days, and she spoke only Spanish. She was warm and friendly and I laughed and smiled at everything she said. I didn't get into a lot of trouble during my visit, and they seemed pleased to have me there. But it ended pretty quickly, and soon I was back in Anderson, living with Joe.

I guess I hadn't learned any kind of lessons on how to behave while I was in Lancaster because I kept screwing up. One day, I had stolen a bottle of Southern Comfort and gotten a bunch of kids drunk in the backyard. My little sister, Suzy, was going to tell on me. She was always telling on me. So I got mad and pulled a knife on her. On my own little sister! I must have been drunk. I tried to scare her; I said I'd stab her if she told. It didn't work. Suzy doesn't scare that easily. Robynn is sort of girly and sweet, but Suzy was tough. So she told on me anyway—about the Southern Comfort and the drunk kids *and* me pulling the knife.

My mom freaked out and called the police, so I ran away. I don't remember where I ran, but I didn't get far. I got picked up by the police and taken to some sort of crisis center. I knew I was in trouble. I was really scared and really confused. But I was also pretty tough. It wasn't like the end of the world or anything. It was just some more bad stuff I was going to have to deal with.

The crisis center was in Redding. It was full of boys and girls like me who'd gotten into trouble. They said things like "My dad's an alcoholic" or "My mom's a drug addict." They came from messed-up places. I began to realize, maybe for the first time, that my life wasn't normal. I told someone about being locked in the closet, and he said that wasn't right. Parents weren't supposed to lock a kid in a closet.

I remember talking to counselors. They seemed nice. They didn't seem mad. They asked me a lot of questions, and from the questions—and the way they looked when I answered them—I understood that things were not OK in my house.

I stayed in the crisis center for three or four days. It wasn't bad. I was locked up, but I knew no one was going to hurt me. I was in trouble, but I didn't think anyone was going to beat me with a belt, like Joe did at home. I could have stayed there a while. It was better than living in the shed.

But I made friends with a girl. She didn't want to stay there, so I decided to help her. We found some way to sneak out of the crisis center. We ran until we were near my family's old apartment. I thought we could hide out in the park near the golf course. There were some homeless guys already living there, so we sort of moved in with them. There was a Safeway supermarket up the street where we would go to steal liquor and food. It went on like that for a few days. It must have been some time in the fall, because I remember I was cold. I hadn't taken enough clothes with me when I ran away from the crisis center. I only had what I had been wearing—maybe because that's all I had when the police took me in. I remember on the third or fourth day after we ran away we were trying to steal some pants and a jacket because I was cold. Later on we went back to the Safeway to steal some more food and we got caught.

This time they didn't take me back to the crisis center. They took me to juvenile hall. There was a hearing, and they sentenced me. That was more serious. Now I was in the system.

2

WARD OF THE COURT

I spent some time being processed at juvenile hall. There were interviews and paperwork and lots of questions. The counselors and the psychiatrists couldn't figure out what to do with me any more than my mom and Joe or my biological dad could. But this was their job, and they seemed to take it seriously. They asked tons of questions. The most important one was: Do you want to go home?

I didn't want to go home. I told the counselors and psychiatrists the truth. They asked, "What are we going to do with you?" and I said, "I don't know. But I don't want to go home." They got it. They said, "You're running away from home. You're running away from the crisis center. You're getting the other kids drunk. You're pulling a knife on your sister. You probably *can't* go home."

They used the traditional two-person cell at juvenile hall. That's where I slept. At first it was me and an Indian kid. Then it was me and a black kid. Looking around, I saw all kinds of kids. Up to then, living in Anderson had meant being around nothing but rural Caucasian families. Now I was with a whole lot of different kids.

That's how I found out I was Mexican. Kids would ask me, "So what are you?" I didn't even understand the question. They'd say, "What are you, Mexican?" They asked me my name. I told them it was Juarez. They said, "So you're Mexican." For the first time I understood there were differences and classifications. I didn't know what my classification was, exactly, but I understood there was some sort of hierarchy.

Being at juvenile hall didn't feel like being in jail. We slept behind locked doors, and everything was hard and cold and made of steel, but it wasn't all that scary to me. I felt more free than I had at home.

At home, I had been scared all the time. I was always worried. I felt like I was going to get hurt, or that someone was going to kill me—usually Joe. My whole life seemed to revolve around trying to not get hurt, surviving, staying out of physical pain. My whole life felt like shit. Unless I was doing something physical, like playing in the park or doing sports, or getting drunk or getting high, I was just alone in my head and worried. I remember feeling like I needed to be taken care of. I needed my mom. And I couldn't have my mom, because Joe was there. I was always in trouble with him, and he was always mad at me, and he was always hitting me. I remember lying there at night thinking of ways to kill Joe, and thinking that there had to be some solution. There had to be something I could do. There had to be a way out.

Juvenile hall seemed like the way out. I was happy there. I was locked up, but I had plenty to eat, and I was free to read all I wanted. I went to classes and did schoolwork. We did arts and crafts, and we had sports, and no one was trying to hurt me.

So when the counselors said I should probably become a ward of the state, I said that was OK with me. I didn't really get what it meant. I didn't understand the long-term implications. Maybe they didn't explain it to me. But I knew that, whatever it was, it had to be better than my life at home. The state had been good to me. Why wouldn't I want to be a ward of the state?

In that moment, I learned a lesson: I made a decision. Up until then, I had been trapped in a place where I had no control and no hope of change. I was just the kid in trouble, who couldn't stay out of trouble, who was going to get caught and punished. But at that moment I realized that I *did* have control, that I could create something new, be something new. I had broken the law, but I had taken control of my future. It gave me a weird sense of energy, like I could create whatever I wanted. Now I had the solution. I had a plan. If things got too tough, you grab the girl, grab some stuff, and run—and see what happens. If I didn't like my life, or my family, or my group, I could break the law in some drastic way and everything would change.

This became a pattern for me. This is how I lived my life for the next ten years.

I wasn't at juvenile hall for very long, but I grew to really love the custodians there. They were gentle and caring and more like a real family than any family I'd ever known. They were only there because they wanted to help kids in trouble. I *got* that. I didn't understand it, but I understood it was real. But they didn't want me to stay there. They wanted to get me placed with a family. They oversaw the paperwork that made me a ward of the court, and then they found me a home.

I was sent to live in a group home with a Christian Scientist family. They had a big white house in a small town in a rural area somewhere outside of Redding. The house was on two or three acres, and one of the acres was all lawn. I remember a black dog playing on the lawn. There were five or six kids in the group home, plus the mom and pop who were in charge of it. The kids were all boys of varying ages and backgrounds. The parents were loving and kind. The man was very strong in his faith. I was interested in what he believed and I loved to read, so he gave me some books. Before, all I had known was the Jehovah's Witnesses. Now I started consuming information about Christian Science. The man and I connected over that. I was studious and took it seriously, and we had long talks.

My information about the Jehovah's Witnesses was a little spotty. I knew that we didn't have holidays and we didn't celebrate birthdays. The deal was we were chosen to work for God, and we were lucky to be chosen, because the world was going to end—any day now, the world was going to explode in a terrible fireball. Then Jesus would rise and we would all be in paradise. After that, we would live together and the animals would talk to us.

I don't think this is exactly what Jehovah's Witnesses believe, but I didn't know much else about it at the time. I heard someone say we were just "jack J-dubs," which probably meant we were Jehovah's Witnesses in name only. But I remember thinking, as I got older, that some of it didn't make sense. I remember wondering, "If we are all together living with the animals in paradise, what will the animals eat? Will they stop eating each other? Will the lions stop killing other animals and start eating grass, like the cows?" But when I asked questions, I was told to be quiet. At this home, though, there was a man who believed something different, and he was happy to talk to me about it.

But it didn't get me to straighten out. I had a regular life with these nice people and these other kids. We went to school. We had activities. We were well fed. We were loved. But I kept getting into trouble. I got into a fight on the football field with a kid who tried to bully me, and there was zero tolerance for violence at this place. The dad at the home went to bat for me. He said he would smooth it all over, but I'd have to mow the lawn—the whole lawn, the whole *acre* of lawn. I did that, and everything was forgiven.

One of the activities at this home was boxing. Thursday night was boxing night. The boys would put on the gloves and everyone would box. Most of us were just goofing around, but there was one kid who really knew what he was doing. One Thursday night, he kicked my ass. He hit me really hard and gave me a bloody nose. It hurt, but more than that it was embarrassing. I was so humiliated.

He made me cry! It was the first time it had ever happened, that I was embarrassed by an ass-kicking. It made a huge impression on me. Maybe it made too big of an impression, because soon after that I did something else stupid at school. I don't remember what it was, but it must have been pretty serious. Suddenly, after I had been there for three or four months, I got sent back to juvenile hall.

I saw all my old friends. I was with the kindly counselors again. I stayed a month or so. I was happy to be back. But I got a reevaluation. The thing that got me sent back must have been serious, because my security level went up a notch. When I was sent to another home, it was a higher-security one.

These people were also Christians, but they were more mainstream—not Jehovah's Witnesses, not Christian Scientists. They were a husband and wife, with a young baby girl, in a different rural area. They were very kind and sweet, and when they took us to church it was full of other people who were kind and sweet, too. We were surrounded by kindness.

The house had a fence around it. The school they sent us to had a fence around it, too. This was a school for troubled kids, and there was security. We were driven to school every morning in the dad's van. He had to escort us in. Then we had to check in, and in the afternoon we had to check out. Going to the bathroom was a serious deal. You had to punch out and punch back in. It felt almost like being in jail, I thought.

There were lots of activities there, and I was interested in that. One of them was waterskiing. I had never seen anything like that before. The only water sport I knew was tubing. Waterskiing was amazing. The speed of it blew me away. But I didn't like living under such tight security, so I hatched a plan to run away. There were three or four other kids in the home. I pitched them my plan and rallied the troops. They went along with it. I told the kids to pack up some clothes.

I had been a thief for a long time. I had gotten good at going around on tiptoe in the dark and finding things to steal. Back home I had stolen a lot of money from Joe's wallet. So I snuck into the foster parents' room and stole some money from the man's wallet. I found the keys to the family van.

I knew how to drive a little; my mom had taught me, in our old 1962 Dodge van with a three-on-the-tree manual transmission. But there was an older kid in the home, and he wanted to drive. So I was the ringleader, but he was the driver. We all snuck out of the house and got into the van, and away we went. One by one, we started dropping kids off. Then the driver and I headed for Sacramento.

Why Sacramento, I don't know. I think there was some field trip we'd wanted to go on, maybe a concert, that we hadn't been allowed to attend. We had this crackpot plan to head to the big city. We were going to meet some other guys and get some money and have a big party.

We almost made it. We got all the way to Sacramento. But we were running out of gas, and we didn't have much money. One of the other guys, not the one who was driving, thought he was a big hoodlum. He said, "We gotta find some people to rob." This guy said he knew the area and knew where to go. On some level, I knew this was a bad idea. These guys were older than me, and this was a little more severe than what I was used to. I tiptoed around in the dark and stole pocket change. But now we were driving around the city looking for someone to mug.

For better or for worse, we never found them. We were still driving around trying to locate some victims when the cops pulled us over. They asked, "What are you guys doing?" We were three underage guys in a stolen van, driving around in the middle of Sacramento. We must have looked out of place. They took us in. I don't know what happened to the other guys, but I got sent to the huge juvenile hall in Sacramento. This was a big deal. I had to walk the line. I knew I was in real trouble. When they locked me up there, I knew I was in big, big shit.

There was a hearing. I was sentenced to four months in a juvenile facility. They gave me an orange jumpsuit that didn't fit. Until then, as a ward of the court, when I did something wrong the counselors were upset but their attitude was that we could give it another shot. But this time I was being given a sentence. I was being punished. I was a prisoner.

I got sent to a rural facility near Red Bluff, California. The kids were not as tough as in Sacramento, not as jacked up. It wasn't as scary, and the staff was nicer. But it was like jail, no doubt about it. I was given a set of blues and whites—blue pants, blue shoes, white shirt—and sent to a special school inside a mobile trailer. I had a job in the kitchen. Part of my job was going to Costco in my blues and whites with this stoner dude, this hippie refugee from the 1970s, for supplies.

I may have been a prisoner, but I was only twelve years old. I didn't see my family during this period. My mom visited me once, when I was first in juvenile hall in Redding, I guess to say good-bye or make sure I was OK. But I never saw Joe or my brother or sisters. After I was sent to the first group home, I never saw my mother. They were doing their thing. I wasn't part of that anymore.

That was hard for me. I always loved my mom and now I really missed her, and I missed my brother and sisters. But I didn't want to go home. If I had been given the choice of moving back with my family and Joe or staying at the facility on Red Bluff, or going to a group home, or staying at the juvenile hall in Redding, I would have chosen *anything* except moving back home. I never wanted to go there again.

I was happy in the Red Bluff facility. I really enjoyed learning, reading, going to school, and hanging out with people my own age. But soon my term was up. I had to go back into the system, back to

Redding. I started being interviewed again to be placed in a home. Now, though, where I could go was classified differently. It wasn't just moms and dads looking for a few boys. Now it was camps and ranches, higher-security places, people who were in the business of running group homes.

I had a few interviews, but nothing happened for a while. I stayed at the juvenile hall in Redding. Then one day a guy came in and I was sent to interview with him. He had a boys' home outside of Susanville, California. His name was Bob Shamrock.

This guy was incredible! I had never met anyone like him. He wore a bright, flowery shirt and rings—tons of rings. He was very polite, very gentle. He smiled and shook my hand, and then he asked questions and actually listened to the answers. He seemed to have strong opinions about things, and he was very passionate about the work he was doing. He gave me a big spiel about his ranch. He made it sound like summer camp, like the Hardy Boys.

So I made my usual pitch, too. I told him about how I had been having a hard time, but I wanted to do better. I had made mistakes, but I now was—he just cut me off. He said, "That's all fine, but I don't want to hear any bullshit. This is about doing things differently. This is a home where you can change, where you can build yourself up and live differently."

It was a fatherly pep talk. He called me on my bullshit, but he wasn't angry. He was just telling me how it was.

I liked him instantly. I wanted to go with him. I would have done anything to get into his ranch. But I felt sure he wouldn't take me. I had screwed up too much. When he left, I just knew I'd never see him again.

But two weeks later, one of the counselors took me aside and said I had been assigned to Shamrock Boys Ranch.

3

SHAMROCK BOYS RANCH

Bob Shamrock came and got me a couple of days later, and he drove me from Redding to Susanville. He was dressed up nicely and he had a big Cadillac, one of several: he had a '56 and a '57 and a '62, all of those beautiful and shiny Cadillacs from the grand sweeping years, with the big fins.

The house was a huge compound, out in the country a few miles from Susanville. There was one main building and lots of little outbuildings surrounded by fields and trees. Across the street was a golf course.

Bob lived in the house with his staff and about twenty boys of all ages and sizes and backgrounds. The staffers were all men, helpful young guys, former military or group-home kids who had graduated from the youth system. The boys slept two or four to a room all over the compound. For meals we got together in one giant dining room. Places were laid at the table and we had pewter goblets. Bob would preside over these massive meals, huge productions put on by an old woman we called Granny. She lived in town with her husband, T-Bone, and she loved Bob and she loved the kids. She was very sweet, and I saw right away that everyone treated her with respect. No one ever talked back to her. It was forbidden. She would bring out the food, and everyone would sit politely and wait. We sat down as a family. Bob stood up and said grace.

I was just shy of my thirteenth birthday when I got there, and it was obvious to me that I was the youngest. I felt really small. Some of the kids were already seventeen or eighteen, and they were massive. They seemed like grown men. They drove cars and had jobs in town. I felt really little, and I was intimidated by them. But I felt really protected by Bob, and I fell in love with the whole scene. Bob was our mom and dad. Bob's attitude was "We believe in working hard and doing sports and kicking ass and having fun!" It seemed like fun, and it seemed like a challenge. I really wanted to fit in and do it right.

But it was strict. There were lots of rules. Bob ran the place like a business because it *was* his business. He had some tough kids sent to him, and he was determined to do right by them. He was a strict Catholic and had very strong ideas about right and wrong. The difference from everything I'd grown up with so far was that he was fair, and his ideas were actually *about* right and wrong. Before that, the rules in my life had just been the rules. We do this because Jehovah's Witnesses do this, or because Christian Scientists do this. The church says so, or Joe says so. Now Bob was offering another voice, but one without the guilt or anger or force. Or shame. His word was final, but it didn't feel severe. He talked the talk, but he walked the walk, too. He never cursed. He never got drunk. He never got angry. He just told you how it was, and that's how it was.

You'd see him every day at breakfast. You had to be up on time and dressed and presentable. If you weren't up, or if you were late to breakfast, someone would come shake you. If it happened twice, Bob would come to your bed with a pitcher of ice water and dump it on you.

Most of the boys went to school in Susanville. I started in there right away, too. Every morning we'd get into a white van with one of our counselors behind the wheel, and we'd all ride to school and go to our classes. In the afternoon we'd get in the van again and come back to the ranch, where we'd hang out and play sports. On the weekend, Bob would arrange big games of football and baseball with the boys and local teams. Physical fitness was very big with him. He thought that was how you took wild city kids and calmed them down—by putting them out in the country, taking them away from whatever was making them crazy, and giving them a safe place to spend all that energy. You played sports, or you worked, or you did both. And you did your chores.

Bob was a huge force in the community. He was involved with the church and with the town. He'd drive down the street in his Cadillac, which was always shiny and perfect, and wave at everybody. He was a snappy dresser, and he was always smiling and friendly like he was the mayor. He went to the same restaurant for breakfast every day, and would eat the same meal: eggs Benedict, wheat toast, and coffee, black (at which point he would announce, "hot and black, like my women"). He was very social and would hold court over those three cups, volunteering his boys for whatever the town needed.

At the house, things were very orderly. There were rules and there were consequences. If you were supposed to be somewhere at seven o'clock, it *had* to be seven o'clock. If you screwed up, you got work duty. You had to clean something or fix something. Bob had a road crew, and the kids who had screwed up had to go into town and clean up a park or pick up trash by the side of the highway.

If a kid had done something worse than just being late, Bob would bring out the belt. He'd say, "Come here, kid," and you knew what was coming. But he wasn't angry, even then. He was the king of cool. You could cry, you could scream and yell, you could whine—

it didn't matter. He had his rules and he had his consequences, and that was it.

If you had a beef with another kid, you could tell someone. If you were being picked on, you could talk to Bob or to one of the counselors, and you wouldn't get punished for asking for help. Bob always told us that we were a family. We were *his* family. He was the dad, and we were his sons, which meant we were all supposed to be brothers, just like in a real family. If a kid was bullying someone, Bob would take one of the older boys aside, one of the popular boys, and say, "That guy's got a problem picking on the younger kids. Maybe you could have a talk with him."

If the beef was more serious, Bob would say, "OK, get the gloves and go to the living room." He'd move the couches and sofas out of the way, and you'd have a little boxing match. Then he would make you hug each other and take responsibility for your part in the beef.

If you'd done something more serious, told a lie or stolen something from another boy, there were punishments. First you'd get excluded from things—you wouldn't be allowed to play in the football game, or you wouldn't be invited for the tubing trip on the river. Next, you'd get something taken away—your radio or, if you were older, your car keys. Maybe you wouldn't be allowed to go visit your girlfriend. Next, you'd get the road crew.

If you couldn't straighten up, you were out. Bob had all the patience in the world for a kid who tried to be good, but not as much for a kid who wouldn't try. Some of these kids were tough city kids who'd been pretty bad. They didn't last very long.

It all felt very safe to me. After an hour, I just knew: Bob wasn't going to lie. He wasn't going to take advantage of anyone. If he said it was like this, it was like this, every time. He was patient, but he was firm. And he was loving, which I'd never experienced before. I had had no idea what had been going on with me, why I was so unhappy, why I acted out so much. But I was starved for affection.

I'd had no one to be affectionate toward. My mother doesn't hug. She's a quick-pat-on-the-back sort of person. Joe's idea of affection was a smack on the head. But now I was around a guy who showed me it was OK to love people and to show them you loved them. He would give you a hug, and let you hug him back. If you were lonesome or sad, and you started crying, he'd hold you and let you cry.

This was a brand-new thing for me. Even when we were being punished, we knew we were loved. Bob would say, "You're a good kid, you've got a good heart, and I love you. I'm sorry you're being punished." You absolutely understood that he didn't stop loving you just because you'd screwed up.

The first time I got punished, he said, "I love you, and it's very important for me that you know this. What you've done is serious, and this is your punishment. But I'm doing it because I love you and I want you to act like a good kid." I'd never felt anything like it. It was the first time I had ever heard anyone say, "I love you" and mean it. With Joe, when you were in trouble, he'd sit you down and say, "Who loves you?" and you'd have to answer him, "You do, Joe." "And who does all this stuff for you?" "You do, Joe." Then he'd beat the shit out of you. With Bob, you could feel the love. If you screwed up, you knew you had disappointed him, but you also knew he wouldn't stop loving you, no matter what. I wanted to make him proud of me.

For a while, it seemed like everything was working. I really enjoyed being there. I couldn't imagine ever leaving. But it was difficult for me to stay good. I hadn't changed all that much. I was still drinking and smoking pot, acting like an idiot, staying out late. It was minor stuff, but it was against the rules, and I kept getting into trouble. I was often on the road crew. I was one of those kids cleaning the park.

I was mischievous. I don't know if it was because it gave me a sense of control or power, or just because I was restless and needed something to do. But I had to try really hard to stay out of trouble. I would find myself wanting to do something but think *that would be wrong* or *I shouldn't steal that*. Normal people don't have to think like that.

I know now that, because I was young, my brain was not fully developed. I know that young boys can't fully understand consequences. And I know that I never thought about the consequences, which I couldn't imagine would be that bad anyway, at least until I turned eighteen. The worst thing that would happen was I'd get sent back to juvenile hall and see all my friends.

So I was good for a while, until I got integrated with the boys. I found the troublemakers. I was good for five or six months. I made a couple of new friends. One of them was Ryan, who came in around the same time as I did. He was a skinny little Puerto Rican guy, brown like me. We had that in common. He became my friend and stayed my best friend for years and years.

Unlike me, he was not a bad boy. He wasn't serious about criminality. He was just a good kid who got into trouble. He grew up with a wealthy adoptive family. For most of his childhood he didn't know they weren't his biological family. He found out when he was fifteen, and he went a little nuts. But he wasn't a bad kid. He just had a big mouth. People beat him up, and he got into trouble, and he wound up with me at the Shamrock place.

After a while, after I got settled in, I started drinking and screwing around, staying out, testing the limits. Some of that was probably not a big deal. Bob understood boys. He understood that if you were taking care of business and doing your stuff—keeping up with your schoolwork, doing your job, coming home on time—then having a beer with your friend was OK. His philosophy was "If you can handle all your responsibilities then you can handle one beer."

It was easy to do. There were a lot of older boys at Shamrock. There was a lot of drug use there because Bob was pretty naive when it came to addiction and the harder stuff. He knew about pot and drinking, but the rest was a big secret. And I found the bad kids in the community, the way the bad kids always find each other. It wasn't hard to get the stuff; it was hard to stay away from it.

As much security as there was around us, and as much love, screwing around had become my life. I'd get up on time and get on the van for school, and I'd be there on time to get on the van to go back home. In between, I went to a rural high school run by people who weren't used to dealing with little criminals. It was easy to get away with stuff. There were hoodlums like me all over the place. The big hangout was the high school. If you wanted someone to hang out with, or drink with, you'd sit on the high school lawn. Eventually, someone would drive by. There was always someone who would buy a bottle for you. Or you could get a ride outside of town, where there was a family who ran a small liquor store. They'd sell liquor to anybody with money. I could get booze from town, or pot from school. Near our school was the continuation school where they sent all the problem kids. It was just a short walk, and that's where the pot was. And in town you could get a twelve-pack of Hamm's beer for a few bucks.

I usually had a little money. I was always volunteering to wash Bob's Cadillacs. He paid five bucks per car. I was very meticulous about it, and I'd wash two cars a week. With ten bucks, I was cool for beer and pot for the weekend. My problem was that I had no control when drinking or using drugs. I would get wasted. I would be the drunk-in-public guy, the guy who gets everyone in trouble because he's too trashed.

This led to some terrible things. There was a counselor at the ranch who was sort of the house dad for our group. He seemed to act really nice to me, and really helpful. He got booze for me. But then he also molested me. After he got me drunk, he would suck me off.

I was only thirteen. I hadn't really had sex with a girl yet. I had all kinds of ideas in my head about sex being wrong and dirty. I was twisted up about it because of what I had been told and what I had heard, mostly from the Jehovah's Witnesses. I knew that what he was doing to me was wrong, but I didn't know what to do about it. I could have told somebody. But who would I tell? He was a trusted employee of the Shamrock ranch who had been there for years and I was some punk kid who was always in trouble.

Over time I got a reputation for being a bad kid. I got thrown off the football team after going through "hell week" because I was fooling around with a girl. Later, I lost my chance to be on the wrestling team because a bunch of the guys on the team had gotten drunk and the coach thought I had gotten them the booze. I actually had nothing to do with it, but I was sort of the go-to guy when something bad had gone down. I just happened to be innocent that time. My life might have been really different had that moment turned out a different way.

There was a world-class wrestling camp at Lassen College, near Susanville. It was a fantastic place, and I loved being there. But the second day of camp the coach started screaming at me and told me to leave. Bob came to pick me up. He asked me what happened, and I told him I didn't know. When we got home Bob called the coach. He told Bob, "Frank took the boys out last night and got them drunk and ruined our practice." Bob said, "That's impossible. Frank was here with me the whole time."

The coach apologized and invited me back, but the damage was done. I was finished with wrestling. Why would I participate in anything run by a guy like that?

But I had always been into sports. As a kid I could play soccer for hours without ever getting tired. I never got cramps or got winded. I never wanted to stop. I would play every position on the field— at the same time—and I'd never stop moving. I had no idea I was a gifted athlete or had anything special in that area until I got to Bob's. He pointed out to me that I was fourteen years old and completely shredded. I didn't realize it, but I had been like that since I was twelve. I just had this extremely developed body, before I ever started doing anything to work on it. Later on, when I started training and lifting weights, my body got really extreme. But at that time it was just how I was naturally. I could have done anything with it, but I was too busy getting into trouble.

I finally did have sex with a girl from the high school. We were both drunk. It was at some house party. I don't remember much about it except that it wasn't special. But then I met someone who was special.

Her name was Connie, but she was called Christy. She was really pretty, maybe the prettiest girl in town. She went to my high school, and that's where we met: I ducked into the girls' bathroom to smoke a cigarette, and she asked me for a drag. The next thing I knew, we were together. We started fooling around, and almost right away she got pregnant.

Right after that, I got into some real trouble. I was out drinking, getting into my usual wasted state—not quite blacking out, but almost. That happened to me a lot. I had no on/off switch for my consumption. Alcohol and drugs just melted my brain. Almost every time I drank, I blacked out. I'd start drinking, and then I'd just wake up somewhere, hours later, with no idea what I'd been doing.

This particular night I was at a party at somebody's house. I started feeling sick, so I went outside to get some air. Then I decided I'd walk home. It was a long way, and it was really cold. So when I came upon a car parked outside a house, with the keys in the ignition and the motor running, I decided to steal it.

That's not quite right. I didn't "decide," exactly. I just saw the car and I knew I was going to take it.

I wasn't in any condition to begin a crime spree, and I think someone must have seen me getting into the car and driving off. The cops caught me right away. I hadn't driven a mile before they came up, lights and sirens on. I drove hard for a while, then turned into a Safeway parking lot. I ditched the car and made a run for it. That didn't work. They were on top of me. Then I was in handcuffs in the back of the car and it was over.

I wasn't quite sixteen years old. Technically, this was my second stolen car, since I helped liberate the van from the group home and got arrested in Sacramento. It was also my sixth or seventh actual arrest. I'd been caught throwing rocks at the train. I'd been caught pulling a knife on my sister. I was busted a couple of times for shoplifting and petty theft. I already had a record. So this was more serious than just a kid acting out because he was drunk and stupid.

Bob Shamrock did what he could. He wrote letters. He tried to get me back to his place. Some of my teachers wrote letters, too. And for months, it looked like I was going to be reassigned to the Ranch, but someone determined that the security level at the ranch was too lax, and I was getting into too much trouble going to school and hanging out. Bob was very respected, but in this case that didn't matter. I got sentenced to 120 days in juvenile hall.

I was held there for a while, and then I was sent to a group home in South Lake Tahoe. This was up one level in security from Shamrock Boys Ranch. But it wasn't horrible. It wasn't like prison. It was a good home. The guy who ran the place was a hippie dude, and he was very kind.

I was doing my time there and keeping things clean when I found out my son had been born. After some complications, Christy gave birth to a healthy baby boy. He was a huge baby, causing her to go into labor early and prompting doctors to fly them both to Reno, Nevada, for an emergency delivery. We named him Frankie Blake. A little while later, Christy brought him up to visit me. I had just turned seventeen. She was about the same age. We decided to get married and try to make a life together when I got out of the group home. I told her I would stay out of trouble and finish my time and come back to live with her in Susanville.

Now I had a goal. I was going to get out and be a husband and father and work to support my family. But I got in trouble again. The group home was a couple of miles from Stateline, Nevada. A group of guys and I rode our bikes over there to the Harrah's Casino. They had an arcade in the basement, and that's where all the local kids hung out. My friends and I were drinking and goofing around. There were lots of kids hanging out who we didn't know. One of them was a Latina girl who was being really loud. One of the guys in our group didn't like it, so he said, "I wish that fat Mexican bitch would shut up!"

For some reason she thought I had said it. So she came up to me and whacked me. I was surprised, so I instinctively hit her back. Unfortunately for me, she had friends. Twenty guys came running and jumped on top of me. My friends ran off. I ended up getting my ass kicked. The fight ended when the casino security people showed up. Luckily for me, it was too much trouble for them: I was in their casino, drunk, and I was a minor, from a group home across the state line. So they just let me go.

I walked home, limping and bleeding and still kind of drunk. But unluckily for me, the police picked me up in that condition and charged me with being drunk in public. That violated the terms of my sentence to the group home. I got sent back to juvenile hall. While it was a lot more like real jail than the group home, I was closer to Christy. We started talking about having a real future together.

Then I was sentenced for an undetermined time to the BAR O Boys Ranch in Gasquet, California, a high-security work camp isolated in the redwoods of far northern California, population 93. I finished the program in the fastest time of any inmate. I was really serious about being a man and a husband and a father.

As soon as I got out, Christy and I got married. That made me an emancipated minor, so I was no longer a ward of the court, and within months I was free of probation. It also meant that if I got into trouble again, I would no longer be tried as a juvenile. I would be treated as an adult, and tried and sentenced that way. But that didn't worry me. Things were different now. My relationship with Christy was for real. She was my wife, and I was a father. We lived in Susanville with our little son.

Because we were first-time, teenage parents, the state helped with bills and food. We moved into a house at the end of a dead-end street, right next to one of those storage-unit rental places. I found a job pretty quickly, working for Payless Drugs. I got another, too, working for a plumbing company. I also mowed lawns in my spare time. I was a hardworking man.

But I was still a thief. Right away, I started stealing. My job at Payless included working at the cash register. I learned how to do that pretty fast. Then I figured out that if someone came in and bought something expensive, I could charge them a lot less, and then they could sell the expensive thing and give me some of the money. So I had friends coming in right away, buying high-priced stuff and paying $10 for it.

I was also stealing cash. The registers all required a four-digit code, and each cashier had his own personal code. I'd peek over my coworkers' shoulders and memorize their codes. Then when it came time to clean up at the end of the shift, I'd volunteer to do the register areas. I'd open the registers with the codes and slip out a couple hundred dollars.

I borrowed some money from a friend and used some of the stolen money to buy myself a car. It was a canary yellow Chevy Nova. I bought it from an old lady who had it sitting in her backyard. I brought a can of WD-40 and a tire pump. I put air in the tires, sprayed the carburetor, and drove the car away. I think I stole another hundred dollars from Payless to pay back the loan. I was rolling!

Not surprisingly, Christy's family wasn't really happy about our marriage. They didn't like the idea of their daughter living with a career criminal who was only seventeen. My behavior didn't help, either. We were both under a lot of stress. We were both still trying to finish high school. She took care of the baby while I worked my two jobs. We were both drinking and taking a lot of drugs. The crummy house we lived in got condemned, and we had to move into an even smaller place. It was like a shed, in the middle of town, maybe three hundred square feet. It wasn't even like a real house. It was like a playhouse for children, which was funny, because we *were* children.

As part of my second job, with the plumbing company, I was helping build a house at Eagle Lake. I had an old friend from Shamrock Boys Ranch helping me. One weekend I invited Christy and my friend's wife to come hang out and go out on the boat as soon as we were finished with the job. We were all drinking beer and the job was taking forever, but soon as we got done we stripped down and hopped onto the boat to pick the girls up on the sandy shore. When the girls saw us pull up, drinks in hand, they wanted to leave— they thought that we had been drinking and cruising the boat all day while they were stuck with the kids on the beach. Christy was pissed at me. She yelled at me. I must have yelled back, because she suddenly hauled off and hit me. Without even thinking about it, I hit her back. She took little Frank and they raced away in my yellow Nova. I went back to the job site and hitched a ride into town.

So now I was a drunk *and* a wife beater. When I got home, everyone was gone. Christy had packed her things and taken off. I called Christy's mom and drove over to Christy's parents' house. It was all dark, but I pounded on the door until her dad came out. He said, "I don't know where she is." I went home thinking she'd be there when I got back, or that she'd change her mind. She didn't. Her parents told me she wasn't coming back. I begged to see her, and after a few days they finally agreed to meet me in a park.

It didn't go too well. They all showed up—Christy's father, her mother, and at least two of the seven kids in the family. Her father told me I was a drug addict and a criminal and not fit to be married to his daughter. We started yelling at each other. He attacked me and tore my shirt. I fought back. Her mother jumped in. Everyone was screaming and beating on me. Finally they got into the car and drove away. That was it for my marriage. Not long after that, I got a court order telling me I had to start making child support payments. I wasn't even divorced!

That was the beginning of a real downward slide. With Christy gone, the brakes came off. I had no reason to be responsible. I had no reason not to be a *real* criminal. I started really drinking and really taking drugs, full time, with no regard for the consequences. What difference did it make?

While I was married, when I lived in the camps, and when I lived with Bob, there was usually a limit to how much I drank. I always had to be somewhere, or do something, that kept a kind of lid on my drinking. I might go out and get drunk, but that didn't happen every day. Now it was every day. There was no reason to remain sober or to control myself in any way. I was also smoking weed, and I started using huge amounts of crystal meth. In those days it was called "speed" or "crank," and I was snorting or smoking at least $100 a day worth of it.

I needed a lot of money, so I committed a lot of crimes. After Christy moved out and took the baby, that's what I did with my time. Sometimes I had an accomplice, sometimes I worked alone. The jobs were always my idea, my plan. We went out every night and committed "jobs"; this was my new line of work.

For a few months I stole everything I could get my hands on that wasn't bolted down. The idea was to steal stuff and sell it. So we'd break into houses and vacation rental homes and steal stereos and cassette players. I thought electronics would be worth all kinds of money, but they weren't. I could hardly sell most of the stuff we stole. I wasn't a very good criminal. So I cranked it up. I started robbing businesses. I broke into an auto-body repair shop and stole some cameras. I broke into a pizza place and stole a VCR and a radio, plus some beer and some pizza sauce. I broke into a storage facility and stole some tools. I robbed a gas station, where I stole $200 from the owner's checkbook and a mini-cassette tape recorder. I snuck into the golf course across from Shamrock Boys Ranch and stole some money. I tried to break into the cash register in a restaurant, but all I got was a Makita drill. I broke into a florist shop and got away with some coffee mugs, some ceramic vases, some imported cheese samplers, and a roll of dimes.

Some of the crimes I must have committed while I was blacked out from drinking and smoking. I don't remember the incidents at all. And I wasn't wearing gloves, which meant I left fingerprints everywhere, which suggests I didn't really know what I was doing. Besides, I stole pizza sauce and imported cheese samplers; I *had* to be high. What kind of idiot steals cheese samplers?

The great Susanville crime spree went on for several months. I had met another girl named Christy, and we were hanging out. This was kind of funny, because her father was the local district attorney and I was a "master" criminal. Maybe that's why she liked me. I was the furthest thing she could imagine from her father.

My wife filed for a separation and got a temporary restraining order against me, so I couldn't see her or my son, and a child-support judgment. I was still working at Payless Drugs and scamming them, but they got camera footage of me lifting twenties from another employee's register. I was fired immediately and escorted to the front door with the promise they would turn the tapes over to the police. I left quickly. Then I got another job, as a fry cook at Taco Bell. I didn't like working at Taco Bell. I resented the way they treated me, so I decided I should relieve them of their money. I had noticed that the drive-through window wasn't secured very well. I figured I could come back after the end of my shift, break the glass, and climb through. I would clean out the cash registers and sneak out. I'd come back to work the next day like nothing had ever happened.

Nothing could have been simpler. I went over there really late one night. I broke in through the drive-through window as planned. I noticed the manager's office door was open. I walked inside and saw that the safe, for some reason, hadn't been locked. I started shoving money into a bag. I felt like I had won the lottery! When the safe was empty, I went out to check the cash registers.

That's when I heard tires screeching. I heard people moving, too quickly. It was the middle of the night, so I knew something was up. I didn't want to trip the alarm, so I crawled back out the drive-through window and started to run.

There were cops everywhere already. I heard them yelling "Stop!" and "Freeze!" The Taco Bell was at the edge of the shopping center, at the edge of a wilderness area. I ran hard for the trees and up into the foothills, the cops running behind me. I knew I could outrun them.

But there was a cliff a little way into the woods, with a creek at the bottom of it. There was a thirty-foot drop to the creek, which was actually part of the Susan River. I jumped. But it was the middle of winter, and the creek was frozen. I hit the ice, broke through into the freezing water, and hit the bottom of the creek. The bag I was carrying broke and a bunch of the money slipped out. And because of the ice, I had trouble getting out of the creek. I had to swim to the other side and crawl out before I could start running again.

The cops got busy. They launched a manhunt and brought out the bloodhounds. But I was still running. I found some railroad tracks and started heading down those. I ran for a long time. I was tired, and I was soaking wet with icy water from the river, and it was January in Susanville. I'd never been so cold in my whole life. Then after a while I started to warm up a little. I started feeling pretty comfortable, in fact. I was a little sleepy. I felt like I was going to be OK. So I lay down on the railroad tracks and started to take a little nap. But then I realized this didn't make sense. I couldn't be warm. I was freezing! It was the middle of the night in the middle of the winter and I was soaking wet. I realized it might be hypothermia. This wasn't good.

So I got up and ran some more. I made my way to a place where I thought I'd be safe. I knew a girl named Tracy. She was the girlfriend of a friend of mine. She was older than me, and she was beautiful, but all I wanted was a safe place to hide. Tracy took me in. She got me dried off and put me in bed.

I might never have gotten caught. I found out later that my body was so cold from the icy water that the dogs couldn't follow me. My body temperature was too low to give off a scent. According to the police report the cops called out an officer from the Lassen County Search and Rescue Team—Officer Daugherty and his dog Zeus. They wanted to catch me, but they were afraid I was going to die from exposure. (I did get hypothermia, and to this day I get cold whenever the weather changes, and I hate the winter.) They gave up after four hours and called off the dogs and the search.

But Tracy had a jealous boyfriend. He was one of my cronies, and we had committed some crimes together. He was pissed that I'd stayed all night at Tracy's house. He thought I had betrayed him, so he called the cops and told them where I was. The cops arrested me and searched my place and found all kinds of evidence.

I was sent to the Lassen County Jail, where I met with a public defender and got the chance to start thinking about what I was going to do next. The public defender seemed to think the evidence against me was pretty substantial. He didn't think I had a chance of beating the charges. Neither did I. So it became a question of minimizing the damage. We decided to plea bargain and throw ourselves on the mercy of the court, and hope for the best.

It didn't seem that serious. I had a history of screwing up and getting caught. So I thought I knew what was coming next. I was going to get the old wrist-slap thing again. I guess I had kind of lost touch with my own activities. I didn't realize how much trouble I had caused, or how many crimes I had committed. I hadn't added it all up.

The state added it up for me. There were a lot of crimes, and a lot of victims, and the cops knew who they all were. It even turned out there had been another investigation under way at the Payless Drugs. Detectives had been looking into a series of things over there. They had reviewed the store videotapes. Something like $3,000 had been stolen. They figured it was all me, and they had the video to prove it.

The judge brought me in for my hearing. The public defender and I had decided to plead guilty to certain charges—the ones where they had me cold—and hope for some sympathy. I told the judge about my wife and son being taken from me, and trying to graduate from high school while working two jobs, and having this drug and alcohol problem. I told the judge, "I just want to go to school and AA or NA to get help." The court records state that I was "polite."

But the victims of my crime spree called for justice. They all came to court. According to the court records, they told the judge things like "If he gets loose, he'll just go and do it again" and "He has no remorse. He should be taught a real lesson" and "Something needs to be done about him—he's an out-and-out thief." The only guy who sounded sympathetic was the security officer at the Payless. He said I seemed remorseful.

I got off the hook on some of the charges because I pled guilty to the others. But that didn't mean I was out of trouble or that I was going to get the old slap on the wrist. The judge fined me $1,500 and sentenced me to six years in the California Youth Authority.

4

JAIL

So I went to jail.

I was used to getting into trouble and then manipulating the situation to my advantage. I wasn't afraid to be sent in front of a judge. I wasn't afraid to go to jail. I'd been in courts and jails almost my whole life. I knew what CYA was. It's like graduate school if you're an adolescent criminal. It's like prison for little kids.

I thought I'd fit right in. I figured I was basically still a kid, and most of the crimes they'd busted me for had been committed before I turned eighteen. I figured I could handle whatever they threw at me.

It didn't start off too bad. I was locked up in the Lassen County Jail in Susanville for three or four months. That was real jail. It was pretty hard-core—all men locked up because they were criminals. After I had been processed, when they keep you apart from the rest of the population, I was put into a two-man cell with a guy who was accused of beating his wife to death with a telephone.

He had been a very successful local businessman whose marriage had fallen apart. He was very high-strung, and the breakup was upsetting to him. He started taking Prozac, which instantly fixed him, except when he'd go into these rages. His wife had moved out and found another place about ten houses away. One night they were arguing on the phone. He said, "Can you hold on a minute?" He walked out his front door, walked down the street to her house, took the phone out of her hand, and beat her to death with it.

"It was the Prozac," he said. "I'm innocent." He was the nicest guy, but he was a murderer. And he was going to sleep two feet away from me, every night.

I was working on my plea bargain. I was trying to figure out which things I could admit to, and how far they'd reduce my sentence. My cellie was also waiting to go to trial. The whole process moved very slowly and took a couple of months, so we got a chance to know each other.

His trial date came up before mine; he had been there for almost a year. He was sentenced to twenty-six years to life. It would have been twenty-five years to life, but he was carrying a concealed weapon at the time his crime was committed, and so that added a mandatory year. He was in the habit of carrying around large sums of money and had gotten a gun and a concealed-weapon permit, but the law didn't care about those details.

When he came back from the sentencing he looked sort of crushed but also sort of outraged. He kept saying, "It's not fair! I had a permit for that gun!" He didn't seem that upset about the twenty-five to life for first-degree murder, but the extra year really pissed him off. I kept thinking, "Dude! You killed your wife." Besides, what was the difference between twenty-five to life and twenty-six to life? Either way, he was out of there. Being a convicted and sentenced murderer meant he had to go to a different part of Lassen County Jail. So I lost my roommate.

Once I had my plea bargain session, it was time for me to move on, too. I wasn't that worried about being sent to the California Youth Authority. How bad could it be? Like juvie, but bigger? Like juvie, but for longer? It didn't seem that scary. A bunch of screw-up kids, like me, who'd gotten busted and put away for a while.

Besides, my wife had started visiting me again in jail. She brought me my son. We rekindled our relationship. She was going to keep visiting me. We were going to be together. The future looked kind of bright.

The next stop for me was the CYA induction center in Sacramento. I didn't expect to be there long; I'd been told I was going to be one of the first one hundred prisoners to be sent to the new "Chad" high-security facility near Stockton. (This became one of the state's most notoriously violent institutions. At the time it was described as a facility for California's "worst of the worst" juvenile offenders. Its real name was N. A. Chaderjian Youth Correctional Facility.)

I knew right away that I was in trouble. I'd had this romantic idea about CYA, that it was just like the adult prisons I'd seen in the movies. I imagined tiers of cells, with everyone quietly doing his time. I imagined something orderly and quiet.

This was hell. This was *Lord of the Flies*. This was thousands of kids who were disconnected from life, who had no connection to anything. They were seriously screwed up—tattooed, like lifelong gangsters, at twelve. I felt completely unsafe.

I was a good-sized guy by then. I had a fair amount of experience in the criminal world, stealing stuff, selling stuff, doing drugs, and making trouble. I could pass for a fairly experienced criminal. And I was near the top of the age range. Though some kids were going to stay at CYA until they were twenty-five, most of them were my age or younger.

But this was a seriously bad environment. I came from fucked-up shit; this was a whole new level. There was heavy gangbanging here. There were serious politics. I was out of my element. I thought I was a man, with a wife and a child. I felt like a grown-up.

But now I had thirteen-year-old kids, really *hard* kids, coming up on me and saying, "Where you from, holmes? Who you roll with?"

"Uh, nobody. I'm from Anderson."

I understood right away that I had to get out. I knew that if I stayed I was going to be in CYA for a long, long time. I'd just get sucked in. I felt like I was past that kind of behavior, in terms of who I was and where I was in my life. In jail, I had begun a new relationship with my wife, and things had changed.

When Christy was first pregnant and then when our son was born, I did everything I could to avoid being involved. I didn't want to feel responsible and I couldn't stop doing drugs. I was high all the time. I was in jail half the time. But now I had this new experience where I was sober for the first time in a long, long time. Everything felt so clear once the drug haze wore off. I felt a new responsibility to my son and to my wife. Christy was writing me letters. I was committed to becoming a real husband and father. When I got out, we could be a real family.

But I knew as long as I was in CYA, I couldn't help her and my son. There were no jobs, which meant you couldn't make money, which meant you couldn't send money. There was no visitation. I couldn't be a dad to my son locked up in that place.

So I went to the counselor and asked him what my options were. He said that because I was over eighteen I could ask to be classified as an adult and sentenced to an adult facility. He tried to scare me off that. The counselor said, "You think you're all hard, and you want to go where the real criminals are. But you're a good-looking kid, and you're young . . ."

He was probably right. He was trying to protect me. It was outside the norm for a youth offender to ask to be reclassified as an adult. He warned me that there would be no coming back. I wouldn't be able to change my mind. But I knew I wasn't going to make it at CYA. My only goal was to get out, be a father and husband, and move on with my life. In the CYA system you can be held until you are twenty-five years old, even if your sentence is less. Unlike in the adult system, where you get a day off your sentence for every good day you produce, in CYA you are subject to periodic reviews by your counselors. They can add what they think you "need" to behave. I was a youth offender. I had a long rap sheet. They might feel like they needed to keep me a while to help me get over that. That might mean staying the full six years. Plus I knew from what I could see around me that I was going to have to fight. If I had to fight, I was going to get more time added to my sentence.

I had already had one incident. It was just after I arrived at Lassen County Jail in Susanville. It was dinnertime, and it was chili night. I had already heard about chili night; the old-timers had warned me about it. The old-timers said it hurt their stomach. But I was hungry, and I had a strong stomach. The chili was served in bowls at the tables. I sat down and started to reach for my bowl of chili.

A big, bearded biker dude, way bigger than me, sat across from me. He looked like he had just came down from the mountains. When I reached over to pick up a bowl of chili, the biker dude grabbed the bowl and said, "That's mine." I apologized and reached for a different bowl. But he said, "That's mine, too."

I knew from the streets what this moment was, and I could feel twenty sets of eyes sizing me up and down and waiting to see what I was made of. So I said, "Oh, here you go" and threw the chili right in his face. Then I jumped up and started beating him on the head with the metal tray. That was a good start, but then it got ugly. He hit me hard in the stomach, and I hit him back in the face with the tray, and then it was on. He grabbed me and threw me across the room. Then he got on top of me and pounded me on the head and back. I started uppercutting him in the balls. The guard got on us and we all fell over. He was still banging me on the head, but I still had hold of his balls. We were both screaming. By the time the guards separated us, we were messed up. It was a successful fight because that guy never bothered me again, and everyone else was very nice to me, too. In fact, after that, the old-timers would bring their bowls right to my seat and spark up some conversation.

At CYA, I was always prepared to fight, always on guard. I knew I was going to get jumped, and I was going to get hurt, and I was maybe going to have to hurt someone else. I didn't want to do that. I had been roughed up a little. I could take a fair amount of punishment. But I didn't like hurting other people. So I signed the papers and filed the writ, and the transfer came through. I was taken out of CYA and sent to an induction center at Tracy, California.

This was another step up. Or down. CYA had been weird. This was really, really scary. It was a real prison, a *big* prison. It was eight stories tall. It was all cells. The cells were filled with men—serious adult criminal men. Everyone was wearing prison orange and moving slowly. The mood was very tense, and very sad.

I remember the first night. I was on one of the lower tiers with easy access, cell block number two or number three, because I was a new guy. I was a fish. That meant they kept me on a rotating suicide watch, in case I killed myself or something. I was alone. Up on the seventh floor there was a gay black guy, and when it got dark he started singing. He had the most amazing voice. He sang "Under the Boardwalk." It was unbelievably beautiful. It made guys cry. You could hear him singing. You could hear guys crying. You could hear guys getting beat up. You could hear other stuff that you weren't sure *what* it was. It didn't sound good.

I remember lying there thinking, "What's a guy with a voice like that doing here? And what am *I* doing here?"

The whole life was new to me. For example, there was the kite. I never knew about this stuff. A kite is a way of sending things from one cell to another. One guy would tie something to a piece of string—a cigarette, a message, a tattoo needle—and send it to the next guy. He'd send it to the next guy. It might start on the eighth floor and wind up on the third floor, just passing along from one cell to the next, on this little piece of string. Some nights there would be kites going all over the place. Everyone sends the kite along. Even if one guy's a white guy and other guy is a black guy and they hate each other, they have to move it along. Everyone's got to move the kite along.

There was also a "telephone" system. There was a way you could take your pillow and stick it in the top of the toilet and suction the water out of the pee trap. It turned the toilet into a telephone. You could lean into the toilet and talk to the cell above you or below you—depending on whether they took the water out of their toilet, too. You could have a whole conversation that way, or pass along a complicated message.

Because Tracy was an induction center, everyone was in his own cell. There was no work. You just sat around waiting for your one hour on the yard, or to go to the chow hall, or for someone to bring you a bag lunch. There was no visitation, either. Maybe that's why there was so much kiting and telephoning. It was the only way for anyone to communicate, and we all had too much time on our hands.

It was a big facility, and the yard was huge. Everyone was in orange, and everyone was broken into groups. This was my first introduction into the racial self-segregation of prison life. In the youth system, I was aware of people being from different places. I was aware that I looked Mexican. It was no big deal. At Tracy, it was much more serious. There were three groups—white, black, and Latino. In that facility, the whites had most of the control. They were the most trusted, and they had the most access. But the blacks had all the power. Everyone was most afraid of them. If you weren't black, you couldn't walk through the black guys' area. But if you weren't Latino, you couldn't walk through the Latino area, either. And if you were North Mexican, you couldn't walk through the South Mexican area. When I first arrived, some old-timer took me aside and laid it out for me. He asked me what I was and who I ran with on the streets. I wasn't sure what I was. He told me I was "other"—not black, not white, not Latino, but other.

"Other" was for the leftovers. "Other" was for Indians, and Pacific Islanders, and Asians. This was the smallest group, maybe 10 percent of the population or less. That's where you'd find the Japanese guy and the Hawaiian guy and the Samoan guy. And me. Mostly they don't bother anyone because they don't have any power, and no one bothers them because they're no threat. But they're also the most exposed because they have small numbers and no protection.

It was tense, like all jails are tense. Everyone is scared. Everyone is angry. You have all these violent men, and everything has been taken away from them. They have nothing left. They have no power, and they're scared. So they grab what they can and are ready to die for it. This is *my* piece of the yard, and you can't be on it, holmes.

I was at Tracy for only forty-five days. It felt like a long time. No one bothered me. No one assaulted me. I was pretty good at figuring out how to survive and be OK. I got some tips. I figured out who went where and what part of the yard to stay away from. I did the time and waited.

At the end of my induction time I was sent to Corcoran. I was in real prison. I mean, *real* prison: Charles Manson was on the yard next to mine. I could do my time, and maybe make something out of it. In real prison, you could get a job. I got a job bending sheet metal. I got an apprenticeship, and I made eleven cents an hour. After a while I transferred out of that and got a job in the kitchen, where I made a little more money. I treated it seriously, like a real job. I had decided to be a provider for my family. I was making as much money as I could and making the best of a bad situation.

I had realized by then that I was not going to be able to manipulate myself out of prison. I wasn't going to be able to talk my way out of doing the time. No one wanted to hear my story. I saw I was going to have to do my time and work the system the hard way. So I decided to play by the rules. I found out you could get an education in prison. I decided to start going to college. I had graduated from that continuation high school up the hill when I was seventeen. Now I had lots of time on my hands. I knew I was smart. I knew I could study and learn. So I learned sheet metal on the job, and I took psychology classes and history classes. I took business classes. I took all kinds of other classes. I figured that one day I was going to get out of jail and I was going to need a trade. I didn't know how to do anything, and I didn't know what I wanted to do anyway, so I studied everything they had.

I also learned about being Native American. My grandfather had told me I was part Native American on my father's side. But I didn't have any sense of the history or the culture until I took a class in Native American history. I learned about the tribes and the ceremonies. I had a connection to something. I got to be part of something other than "other."

The time went slowly. It was hard for me. I was lonely. My wife hadn't visited me since I left Susanville. She had stopped writing me, too. I found out from a friend I'd known at Shamrock Boys Ranch that she had gotten pregnant. I wrote to her and said I didn't care about the other guy, and I didn't care about the baby. I said I'd take care of her anyway, when I got out. I asked her to please write to me.

She sent me pictures of our son, little Frankie, and included some scribbles from him. But she couldn't visit me. It was too far. I tried to get myself moved to Susanville prison, which was only seven miles from where she was living with the two children. But there was a problem: there was an arrest warrant out for me. It turned out it was for back child support! I hadn't even known about that, but now it prevented me from moving to be close to my family.

For a couple years I stayed out of trouble and followed the rules, so I accrued points for good behavior. My classification dropped from IV to II. I got transferred to Avenal and then to Jamestown. Life should have been easier there. But it was still prison. I got into a fight with a guy in the bathroom. He thought I'd taken something of his, though I hadn't. He came up on me at the urinal and threw a punch. I slipped the punch and then I decked him with a right uppercut to the eye that laid him out unconscious and crushed my knuckle. It was over, just like that.

I wasn't especially good at fighting, but I was starting to get strong. I had started lifting weights when I lived with Bob at the Shamrock Boys Ranch. I continued in work camp and then prison. I got good enough at it that I started training other guys. They wanted to know how to get big, so I spent some time training them in conditioning their bodies with weights. I could talk to them about the mechanics of their bodies, and why their form was correct or incorrect. It helped that I read anything and everything on the subject and had plenty of time to read.

Up until this point, I had been good at staying out of trouble. But it didn't last. I got into a bad fight.

Jamestown was a minimum-security facility. It wasn't as tense as Corcoran or Tracy, but it was still very segregated. I was still with "other." The races didn't mix, and one group didn't mess with another. But there was only one TV. So every night was designated. Each race got a night of TV in rotation with the other races.

It was our night, "other" night. I was alone in the TV room watching some show. Then a group of black guys came in. *In Living Color* was scheduled to be on. The show hadn't been on the air that long. It was the only sketch comedy show on TV that was made by blacks for blacks, and it was really popular in prison. So these guys just came in and changed the channel.

I said, "Hey, it's our night."

They said, "Nah. We're watching this."

There were eight of them. I knew they'd kill me if I fucked with them, so I just left to make a plan. I took a bunch of sharpened pencils and stuck them in my sock, where I would have easy access to them. Then I went and found a mop handle, which makes a pretty good club. You can also do some pretty serious jabbing and stabbing with it. I went back into the TV room and just started swinging. I pulled a pencil out of my sock and stuck it into somebody. I landed a couple of blows with the mop handle. But there were still eight of them, and no one jumped in on my side. They got on me pretty quickly, wrestled me down, and took away my weapons. I hurt a couple of guys, but they hurt me back. The guards came and broke it all up.

I got two months in solitary. I probably could have shortened that, or missed it altogether, if I'd told them what had happened. But you can't do that in prison. You can't tell on anybody, ever. So when the guards asked me what happened, I said, "I slipped and fell." When they asked me about the eight black guys, I said, "They slipped and fell on top of me."

The guards were concerned that it was the beginning of some kind of gang war. But I refused to tell them anything, so I got two months in solitary with no release date set. I didn't have to do more than a month, though, because someone from the dorm, maybe someone from "other," came forward and told the guards what had really happened. That was good, because I got sent back to the yard. But it was also bad, because it looked like I must have told them what happened. Because the guards figured it was a gang thing, they put me back on the yard and sent all eight of the black guys to different prisons to separate them.

That was bad. I was in deep shit, and I knew it. A snitch is the lowest thing you can be. It doesn't matter what color you are or who you roll with. If you're a snitch in prison, you're going to get killed.

I was back working in the kitchen when they came up on me. I was sitting with my book, back to the wall, alone at a table. Fifty guys came into the kitchen. They were black guys and Mexican guys and white guys, all together, and they were pissed. One of them said, "We are going to kill you, you rat." I put my book down and said, "I've never ratted anybody out. I didn't tell anybody anything. But if you're here to kill me, we better get going." I put the book down and stood up.

For some reason, they changed their mind. They turned around and left. Nobody bothered me after that.

Time passed. I took my classes. I taught weight training. My body developed. It was something people noticed. Guys asked me about it—"How can I look like that?" I started thinking maybe I could do something with my body when I got out of prison. I didn't know what, exactly.

I had always had it in my head that I was going to be some kind of entertainer or showman. But I didn't have any actual entertainment skills. I wasn't a singer or an actor or a comedian or anything. But I wanted to entertain. So I thought I'd use my body. I thought I'd be some kind of a male dancer, an exotic dancer or something. Or, if that didn't work out, some kind of fighter. But I didn't have any real information about that. I didn't know any fighters. I hadn't trained for fighting although I had a childhood fantasy that I was a world-champion boxer. I know some people have said that boxing and martial arts exist so that belligerent, angry guys have someplace to go. I wasn't one of those guys. I wasn't looking for a fight or a fight scene. I never equated fighting with anything other than animosity and problems. But I had this body and I was really strong. By the time I got out of prison, I was huge. I was pumped up to about 210 pounds and I looked awesome. It seemed like I could do something with that.

I had managed to stay out of any more trouble at Jamestown and was eventually invited to be a trainer for the fire crews, convicts who went outside the walls to fight fires. It was a dream job that I was never able to qualify for because of the child support order issued against me. When my time was short, I got sent to Folsom, and I was paroled out of there on April 5, 1994. Of the six years that I had been sentenced to, I had been locked up for three and a half years. The state of California paroled me out into the care of Bob Shamrock.

Bob had come and visited me in prison. Other than my wife, he was the only one. I hadn't had any contact at all with my family, not for years, except for the one visit in jail when my mom came to see me. (Joe was with her. He stayed in the car.) It was as if we were all just done with each other. Joe was able to semi-retire once the rest of the kids left home, selling the house and touring the US in a motor home. They sent postcards from their travels and escapades. Utah, Nevada, Louisiana: beautiful places that I was sure I would never see.

But Bob came. He encouraged me to stay out of trouble, to take college courses, to take care of my body. When my time was getting short, he told me he had a plan for me. He wanted me to join Ken Shamrock at a gym he ran in Lodi, California. It was called the Lion's Den.

Ken was his adopted son. He had been at Shamrock Boys Ranch for three or four years and had gone on to a career in professional wrestling. I hadn't known him at Bob's place. He was older than me, and he'd left just before I got there. He had already had a checkered career. When he left the boys' home, he went off to Shasta College in Redding, California, but that didn't work out somehow. He started making money by squatting in bars. He used to sit at the bar and say, "I'll fight any man here for a hundred dollars." He was a real tough guy. I would be scared to death to do that! But Bob told me he'd come home every night with $500 or $600.

Later on, he got work as a bouncer. One night he pulled a guy into the street and started fighting with him. The guy had a friend, and the friend got a crowbar. Ken hit the first guy so hard that it broke his jaw and drove part of a bone into his brain. The guy was a very talented college linebacker who was in line for a career in the NFL. That punch ruined him and destroyed his career. He sued Ken and won some judgments against him. Bob told me it cost Ken a huge amount of money; it took him years to pay it off. Bob would always tell me, "Never hit anybody in the street!"

I think it was after that fight that Bob took Ken to a wrestling training camp in Sacramento. He pushed him into that as a career. Ken trained under the wrestling brothers Buzz and Brett Sawyer and made his wrestling debut under the name Wayne Shamrock in 1990—around the time I was in the middle of my prison sentence.

I didn't know too much about Ken or what he had been doing. But I was flattered that Bob wanted to make a place for me. So one day after I got out of Folsom Prison I headed for Lodi. I was twenty-one years old, and I had nowhere else to go.

5

THE LION'S DEN

Ken Shamrock was a lost boy like me. He had no place to go and no one to claim him. He had no mother and no father. Like me, he'd had a really difficult childhood, maybe worse. His mother was an uneducated vagrant. She had three sons by at least two men. She was a drug addict who'd leave her boys alone to go out and do her thing. Ken ran away from home when he was really young. He was on the streets when he was ten years old. He used to fight for food. He had come into Bob Shamrock's care when he was about fifteen, and he stayed until he was eighteen. When he became an adult, Bob adopted him as his own legal son, and Ken took Bob's name.

By the time I was released from Folsom, Bob was on his own, too. Bob told me his wife had been a young woman who had never been with another man besides Bob. He was on the road a lot, interviewing kids, bringing kids back to the ranch. She was at home alone in a house with all these boys. Bob said she hooked up with one of the young men and they ran away together. I heard Bob was willing to take her back, but she moved to Hawaii and never returned. That was it for Bob and marriage. He never had another lover or girlfriend. He took all his love and put it into his relationships with Ken and me.

A lot of that was managing Ken. Ken was a wild man, frequently getting into trouble and forcing Bob to come to his rescue. Ken had gotten involved in pro wrestling. He and Bob had left Susanville and moved to Reno. Ken had trained with Buzz Sawyer and others and began wrestling professionally in 1990 under the names Vince Torelli and Wayne Shamrock. (His actual birth name was Kenneth Wayne Kilpatrick.) Later, he simply went by "Shamrock" and called himself "Mr. Wrestling."

Ken was older than me by about eight years, and we could have passed for brothers. We both have a kind of Mexican Indian look. We have really similar bodies. And we were both really damaged children who never had anybody show us much love or respect or kindness. So we really responded to Bob and the attention he gave us. Especially Ken. What he and Bob had was very special. It was real love, an all-or-nothing love, like a man has with his son. It was deep.

Bob was into the Adonis. He understood and appreciated the male body. He understood clothes, decorating, and fine cars and was really into bodybuilding. He wanted his boys to be athletic and to look athletic in a very specific way. Ken and I had that look.

By the time I showed up in Lodi, Ken was leaving professional wrestling and getting involved in this thing called Pancrase. It was from Japan, and it involved certain kinds of wrestling mixed with certain kinds of submission holds. The name comes from the Greek *Pankration*. It was one of the original Olympic sports and might be the world's oldest known form of organized fighting. Ken had already had some success with the Pancrase organization and was building a team of American Pancrase fighters to take to Japan.

I arrived at the Lion's Den gym on April 7, 1994, two days after I got out of Folsom. I don't think Ken was very happy to see me. He wouldn't have had any reason to be. We weren't friends. We didn't even know each other. He was just doing what Bob said to do—just like I was.

We didn't have anything in common. I wasn't into sports, and Ken was a superjock. I was a long-haired stoner. He was a clean-cut family man, married and the father of several boys. I was a criminal coming out of prison. He was a hardworking citizen. We were complete opposites, except physically. But maybe Ken saw me as competition. He shouldn't have; Ken was Bob's number-one boy. Of all the kids Bob had brought into his group homes—and there were literally *thousands* of boys—Ken had been the only one he ever adopted. I was one of Bob's favorite kids, but Ken was the *one.*

The Lion's Den was in a crummy, run-down building behind a car stereo shop that didn't look like much. Ken was doing OK as a fighter, but he wasn't famous yet. But he was making a living out of it. He was training a group of guys for Pancrase—Vernon White, Scott Bessac, Jason DeLucia, and some others. They were all hanging around the Lion's Den when I showed up for my tryout.

Every gym has tryouts. It's not unusual for a new guy to show up and want to get involved. The people running the gym will give him a shot. That's how all fighters begin. I was the only guy who showed up that day looking for a tryout. Bob had told Ken to expect me, so he knew I was coming. He obviously wasn't happy about it. But he agreed to let me test.

The first part was physical conditioning. While Ken and some of the other guys watched and counted, I did 500 sit-ups. Then I did 500 squats. Then 500 leg lifts. Then 250 push-ups. They kept a bucket nearby. This was the "puke bucket." I learned later this is part of the tryout process. It's not unusual for guys to throw up during the physical conditioning part of the test once the body goes into shock from the exertion. It's not bad to throw up. It's good. You push yourself too hard, you get sick, and you throw up—and then you keep going. That's part of the tryout. If you're not trying hard enough to puke, and if you don't keep going after you puke, you're out.

That's the purpose of the entire exercise. It's designed to weed out the guys who don't have what it takes or who don't want it bad enough. The tryout process is very structured, and it's brutal. It's not designed to teach you, or encourage you, or welcome you into the family. It's designed to break you and make you quit. I got the feeling real quick that Ken was going to try extra hard to make me quit.

I passed the physical conditioning. Then it was time for the sparring.

Ken's guys put me in the ring for the first time in my life. No one told me what to do or how to do it. They just put me in the ring and told me to get ready. Then Ken got in the ring with me. I saw right away that he was not going to take it easy on me. It was already clear he didn't think I was going to make it. Now it became clear that he didn't *want* me to make it. He wanted me to fall apart. So he got me in the ring and told me we were going to spar for twenty minutes straight.

I got creamed. For twenty minutes, I stood there swinging my hands around while Ken beat the crap out of me. First, he hit me so hard with a palm strike that he broke my nose. I started bleeding all over the place. I thought maybe we'd stop, get me cleaned up a little, or let me rest a little. No. We kept going.

A little later, he knocked me down. I was on all fours, trying to catch my breath. He punched me so hard in the side that he broke two of my ribs. When I got up, he hit me some more on my broken nose and my broken ribs. When I fell down, he got me in a wrestling hold, and then hit me some more where he'd broken my ribs. It was the most painful thing I'd ever felt in my life. But he got bored with hurting me that way, so he got me in a choke hold and threw me around the ring like a rag doll for a little while.

It went on forever! Twenty minutes is a long time in the ring for anyone. For a beginner, it was an eternity. I kept thinking it was

over, and then it was never over. It just went on and on and on, and
I kept getting hit harder and harder. Ken looked sort of bored and
disgusted by the whole thing. He'd stop hitting me for a minute,
and then he'd start squeezing me and choking the life out of me
again. I had no way to defend myself. I had no idea of where to
be or how to move. I didn't even understand the concept of range.
Until I got kicked in the face—then I understood.

I'm sure Ken expected me to quit without making him do anything but box me around. But I didn't quit. So he knocked me down,
wrestled me to the ground, and held me there. He got me in a leg
lock and started twisting up my legs. I had no idea how to get out of
a hold like that and no idea how to protect myself. So I didn't. Ken
kept twisting. The pain was incredible. After a minute I felt all the
tendons in my left knee pop and rip. It was *horrible.* I felt like I was
dying. I thought I was going to pass out. Then there was this vivid
moment. I heard one of Ken's guys say, "Didn't anyone tell this guy
he could tap out?" I was screaming with pain, but I heard that, and
I said, "What?"

"You can stop anytime if you just say 'tap.'"

So I yelled, "Tap! Tap!" and the fight ended.

We had gone the whole twenty minutes. I had passed the tryout.
Ken walked out of the ring looking disgusted. I crawled out after
him. Someone drove me to Ken's house and took me upstairs and
put me in a bedroom. I passed out and slept for the next two days.
When I finally came downstairs, I actually had to slide down the
stairs on my ass because my legs wouldn't work. It would take two
weeks of icing and heat on my knee to walk without a limp and
another two weeks before I could take a full breath without the rib
pain sending me to the other knee. That's the shape I was in when I
started my training at the Lion's Den.

Ken had trained as a fighter in the old-fashioned Japanese tradition, in which you begin training not as a fighter but as an appren-

tice—almost a slave. So that's the training I got, too. For the next few weeks, all I did was clean the mats and carry the other fighters' bags. I learned to serve. After a while, because of my size I became the warm-up guy. I'd get in the ring and guys would warm up—by beating on me. I'd spar with them and they'd kick my ass until they got bored. Then I'd have to go clean the mats and carry their bags.

That went on for several months. No one was training me or teaching me anything. I'd get the snot beat out of me, and then I'd clean up the gym and pack up everyone's gear and go home. I didn't grasp anything for a long time. I didn't know anything about sports because I'd never been on a team, with a coach, long enough to learn anything. I didn't understand wrestling and fighting as a sport or a discipline. I only understood street fighting—twenty-second fights in which you hit a guy and he hits you and someone falls down and everyone runs. But I didn't know how to fight a real fight.

But I was picking up stuff. I learned the ten positions of Pancrase. They were all on the ground. The system was all grappling. It was old-school submission wrestling. The positions all had Japanese names. Ken had simplified them by giving them numbers, and we learned those.

But Ken was not a teacher, he was a fighter. He fought all the time, and he was successful. But he had no patience or skill for teaching. He was a bully. He had trouble articulating stuff. He could show you things, but he couldn't explain them. So he taught in the old way, like he'd learned in Japan. "I want to show you this technique. Give me your leg." And you'd scream "Aaaaaggghh!" while he twisted your leg. Then he'd make you hold *his* leg, and he'd say, "This is how you get out of it." And you'd scream "Aaaaaagggh!" while he kicked your face.

It was more like a gym than a martial arts dojo. There was no training in the modern sense; it was just guys working out and fighting. No one was in very good condition by today's standards.

We had no concept of cardio. We wrestled and drilled for an hour, then ran two miles. We did some weight training and some sparring, but that was it.

Most of the guys didn't live like athletes or martial artists, either, especially Ken. He had this rock 'n' roll lifestyle. He was a married man and a good father, but he was living it up and doing his own thing, which involved a lot of partying. He was working on his career and training himself.

I didn't like Ken's party scene. It was pretty hard-core, with a lot of sex and drugs, and it all seemed very fake. I didn't see any real future mixing hard partying with training but I didn't have anyplace else to go. I didn't have any skills to make a living with. I didn't know how to do anything. Ken obviously didn't want me there. But Bob Shamrock was the only man who seemed to care anything about what happened to me, and he said it was a good idea. I understood this was an opportunity, and I was a guy with no opportunities. So I stayed with it.

All the while, I was watching and learning. I had learned how to be a student in prison. I had learned how to pay attention and take notes. Watching the other fighters, getting my ass kicked, I began to see things. When I figured something out, I wrote it down. I drew pictures of the moves and the holds. I took the same energy and mind-set that I had used in prison and added it to the martial studies.

I'm not sure how I got it, but I already had a martial arts mentality. I was driven to protect myself, seek excellence, and help others in a shared purpose. And I began to realize that this fighting thing could be a sport, with real skills and real techniques that I could learn. Ken beat me up so easily at the tryout that I was humiliated, but I was also intrigued. I was challenged. It seemed like if I did the physical part, and paid attention, and studied, I should be able to figure it out.

I had an advantage because I didn't have anything to *un*learn. I was a blank slate, with no preconceived notions of how to wrestle or how to box. If someone told me how to do something, or if I figured something out, I just did it. It was challenging, and I respond to challenges, but it was kind of terrible, too.

Other guys would come to the gym and ask to try out. Ken would put them through the same thing he put me through. It was so ridiculously hard that almost no one made it past the conditioning part, with the five hundred sit-ups and five hundred leg lifts. If they made it to the sparring part, they'd crack at the beginning of that. Ken insisted on it. We'd be put in the ring with the tryouts, and if we didn't kick their asses, Ken would kick *our* asses.

After a few months, I started thinking maybe I could do this thing. I discovered I was a gifted athlete. Plus I was smart. Most of the guys in Ken's organization weren't either of those things. They were really tough, but that's all they were—just tough, angry guys who knew how to take a lot of punishment and who liked dishing it out. I realized after about six months that I might actually have a shot. Then one day I got Scott Bessac in a choke hold and made him tap out. That was huge. I had finally beaten somebody.

In the fall of 1994, Ken and the Pancrase guys in Japan decided it was time for me to fight. They wanted me to leave Lodi and the Lion's Den and finish my training over there. So I flew to Tokyo and joined the Pancrase organization.

6

JAPAN

I moved to Japan in late 1994. It was the middle of winter in Tokyo, cold and damp. I was taken to a big tin building in a suburban neighborhood in Yokohama, in Kanagawa Prefecture, about an hour by train from downtown Tokyo. The houses were all packed tightly together, and the air smelled like raw sewage.

The tin building was my new dojo. There were mats here and there on the floor, and there was a fighting ring in the middle. Around the sides of the building were very Spartan dormitory rooms with nothing in them but a mat on the floor and some blankets. There was a partitioned area with a rice cooker, a refrigerator, and a huge cooking pot. That was the kitchen. The toilet was outside the building and was a traditional Japanese squat toilet, which is just like an outhouse over a trough.

This was my home and my gym. This is where I worked and trained, along with the other Pancrase fighters.

Every day was the same. I got up at eight. We'd get breakfast, which was a kind of rice stew called *chankonabe*, or just *chanko*, a sort of goopy rice soup in a huge pot with vegetables and bits of fish in it that would stew all day. The fighters would start coming in around nine. The young boys who lived at the dojo would do their training while the fighters did their warming up. Then the wrestling part of the training would start around eleven. We'd have a break for lunch a couple of hours later, and we'd all eat some more chanko. Then we'd have an afternoon session. We'd break for dinner and eat chanko again. Then there was an evening session. At night, you'd have to clean the gym. Then you'd roll up in your blankets and try to get warm and get some sleep.

The young boys were at the lowest level at the dojo. They were all poor farm boys from the provinces whose families had given them to the dojo to train. They lived there and worked there. It was their whole life. They hadn't had much schooling. They didn't have much future back home in their poor villages. This was their shot.

They had to do all the really hard work—the cooking and the cleaning. I was one level above them because I was a foreigner. They didn't really know where I fit in. They didn't know what to do with me. When I decided I couldn't eat chanko for breakfast (I just couldn't eat fish for breakfast, yuck), they let me start taking just the rice part and put milk and sugar and bananas in it. They wouldn't eat it, but they didn't stop me from eating it.

I slept in a room with a fighter named Ito. *Ito-san.* He was the most senior young boy in the dojo. He had been there long enough to have his own room. He came from a poor country family, and he'd been a wrestler in school. When Pancrase got started as a sport, he tried out and was invited to move to Tokyo. He had lived there three years already, doing nothing but serving. Now it was his fourth year, and he was going to turn pro, like me, and start having actual fights.

The Pancrase organization was only a few years old. It had been created by three Japanese catch wrestlers: Minoru Suzuki, Takako Fuke, and Masakatsu Funaki. They had all been professional fighters in an organization called Fujiwara Gumi, then had broken away to do their own thing.

Pancrase is real fighting, not fake wrestling like the WWE in America. The rules were pretty simple. Fights were ten, fifteen, or twenty minutes for non-title bouts, thirty minutes for title bouts. Wins are by knockout, submission (with or without a tap out), or on points. Each fighter has five "escapes" at the beginning and can use one to grab the ropes if he's in a submission hold. After five escapes, he loses. Closed-fist strikes to the head were not allowed—but open-fist hits were—as were kicks, knees, or elbows to the head.

The organization idolized Karl Gotch, who was seen as the father of pro wrestling in Japan. He was a Belgian wrestler from a Hungarian family, and he had studied world wrestling styles, especially some East Indian disciplines and training techniques. He had wrestled on the Belgian team in the Olympics and then come to fight in the United States. He was also held for three years in a Nazi concentration camp, using the Indian conditioning training to keep himself alive and strong. Later he moved to Japan, where he was a huge star—they loved his spirit of survival. When he retired, he started training Japanese fighters, including Yoshiaki Fujiwara, who founded Fujiwara Gumi, which trained all the Pancrase fighters.

Gotch's and Fujiwara's pictures were on the wall at the entrance to the mats. Every morning we would have to line up and bow to them before beginning our workout. But the master of the dojo was Masaru Funaki. He was, to me, the ideal of the martial artist, a charismatic leader with a brotherly tone. When teaching, Ken had been like an animal. Funaki was gentler. Ken would show you an arm bar and almost break your arm doing it. Funaki would show a new move and say, "This uses less energy" or "This will scare your opponent" or "This will make you confident." No one had talked to me like that. No one ever criticized me by saying, "That works, but this works better."

A lot of our day was spent conditioning. That was the Gotch legacy. He was a freak about conditioning. His theory was that if you conditioned enough, no one could beat you. Maybe that's why the Japanese loved him so much. It was all about repetition and ritual. We were like an army. We'd do three hundred squats in a row, all counting out loud, all together. Then we'd do the exact same number of sit-ups, and the exact same number of push-ups, and so on.

We did that all day, six days a week. On Sunday, the young boys slept. They didn't go out, or hang out, or visit their families. They stayed in bed. I was left on my own.

There wasn't really anyone to hang out with other than the young boys. I couldn't talk to them anyway. English is the second language in much of Japan, but these were rural country boys who hadn't had much schooling. None of them spoke English at all. Funaki and Ito spoke just a little. It was really lonely for me. I tried to learn Japanese for the first few weeks, but it was too difficult. Japanese is one of the toughest languages out there to learn.

It was weird. I had been in prison only eight months earlier, but *this* made me feel more alone and isolated. In prison, at least there were people to talk to. Here, I felt like I was totally alone.

So I got into the habit of borrowing a bicycle on Sundays and pedaling down to the Shin-Yokohama train station. I'd park the bike and go hang out inside. If I saw anybody who looked like they spoke English, I'd say hello. I tried to make friends that way. If I saw a white person, I'd say, "Hey! How's it going?" I didn't make too many friends that way.

There was partying at the dojo, but I wasn't really part of that. I was still in that weird class status where no one really knew who I was, so everyone deferred to me as a higher class. I would have to speak up if I wanted something. The fighters would all drink heavily after a fight. The young boys weren't allowed to drink, and the rules in the dojo were very strict. No one broke the rules if

they wanted to stay. One kid told someone no one day during training. It was all very quiet and subtle, but two hours later his family
arrived to pick him up, and no one ever saw him again. There was
no sneaky drinking or drugging there, like there had been at the
group homes where I'd lived.

But in the Japanese culture you are not allowed to *refuse* a drink.
So after the fights it was a tradition for the fighters to get the young
boys drunk. Then the young boys would screw around and act like
idiots. One of them fell off a beam one night, broke his neck, and
died. After that, they hung his picture in the hall, and we bowed to
him, too, every day when we began our training.

The other difference between my life in Japan and my life in
prison is that in prison you always know what's going to happen
next. In Japan, I had no idea where anything was going. I was just
training. I didn't know the plan. It was just one day to the next,
training hard without any idea of what I was training for.

Then, after several months of training, I was told to prepare for
my first fight. It was scheduled for December 18, 1994. I didn't know
who I was going to fight, but I was told to get ready. We traveled
to Tokyo. A little while before the fight they told me I was going to
go up against a Dutch guy named Bas Rutten. This was insane. Bas
Rutten was one of the top fighters in the world at that time. He was
a veteran, six or seven years older than me. He was also a lot bigger
than me—six foot one and about 205 pounds to my slimmed-down
five foot ten and 185 pounds. I had basically no chance of beating
him. Bas was favored to win the whole tournament. It was my first
fight! I was just the appetizer portion. I was sure I was going to get
killed.

It was supposed to be a ten-minute match. I was wearing black.
He was wearing red. I had hair. He was bald. My brother Ken had
come in from Lodi, to fight and to watch me fight. Funaki was there,
along with all the other Pancrase guys. This was a tournament fight

to crown the first Pancrase champion and bring some credibility to the year-old league. I was making my big debut.

We came out to the ring. I was completely scared. I could feel the lights in the building like electricity running through me. Then the referee shouted, "Fight!" The bell rang. The crowd started screaming, mostly in Japanese, except for some American who kept yelling, "Punch his head!"

I felt his strength, right away—this superhuman, experienced strength. He was very muscular and wiry, and his muscles were incredibly dense. Mine aren't like that. When I get big, I get these full, perfect muscles, which are very good for fast reactions and fast recovery. They're very elastic, so I don't get many injuries. But they're not that strong. They don't have that density and that super strength. Bas's strength, compared to mine, was enormous. When I hit him I felt how strong his body was. So I knew he was going to hurt me. I knew he was going to win. I was afraid it was going to be serious—I was afraid I was actually going to *die*. He seemed really dangerous to me. Then he hit me really hard five or six times and I was sure of it.

Because of that, I fought like a crazy person. I had nothing to lose. I didn't pace myself. I threw everything I had, just to try to keep him from murdering me. But first he had to mess me up some. Right at the start of the fight, he got me with a front kick to the face and broke my nose. He got me right on the tip of it with his shoe and snapped the cartilage.

My plan had been to get him on the ground. I tried really hard to do that, but once I got him down, it didn't work right away. He threw a front choke on me and said, "Aha! I've got you!" But I could feel myself slipping out of the choke before he was finished saying it. I snapped free and we grappled. A minute or so later, I got him in a headlock. He started saying, over and over again, in his heavy Dutch accent, "That will not work. I am so strong."

He wasn't actually talking to me; he was talking to himself. He was trying to pump himself up. I thought, "OK, this guy's crazy." That made me fight harder—not better, but harder. I kept taking him down, and taking the better position. The next few minutes happened like *that*. They rang the bell again and suddenly it was over.

I went to my corner. Ken said, "OK. You did good." *Good?* I was just happy he hadn't killed me. I said, "He broke my nose!"

Then the decision came down. I had won.

It was a huge upset. I wasn't supposed to win. I was just the bag boy. I was the guy who carried everyone's equipment, or the warm-up you beat on while you got ready for your *real* fight. People knew I was Ken's brother, but other than that I was relatively unknown. It was a huge victory.

In those days, everyone on the card was scheduled for several fights. My second one was with a guy named Manabu Yamada. It was supposed to be a twenty-minute match, but it was over in about eight. He got me with a leg lock and finished me. Then he went into the finals and fought against Ken and lost. Ken was named first champion of Pancrase.

It didn't matter to me that I didn't win my second match. I was on the map. I had fought my first fight, and I had won. I became an instant superstar in Japan.

We all went out that night to the Roppongi section of Tokyo— Bas and me and all the other fighters—and drank like fish. We went all night long. That was the tradition. In Japan, after a fight, you drink. The moment the training is over, you celebrate. I had been doing nothing but training for months and months—no drinking, no smoking, nothing but hard training. Now the event sponsor took us all out for an evening on the town. We sang karaoke and drank gallons of whiskey.

I became friends with Bas that night. I would make a lot of friends that way, bonding after a fight. That's a human tradition. Whenever two people share a stressful event, it brings them together. It gives them something relevant to share.

I was just blown away. The whole experience was huge for me. Training in Japan, fighting in Japan, winning my first fight were all huge. Just *being* in Japan would have been the biggest thing that had ever happened to me. I was a small-town kid. I'd never been anywhere in my whole life. Travel, to me, meant getting into trouble and going to a new group home. Taking a trip meant being in handcuffs, riding on a bus, going from one jail to another. So this was gigantic.

I was on top of the world. I was blown away for weeks by the experience. I got my paycheck, and I went home with $1,800 in my pocket. To me, that was a fortune. I was rich! But when I got back to the United States in December, I learned the IRS had put a lien on my wages. I owed $4,000 in back child support, so I had to work out a payment plan for that debt. I didn't get all the money. But I was now a professional fighter.

7

PANCRASE AND THE
ROOTS OF MMA

After my first victory in Tokyo, I was placed on the Pancrase circuit. The fighters were all scheduled to fight every six to eight weeks. Fighting became my life. I'd stay in Lodi, living at Ken's house, training at the Lion's Den. Then I'd go back to the dojo in Tokyo, work out for two or three days to break the horrible jetlag, and prepare to fight. Afterward, I'd come back to Lodi. After a few months, I moved out of Ken's house and moved in with another fighter, Jason DeLucia.

It was a good time. I felt like I had arrived. I was part of something: working with Ken, training at the Lion's Den, beginning to train other fighters there, too.

Bob Shamrock was proud of me. He asked me if, like Ken, I wanted to become his adopted son. I was humbled and flattered by that and I said yes. We did the paperwork and I officially changed my name from Frank Juarez to Frank Shamrock. I got a new birth certificate that lists Robert Conrad Shamrock as my father. The line that reads MOTHER is blank.

The Pancrase people gave me a contract. Each month, they'd put $5,000 in my new bank account. I got a credit card. This was the first time I'd had anything like that. I bought a car. I started to realize this was how people actually lived. This was what people *do*. I had been mowing lawns and doing odd jobs and stealing things since I was nine years old. But this was the first time I actually had money in my pocket and money in the bank. I began to think this could be an actual job for me, a career.

But there were parts of the job I really didn't like. Weird as it is to say it, the thought of hurting other people as part of my job seemed bad to me. For the first ten fights or so, I mostly worried that I was going to get killed. But after that I mostly worried that I was going to kill someone else. I was really afraid I was going to hurt someone. I think it was because I had come from a home of physical abuse, and I viewed anything physical toward another person as violence. Maybe I was afraid of that kind of power. Anyway, in some fights, I could feel myself pulling back.

In the Pancrase organization, I was among real martial artists. It was an art and a sport. There were a lot of official rules, but also a lot of things you just didn't do. You could legally hit a guy when he was on the ground, but you didn't. It was not cool.

Maybe because the sport was so small, I knew everyone I was ever going to fight. If I fought a guy tonight, I was going to fight him again in six weeks. So we all followed these unspoken rules. We beat the shit out of each other, but we didn't want to *injure* each other. There was more honor and respect in it than that.

We fought all over Japan. The touring circuit took us everywhere from Kobe to Sapporo. We mostly fought in ten-thousand-seat arenas. Some venues were as small as two thousand seats. Some were as large as fifteen thousand. We played Korakuen Hall in Tokyo because that's where all the wrestling and boxing events in Tokyo are held. We played NK Hall, near Tokyo Disneyland. After an earthquake in Kobe, the whole city had toppled over except for this brand-new shopping mall. So we came down the escalators and held our fights right in the mall.

We were treated like royalty, like rock stars. We were modern samurai. I was a big celebrity—over there. At home, I spent all my time training hard in a sport that no one knew and no one really wanted to see. But I'd go back to Japan, and we were big and everyone knew us. They respected us. Everyone knew that pro wrestling was fake. We were something new, this new kind of hybrid fighters, and we were famous.

I missed a lot because I didn't speak Japanese and I didn't really get all the cultural cues. Girls would come up to me, after fights or in the street, and give me their business cards. I thought that was a little weird. Then a friend of mind looked at the card and said, "This isn't a business card. It's a *personal* card. That means she wants to spent personal time with you." After that, I was a young man on a mission to meet as many women as possible. I had always been the goofy, out-of-place kid who never knew anyone at the party. Now I was the star. I really enjoyed it. Being with American girls I had felt all these layers of weirdness and guilt and shame. That wasn't the case with the Japanese girls I met. They were eager to come over and take care of me and cook me noodles and sleep on the floor while I slept in the bed. They viewed their role in the relationship very differently than American girls. They'd buy me things. I had a whole bunch of Japanese women fans who bought me gifts—T-shirts and underwear and all kinds of weird stuff.

Back in Lodi, life wasn't that colorful. I was training hard and beginning to train other guys. I always read a lot. I became obsessed with *The Book of Five Rings*, which is an ancient Japanese book about martial arts. It is basically a textbook on how to live the simple samurai life. The writer was a Japanese samurai warrior from the 1600s, and the book has lessons about how to live, how to train, how to fight, and how to win.

But I was also reading books about serial killers. I got kind of obsessed about those—the more vicious, the better. I'm not sure what that was about. On some level, maybe it made me feel better about what I was doing. I still hadn't dealt with the whole business of hurting people for a living. It was hurting me, to be hurting people. So the books made me feel like less of a monster. I mean, at least I wasn't cutting people into pieces, filleting their faces, or hanging them off a fence.

Meanwhile, I was learning how to live. That was my real education. I'd read these books and exhaust my body and learn from my own mistakes. I'd train all day, go out and drink all night, and then get my butt kicked bad the next day. Lesson: I better not drink all night if I don't want to get my butt kicked. That was my whole education: screw up, get hurt, learn a lesson, do something different the next time.

My second fight was a Pancrase event in Nagoya, Japan. It was only about a month after my first fight. I fought Katsuomi Inagaki and won with a submission hold after six minutes. Two months later, I fought again, in Yokohama, against Masakatsu Funaki. I lost. Funaki was the big cheese in our dojo. He was like the Ken Shamrock of Japan—an older guy, very tough, very respected. He was the guy who had trained Ken. He was a cofounder of Pancrase. He was the first man who gave me some idea of the spiritual aspect of martial arts. So it was to be expected that he beat me.

But a month after that I fought again, in Nagoya, against Minoru Suzuki. I beat him. He was another cofounder of Pancrase. He had been named second king of Pancrase, which was the equivalent of champion. (Ken was the first king, and Suzuki had beaten Ken and taken the crown a year before this. A month after I beat Suzuki, he beat Ken again.) It was a huge victory.

I fought six more times that year—eleven fights in one calendar year! One of them was a rematch with Bas Rutten. A few things had changed since our first fight. I had gotten a little complacent about training. You see that happen with fighters. After they win a few fights, they want to train a bit less. In my case, I had met a really pretty girl. I started seeing her regularly whenever I was in Japan for a fight.

In the beginning, I was very serious about training. I wouldn't do anything before a fight. But after a while it got to where I'd even go over to Japan a little early—not for extra training, but so I could start partying with my girlfriend in Japan. I had always smoked pot but I started smoking hash a lot in those days, mainly because it was the only hard drug that you could buy in the Japanese subways. And I was drinking quite a bit. I remember thinking one night, "Hey, you gotta fight tomorrow!" I had another glass of wine and said, "Ah, you'll be fine."

The second fight with Bas was in Tokyo, about six months after I beat him. I felt pretty comfortable going in. I was a superstar! But I realized after about five minutes that I was in trouble. My strategy was to get him down—Bas is from Holland, and those guys are all really good strikers—and finish him on the ground. But he was even stronger than I remembered him being, and he had much better conditioning. I was getting tired, and I could see he wasn't. I realized I didn't have the gas to finish the fight. I knew he was going to kick my ass unless I figured out a strategy to win.

The takedown strategy didn't work. He anticipated it, and I hadn't really developed my takedown skills yet. I attempted something, and he saw it coming, and we literally *flew* out of the ring, between the ropes and into the first row.

I whacked my head. I was dazed. There was no way I was going to be able to beat him. So I went to Plan B. I would get him mad and make him hit me in the face.

You get points against you in Pancrase for various things. I had one against me for getting knocked down early in the fight. I figured if I could get Bas mad at me and get him to lose his temper, he'd forget himself and make a fist and punch me with it. Then he'd lose a point for hitting me in the face. I knew I could survive that; there wasn't much time left. It was a fifteen-minute fight. I knew I could take whatever he could dish out for the last few minutes.

As soon as he got me into the next hold, I started making these clown faces at him. I stuck my tongue out at him. I called him names. And it worked. He went insane. He's a very emotional fighter to start with. He has a problem with his temper. At that time he always had a big *R* written on his hand before the fight. The *R* was for *relax*, because he'd get all tense and angry and use his energy the wrong way. That's why I knew I could make fun of him and get him to lose his temper. I had asked him about the *R*, so I knew.

He lost his temper, and he started bashing me in the face with his palm, totally legal. He hit me a bunch of times. It was a bad strategy, but it worked and he got pissed and closed his punch. I used my face as a battering ram against his fist and he got a warning and lost a point for the illegal strike. We got to the cards. It was a split decision. He got the point for the knockdown. I got the points for him hitting me in the face.

A smarter fighter would have said, "Dude, you can't use your face like that." Other people got what I was doing, but they thought it just wasn't cool to make fun of someone. But I had to do something. I knew I couldn't beat him down. I wasn't going to just let him beat *me* down. So I found some psychology and made a little tweak.

I learned the same lesson about conditioning when I was fighting Allan Goes, a Brazilian fighter. We didn't know anything about

Brazilian fighters except they had some sort of grappling style. Because we were Pancrase and we were fighting and training in the Japanese tradition, we didn't worry much about anyone from outside the system. Any time you were scheduled to fight someone who wasn't Japanese, you figured it was going to be an easy month. You didn't train that hard.

It was Allan's first professional fight in a ring, but he had fought in a lot of street fights and challenge matches in Brazil—fights where you show up to another school and duke it out with the top guy. I was hanging out, I was goofing around. I was screwing up in every way possible. I thought I had nothing to worry about.

When the match started, Goes threw me on the ground and kicked the shit out of me. It was going to be a little harder than I had thought. I managed to get away from him and we grappled. When he was on my back he fishhooked my eyeball—which was really illegal, but the referee couldn't see it. He used that to put me in a rear naked choke. It was scary and not at all part of my plan for the fight. Somehow, before I went to sleep, I got to the rope and escaped. We started in again. I got him in a leg hold. I thought he'd quit, but he didn't. So I pressed it. I turned his ankle. I could feel all the tendons rip. The pain must have been unbearable. But he broke free somehow and got to the rope.

It turned out I had broken his leg. The fight went to the cards and ended in a draw.

My record was OK, but I wasn't learning the lessons I should have been learning. I fought Bas again a third time and lost about ten minutes into the fight. I got really tired. I had tried to get him on the ground, and failed. My only skill set in those days was on the ground, and he figured out ways to stop me from getting him down. I was getting desperate, so I tried a shoot to his knee. Somehow I got my forehead involved, and I hit his knee really hard with my eyebrow. It opened up a cut and the fight was ruled a TKO. It was a fluke, but honestly I was pretty tired, and I wasn't going to make it. He beat on me pretty bad in that fight, and I would have had a hard time beating him.

I had an easier time with a few other fights. I had a second match against Funaki, the master of Pancrase. I got him into the same hold he had beaten me with, a toehold, about ten minutes into the fight. I got a win by submission. There was no way, though, that I beat him. I couldn't have comprehended that at the time. I was fighting my ass off. I was fighting for my life. But I didn't really know much about fighting. I did not understand that someone else's skill level could be so high that they could let me win without me knowing it. Later, when my skill level was as high as that, I knew something fishy had happened. I think Funaki let me get him into that hold and let me beat him.

Pancrase was still new. The founders knew they had to have more drama. They had to bring up the young fighters, and they had to have compelling matches. They knew it was important for young Frank to win a fight or two and be seen as a challenge to the old men. I think it's possible that Suzuki put me over, too. I beat him twice, once on strikes and once on a knee bar. I was named king of Pancrase after the second one. But maybe he let me win.

I had already declared that I would beat everybody. My first interview with a sports reporter was around that time, in 1995. I told him I was going to be king of Pancrase, just like Ken had been. He asked me about the no-holds-barred (NHB) fighting (the original name for MMA and UFC) that was just starting to take place. I said there was *no way* I was going to do any of that stuff. It was way too violent and way too crazy and way too dangerous for me.

I went on to fight other fights with Pancrase, all over Japan. I beat Takafumi Ito, Ryushi Yanagisawa, and Osami Shibuya—all guys I had trained with at the Yokohama dojo.

The Shibuya fight had one weird element to it. He was the latest big thing at the time in Japan. He was experimenting with steroids,

I think. He had muscles growing out of his ears. I knew he didn't really know how to fight, but he was incredibly strong. I had moved into this lazy, partying stage of my Japanese experience. I had fought six or eight fights. I was doing well. So I was screwing around. I wasn't training so hard. I wasn't preparing so well. I went into the fight with Shibuya really dehydrated. The fight went on longer than I expected and the dehydration caught up with me. I was dry. I couldn't swallow. I felt like I was dying of thirst. All I could think about was getting something to drink. I was getting tired, grappling with this big steroid-pumped guy. I couldn't finish him.

Then I suddenly saw that he was wet. He was all sweaty. We were down on the floor and I was hanging onto him for dear life. There were these big golden drops of sweat on his neck, these glorious big drops of water. So I just licked them off his skin. I sucked those drops down. It worked. I got the hydration I needed. Three minutes later I got him into a shoulder lock and won the fight. I don't think he ever knew what I did. I didn't tell him. It seemed like the kind of thing you should keep to yourself. But I figure, where there's a will, there's a way. That's how you can tell if a guy *really* wants to win a fight. Will he do anything? Lick the sweat off some guy's neck?

I fought some other guys, too. I beat an American fighter, Vernon White, who was recruited into Pancrase by Ken a couple of years before me and who went on to have a long career. He was the first person I fought who was also a training partner. Then I threw my forehead into Bas Rutten's kneecap and lost the king of Pancrase title.

Things back home were weird. Ken had lost his king of Pancrase title to Suzuki a couple of years earlier. He was becoming disenchanted with the Pancrase organization. They wanted him to "lose" his title to another fighter so that if he lost in the UFC it wouldn't make Pancrase look like the weaker league. He had fought in a few

Ultimate Fighting Championships, going back to 1993 and the first-ever UFC events. The Brazilian Royce Gracie beat him by submission in less than a minute in their first fight, setting up a Gracie-Shamrock rivalry that continues to this day. By 1996, he had stopped fighting for Pancrase altogether. A little while later he signed a contact with World Wrestling Entertainment.

But a lot of his Lion's Den fighters were still Pancrase guys, and someone had to train them. This increasingly became my responsibility. The master plan seemed to be that Ken would go do his thing and I would stay home and take care of the business. I was a good teacher, but I didn't really know what I was doing yet. The sport was evolving. We had all these guys who had been good at one discipline—who were good boxers or good wrestlers—and were now trying to become mixed martial artists. No one had taught me how to do that or how to teach that. I only knew what ten fights and a lot of mistakes had taught me. But I was personable, and I could sign people up for classes, and I took the job seriously. The Lion's Den was successful. We had a strong fighting camp, with some amazing guys fighting with us—Jerry Bohlander, Guy Mezger, Tre Telligman, Jason DeLucia, Mickey Burnett. Those were some very tough young guys.

I wasn't teaching them the way Ken had. I didn't have my thumb on them. His system was: if you were breaking the rules, or not respecting the system, he'd bring you in, tell you what you had done wrong, and then make you get in the ring with him. Then he'd beat the shit out of you. You trained hard out of fear, out of the knowledge that he would beat the shit out of you if you missed a training session or showed up late.

I was a little subtler. If a guy was screwing up, I'd get him in the ring and wrestle with him and tire him out and make him keep going until he puked, and then make him go some more. If a guy showed up late, I'd say, "Hey, you're ten minutes late." Then I'd let him warm up and get him into the ring. Thirty minutes later, when he's vomiting and bleeding and about to pass out, I'd say, "Take a break. And by the way, we are *never* late to class."

After a while, I stopped doing even that with most of the guys. They were professional fighters. This was what they were doing for a living. They were adults. My attitude was, you're a pro. I'll help you, and good luck to you, but I'm not going to keep my foot on your neck.

I was a little distracted. I had met a woman, and we had gotten pretty serious. Her name was Angelina Brown. We met in Hawaii, when I was there working as the trainer for some of Ken's Lion's Den team. We were in Waikiki because some of the guys were fighting in a Super Brawl match. I went to work out in a Gold's Gym while the fighters were cutting weight, and that's where we met.

She was super athletic and really good-looking. She had just graduated from UCLA with a degree in marketing and had gone to Hawaii to work with T. Jay Thompson, the promoter of the Super Brawl fights.

I was already seeing someone else, a former Miss Teenage Hawaii named Angel. She had been my sort of unofficial Hawaiian girlfriend; I saw her whenever I was over there. But I met Angelina and that changed. Angel was out. Angelina was in.

In January 1997 I was scheduled to fight John Lober. I had trained a bunch of guys for Super Brawl fights, but now I was getting my shot. Ken or Bob, with their Super Brawl relationships, had arranged the fight. I didn't have a lot of time to think about it or prepare for it. It just sort of came up. I had seen Lober fight a few times. He was known as John "the Machine" Lober because he had a reputation for being able to take a tremendous beating and just keep plowing forward like some kind of robot. He could just keep going. But he didn't scare me. I figured that with my submission holds I could annihilate him. I'd get him down, get him in a hold, and he wouldn't get up. I saw the whole thing play out in my mind. I trained medium hard. I wasn't worried. I was on the beer and oatmeal diet, which meant I was drinking more and eating more than usual. I got really big and puffy looking, but it made me sort of slow and sloppy. I weighed two hundred pounds, but physically I wasn't ready. Mentally, I was OK but not great. I had lost my last two Pancrase fights, to Yuki Kondo and Kiuma Koniuka. That part of my life seemed to be ending. I didn't see any future in Pancrase anymore—the company treated me differently after Ken left for the UFC. But my relationship with Angelina was going strong. She liked the fighter's life, or at least she liked being the fighter's girlfriend. She seemed really into it. She liked being in the limelight, or at least near it.

The Lober fight was held in Honolulu. It was a straight-time fight, one round, thirty minutes, no holds barred—very different from what I'd been doing. For one thing, there was more striking and boxing. There was no rule about closed-fist hitting to the face. I hadn't had too much experience with that kind of fighting. I didn't think it would be any big deal, though. I'd been hit in the face before. I'd been kicked in the face. I'd had my nose broken a couple of times.

John was a stocky white guy with a shaved head and a goatee, with "Machine" tattooed on his stomach. He had just come off a draw against Igor Zinoviev, who was very tough. I should have been more scared than I was. But I had confidence. I came out strong. For the first three minutes, I kicked his ass. I had him on the ground in the first ten seconds, and I held him there a long time. I had him pinned, and he was struggling, and I was head-butting him hard. I landed a heel to his face that must have hurt.

Then I got tired. My plan wasn't working. It was taking too long to work. I had him in a submission hold, and he was supposed to give up, but he didn't give up. I realized he was not a sportsman.

This wasn't Pancrase. I was going to have to do something serious, like break his arm or leg. So I did. I broke his ankle. I hit him so hard that I knocked out two of his teeth. But it hardly even slowed him down. He wasn't going to give up. His tooth was literally on the mat, and at one point he took out his mouthpiece, threw the other tooth into the crowd, and went back to fighting! He must have been on drugs. It was insane for him to keep going.

After three minutes of totally dominating him, I was so tired I couldn't get my hands up. He started beating on me, and he kept beating on me for the next twenty-seven minutes. He hit me with a left jab that knocked me down, and then he hit me hard with his right a bunch of times. He knocked me down again with a left. He used my head like a punching bag.

We went the whole distance. Then the judges conferred. When they were done talking it over, I had lost by a split decision. Two of the judges were jujitsu guys, and they'd called it for Lober. I wasn't all that surprised. I was disappointed, but I was *already* disappointed by the way I'd fought. I had wanted to finish him, and I thought I was going to. The judges weren't wrong. If I'd been judging the fight, I'd have gone that way, too.

Lober was smiling, even though his front teeth were gone.

Angelina didn't seem upset that I was all beat up and my face was all mushy. But I was. I felt humiliated and embarrassed. Plus there was the money. I had been on salary with the Pancrase organization, so a victory didn't mean getting paid more. But this was different now that I was a prizefighter. I got $10,000 for fighting, but I would have gotten another $10,000 for winning. At that time in my life, $10,000 was a lot of money.

I wasn't injured. I was drained, emotionally and physically, but I wasn't actually damaged. The part that hurt the most was my pride.

We were staying in downtown Honolulu. I couldn't sleep and was up early the next morning. I put on some clothes and left the hotel. I walked across Waikiki, and then hiked as far as I could up Diamond Head—which wasn't very far because I was so beat up. I had a jug of water and a cell phone. I decided to sit down and think things over. I ended up sitting there for a couple of hours.

I turned the fight over in my mind. I thought about why I'd lost. I realized that I should have won. I *could* have won. Several times I'd been in a position to break Lober's arm, or break his leg, and I hadn't done it. I hadn't been willing to injure him. I had wanted to fight him, and I wanted to beat him, but when it came right down to it, I hadn't been willing to actually *hurt* him. I realized I had a problem. I had a lot of guilt and fear about hurting people. In sports, as a kid, I hadn't wanted to hurt anyone. I was always worried about it. I think it may be because I had been hurt a lot myself. It also came from my fear of what would happen if I hurt someone—my fear of Joe's anger, of what Joe would do to me if I hurt someone and caused trouble, or if I fought back and hurt him.

I understood that was why I had lost the fight. It was a revelation, an awakening. I hadn't been emotionally ready, and I'd let myself be beaten. I felt completely devastated: emotionally, physically, and financially. And I saw that it was completely unnecessary. I could have won. I didn't have to lose. I just had to change my mind about what I was doing.

I came down off Diamond Head a different person. I made a decision that, in the future, I was going to approach fighting in a different way. When I fought again, I would understand that the other guy was agreeing to fight me. He was offering to fight me, and participating in fighting me. I wasn't taking advantage of him. We had agreed to play a game, and there was going to be a winner and a loser. There were rules, and we were going to play by the rules. If someone got hurt, it wouldn't be my fault, it was part of the agreement. Coming off the mountain, I knew. I had that moment, and very few people ever have that moment, when I absolutely *knew.*

This is what I'm going to do with my life, and if I die doing it, I will die doing it.

I accepted it totally, and it was incredibly exciting. I came down the hill ready to roll. You could have sparked lightbulbs off my fingertips. If sawing off my arm had been the solution to fighting and winning, I would have sawed my arm off and come out with a nub, ready to roll. I was that committed.

I went back to the hotel. To this day, I've never been back to Diamond Head. I've never needed to go back. I had my moment, and I understood.

That was the true beginning of my life as a fighter.

8

GOING SOLO

Almost nine months passed before I fought again. The loss to John Lober had created some drama and some problems. Ken had been in my corner for that fight. He had been a big supporter, and he thought I was going to destroy Lober. I think he was kind of disgusted with me that I lost so badly.

He saw that I was screwing around in training and in leading the team. Ken was off doing WWE and pro wrestling at that point. He wasn't happy about what was going on back home with the Lion's Den. I thought I was doing everything for the team, and the gym. But I believed what we were doing in the gym and in our training was not the best way. We were working with old ideas, on an old model, but we were fighting in a new sport. I felt we needed a new approach. I voiced my concern about this. I was very vocal, and I kept on talking about it, saying what I believed. I kept telling the guys, "Look, we've got to change. There's a better way to do this." I tried to tell Ken, but no one tells Ken anything! Ken wasn't interested in my ideas about change. He wanted me to run his gym and train his fighters his way.

We were invited to participate in a thing called Rings Extension Fighting, which was a kind of Japanese hybrid fighting. I took over the training of some of the guys from the Lion's Den. They were all really out of shape. *I* was out of shape. I started to have some ideas about conditioning. I felt we should be doing more in that area. Maurice Smith went to Tokyo to fight a guy named Tsuyoshi Kohsaka. Maurice did pretty well, too, but Kohsaka seemed to be carrying him the whole way, and Kohsaka won. Pete Williams fought a fighter named Joop Kasteel and beat him but it was not a spectacular fight.

Kohsaka was the up-and-coming star in Rings, and I was looking for a fight for me, so I contacted the organization. They set me up with Kohsaka for September 1997. We fought in Tokyo. It was a thirty-minute fight, one round, no breaks. I didn't fight all that well and I got tired. But I won by decision.

Ken became much more vocal in his criticism. He was pissed off that we hadn't done better with the Rings fights. I was starting to feel weird about my position in the family. I was working hard. I was doing my job. But he was riding me all the time.

I had another fight scheduled, in Texas, against an American fighter named Wes Gassaway. I had taken some time off after the Kohsaka fight. That one had taken a lot out of me, and I hadn't trained very hard. Wes was a weight class above me, but he had no submission ability at all. I knew I could get him down and submit him without any real difficulty. But I found myself getting really tired after about two minutes. Gassaway was super-strong, much stronger than I expected. He hit me a couple of times in the head, and it really rang my bell. I got hot. I felt dehydrated. Partly that was Texas, and partly it was my lack of preparation. But I remember trying to hit him and feeling exhausted. I won the fight, but it was ugly. I came back home depleted. I remember Guy Mezger saying, "Maybe you should take a break or something." He could see I was worn out.

Ken finally snapped. He came in one day while I was training at the gym, running one of my classes. He just burst in, and in front of the students said, "I need to talk to you, *now.*" Then he started yelling at me, calling me a crappy trainer, saying my guys should have won their Rings matches. He was angry at me for fighting, too, in addition to training. He told me, "You don't have what it takes. You're not going to be a world champion. You are never going to be a champion. You need to quit lying to yourself and stick with what you are good at, teaching people and running my gym."

That was devastating to me. Ken and I were not close. We never really had a brotherly relationship. But he was my mentor. He had been my trainer. He was my employer. He and I were connected by Bob, our adopted father. We were supposed to be some sort of family. But now I realized that he either didn't believe in me or he was afraid of me. He didn't want me to be who I thought I could be. Plus he was really angry. When I tried to talk to him, he got even angrier. He grabbed a computer and threw it at me. Then he screamed at me for the next ten minutes.

It was time to go. I couldn't keep working for him.

I was still living in Lodi, in an apartment I was sharing with Jason DeLucia. I was doing OK financially. I had been making good money. My Pancrase salary was $5,000 a month. I had almost no overhead. I was driving a car I'd bought from Ken, a 1990 convertible Camaro that I'd painted purple. But the money was just disappearing. I was training all the time, and eating every meal in a restaurant. I never thought about the cost of anything. In Lodi, we lived in our little apartment and trained. In Japan, we lived like rock stars. We'd fight, and we'd go party, and everything cost a fortune. A beer was ten bucks! And we drank a lot of beer. So even though I was making a lot of money, I was always broke. By the twentieth of the month, I'd be down to seventy-eight dollars again. Every month.

I wasn't sure what kind of future I would have without Ken and the Lion's Den. I figured I'd better talk it over with my dad.

Bob Shamrock was living at a house in Lockford, about twenty miles from Lodi. His big group home in Susanville had been closed down. He had a smaller group home now, with only five or six boys in it. It was a little house on a suburban street, in the middle of grape country.

Ken had a ranch up the road, three or four miles away. It was a giant spread, five or six acres, with a swimming pool. He lived there with his wife and sons, and he had a second house on the property where his in-laws lived. He was doing very well financially. He had money coming in from the Japan contracts. He had his own money from the wrestling and fighting he was doing. He was making a little money from the gym. He was having some good paydays.

It was the afternoon training time. I knew Bob would be at home, and he'd probably be alone. So I drove out there. I told him what had happened with Ken, about him freaking out and throwing the computer at me. I told him this had happened in front of his students, while I was teaching his system and philosophy. I did not agree with demeaning and embarrassing people in front of others. How could I follow this person who treated me this way and speak on his behalf? How could I represent these ideals?

Bob didn't seem that worried about it. He said, "I'm sure it will be fine. Everything will work itself out." I didn't think so. I told him I didn't think I could continue working with Ken. I told him I had a vision about the sport, that I was going to be the best in the world, and I thought that I had to go off on my own and pursue it.

Bob didn't see it. He told me he loved me, but he didn't share my vision. "I don't think you're a fighter—not a cage fighter," he said. "You're an athlete and a sports guy. But you're not a fighter. You don't have the killer instinct. You will never do as well as Ken."

He thought I should stay with the Lion's Den, patch things up with Ken, and just go on. I didn't want to hear it. In my heart, I knew he was partly right. I *didn't* have the killer instinct, not yet. But I thought he was wrong. I told him I was going to get my stuff and pack it up and go. "OK," he said, "But I worry about you." He gave me a big hug, and squeezed my arm, and said good-bye to me.

Maybe he didn't think I was really going. Maybe *I* didn't think I was really going. On some level, I couldn't see leaving Ken and the Lion's Den. It was all I knew, other than prisons and jails. It was my home, and my family, and my income. It was everything to me. But I thought maybe I could just train on my own and not have to listen to Ken and all his madness.

I found out right away that was not going to be possible. I wasn't going to the Lion's Den, but I tried to stay in touch with the guys. I didn't want to let anyone down. I knew they had fights, and I had been training them. So I called a couple of guys and asked them how they were doing and if they needed any help. They were kind of cryptic and strange with me. I got a weird vibe. I called another couple of guys and got the same vibe. I called another guy, and asked, "What's going on?" "I can't train with you anymore," he said. I called another guy back and got the same thing. Ken had told them not to work with me anymore.

So I called Bob. I told him Ken was shutting me out. I asked him what was going on. "It's different now," he said. "You chose to leave. You left the family. If you're not with the family, then technically you are not part of the family." So it was over. My adopted father and my adopted brother were finished with me. I was on my own.

I loaded up my Camaro with my clothes and my blue boxing gloves and I went to Los Altos, a little town outside of San Jose, where my girlfriend, Angie, was living. She had a house there in the Los Altos hills. Her parents had moved out and were living in Santa Cruz, so we moved in.

The only guy associated with the Lion's Den who would take my calls was Maurice Smith. He had been a champion kickboxer when he came to the Lion's Den. He was going to train with Ken. They became friends. He was going to teach Ken striking, and Ken was going to teach him grappling. But when it came time for that, Ken was busy, so he had me train Maurice in grappling styles.

Over the next year or so, we became friends—good enough friends that when I left Bob and Ken, and no one was allowed to talk to me or train with me or work with me, Maurice defied them and said he would support me. He came on board as my coach.

I was pretty educated about bodybuilding, and I had learned a lot about certain kinds of wrestling and grappling and fighting—mostly by trial and error. I knew nothing, basically, about conditioning. But I knew that I got tired in fights. I knew that managing my energy and managing my fatigue was a huge part of what happened in fights. I'd find myself thinking, in the middle of a fight, that I could do a certain move or try a certain strategy, but that it was going to take a huge amount of energy, and if it didn't work I'd be screwed. I knew there was a point in almost every fight, at something like six minutes, when I would start thinking, "We gotta wrap this up *fast*."

Maurice was light-years ahead of everyone else in this area. He was a great fighter himself, and would later be UFC and IFC heavyweight champion—belts that I would help train him to win. He knew what fighting was all about. He had been working with sports doctors. He had a lot of information about vascular training and building up his system. So he started me doing that. We started doing treadmills. We started doing interval training. This was all new in 1997. No one was doing this. All we knew about conditioning was "go run two miles."

We experienced almost immediate results. Within a few weeks, I found that I could wrestle for two hours and not get tired—*never* get tired. This was revolutionary. Almost everyone who was fighting in the sport that became MMA was basically fighting in a judo style, jujitsu style, or Greco-Roman wrestling style. It was an anaerobic kind of fighting—a series of short, violent movements with rests in between. Something like boxing or kickboxing is the opposite. It's very aerobic. You never stop moving. You maintain a consistent heart rate the whole time.

With Maurice, I began to develop that kind of fighting system. I was building my cardiovascular system and creating a new, dynamic kind of fighting style to go with it. I had already developed all the holds from what I'd learned working with Ken and my teachers in Japan. Now Maurice was teaching me all the strikes. And I was bringing in this new kind of athletics and creating moves on the fly.

The fight with Enson Inoue in 1997 was the first fight in which I got to apply it. The fight came together quickly—too quickly. I got a call, and suddenly I was negotiating to fight in Japan in eighteen days. So I showed up at the American Kickboxing Academy in San Jose and told Javier Mendez I was going to fight Enson Inoue in Tokyo. In eighteen days. He shook his head and said, "This is not good." But he showed me some things. He taught me some stand-up techniques. I added those to what I'd been taught by Maurice, who by now had officially signed on. He became my trainer, my brother, and my main guy.

We rolled into Japan. It was the end of the year, and it was cold. We were fighting at NK Hall in Tokyo. The arena was set up like a rock show. They had these eight-foot-tall speakers. I came out on a platform that lifted me up like a rock star. I was wearing this little kimono that I'd bought in a tourist shop. And my sneakers. It was insane.

The fight was called VTJ-1997, for Vale Tudo Japan. Vale Tudo was a Brazilian style of fighting. The name means "anything goes," so it's a kind of no-holds-barred fighting that includes very few rules.

I knew Enson Inoue pretty well. I had seen all his fights. He was a Japanese American, born in Japan, who had already had a lot of success in Shooto and Vale Tudo fights. He was a black belt in jujitsu, and he was big—like 220 pounds big. And he was a killer. And this was a closed-fist striking fight. I hadn't really done that, and I was afraid of the unknown. I was pretty sure he was going to beat me to death.

I hadn't really gotten over my sense of fear about fighting. I had conquered my fear of hurting the other guy, but I was still going into my fights afraid that I was going to get hurt, or even killed. And I was really afraid of this guy. He had more than thirty pounds on me, and he seemed really big and strong. He seemed like Ken, who could smash me.

To create more tension, I had been contacted by the UFC about a week before the fight. They said they wanted to do something in Japan. They had created a new middleweight division. Enson and I were among the top guys in that weight class. So they decided that the winner of our fight would go on to fight Kevin Jackson for the Middleweight Champion of the World UFC belt. That fight would be less than a month after my fight with Enson. So that added a little more pressure.

The fight started hard. Enson came out and hit me and knocked me across the ring. I bounced off the ropes and we were on the floor in about the first ten seconds. We stayed down for half of the first round. I hit him pretty hard a couple of times. He didn't hurt me. He spent half the round on his back, waiting for me to do something. But he was so strong.

The second round went differently. He hit me hard and we both went down. It was brutal. It was just a knock-down, drag-out fight. He was kicking the shit out of me, and I couldn't really do a lot about it except hold on.

Enson kept glancing at his corner. It seemed like he didn't know what to do with me. Then there was an amazing moment, about four minutes into the second round, when suddenly, while sitting on my chest punching my face and the side of my head, he looked at me—right into my eyes like a best friend. We were trying to kill each other, but we both stopped at exactly the same moment to take a breath, and we looked at each other. Our corners were arguing. Maurice was making fun of Enson's corner. He was taunting them, like a child. Whatever they said, he repeated back at them. He was mocking them. They were shouting at him, "Don't say what we're saying," and he was saying, "Don't say what we're saying!" So we both smiled, and Enson started laughing.

Then he went back to trying to kill me. He was mounted on top of me, throwing elbows into my head, and then he was throwing fists into the side of my face. There was one very bad moment where he sort of folded me over when I tried to knee him from the standing clinch. I had my arms around his waist, and my head pushed up under his chin so I could knee his thighs. I guess my hips got too close to him and he was able to step behind my knee and bend me backward and end up sitting on my chest. Whatever he did, it killed my lower spine. It gave me a huge jolt and took all the power out of my body.

My spine had been messed up from way back. I was at the group home in South Lake Tahoe, playing a lot of basketball in high school, when my leg started tripping up, and I thought it was kind of weird, but I kept playing. Then my leg started going numb. They sent me to a doctor. He checked me out and said, "You broke your spine when you were little. You have scoliosis. You'll be in pain for the rest of your life. There's nothing to do about it except fuse some of the vertebrae." He told me I would lose a lot of flexibility, but I wouldn't be in much pain. He also said I had to avoid all contact sports. I freaked out about this news. I thought of myself as an athlete. No contact sports? I couldn't imagine being crippled for the rest of my life. I was just a kid!

So I went to see a chiropractor for a second opinion. He said, "You have a genetic problem, and you must have also fallen and hurt yourself. Now your back is curved in an *S* shape to absorb and distribute the impact of jumping. Your spine has a natural curve but not in that direction. But I can fix it for you." When I was a kid, I had gotten hurt a couple of times pretty badly. One time I fell off a roof. Another time I fell out of a tree and landed flat on my back. Joe had told me not to climb on that stuff, so I didn't tell anybody what happened. I just sucked it up.

The chiropractor worked on me and gave me some herbs and twisted my back and said, "You have to stand up for the next twenty-four hours." He said if I were to lie down and relax, my back would pull right back into that *S* position. The numbness went away immediately and the pain left over the next few days. I went back to see him once a week for months after. I never forgot the exercises that chiropractor showed me.

Now my back issues had come back to haunt me. There was a moment when I thought it was all over. Then the moment passed. I realized Enson wasn't going to kill me and that I could escape. I decided that actually *I* was going to kill *him*. Then I broke free and we were standing up, and it was rock-'em, sock-'em. It was just two guys murdering each other—especially him murdering me.

But something was happening. I wasn't tired, but Enson looked exhausted. I felt like I could go forever. And though he had hit me a lot, I realized he wasn't going to kill me. I realized he had thrown everything he had at me, and I wasn't going to die. I felt like I had gotten really close to death a couple of times, and it hadn't actually *hurt* me.

After that, things happened fast. He hit me a couple of times. I hit him a couple of times. We staggered around. I threw a knee. He got in an uppercut. Then at about seven minutes in, I exploded. I hit him really hard a couple of times with my right hand, and then again super-hard with my right knee. He went down. I went down on top of him.

And then suddenly the ring was full of people. Some one pushed me over from behind, and almost knocked me between the ropes. The announcers started screaming, "TKO!" Maurice was in there trying to keep Enson's guys off me. The fight was ultimately ruled a disqualification. Enson's brother Egan had rushed into the ring and tried to get at me.

In the post-fight interview I look really happy and comfortable. "I feel good," I said. "Enson was very strong and he got the mount, which was very dangerous. But I feel good. My striking was strong. He surprised me with his power, but I'm OK!" I don't speak Japanese, but if you watch the video for the film, Enson's comments have subtitles: "Woe for me, woe! Again the agony! Dread pain that sees the future all too well. Behold ye, yonder on the palace roof. The specter-children sitting—look such things as dreams are made on, phantoms as of babies . . . Horrible shadows, that a kinsman's hand hath marked with murder, and their arms are full, a rueful burden. See, they hold them up, the entrails upon which their father fed!"

Uh, yeah. I don't know what any of that means, but Enson looked completely destroyed. He sounded like he was crying. Later on, when I went to see him, he *was* crying.

Winning this fight qualified me for the next fight. The UFC invited me to the match with Kevin Jackson that would decide the middleweight champion of the world. The whole question of weight class was partly political. Mixed martial arts fighting was having a hard time getting on the map in America. We had been on the Time Warner cable channel for a while, but we had gotten kicked off. We weren't getting network support. Senator John McCain had turned the subject into a real soapbox for himself. One of the complaints he made about MMA was that it wasn't a real sport, like boxing or wrestling, because it didn't even have weight classes. So the UFC decided to create some weight classes. It was necessary in order to keep the sport moving forward.

I came home from the Enson fight to my new home with Angelina in Los Altos. She had found me a new wrestling coach, a guy named Eric Duus. He was the only guy in the world who could beat Kevin Jackson in a wrestling match. I did some more training with Javier Mendez. I trained with Maurice. I also began studying Bruce Lee's philosophies in Jeet Kune Do, in particular the idea of being like water.

I felt confident. I knew I was going to destroy Kevin, even though he was undefeated, and even though he had annihilated everyone he'd fought—including John Lober, who'd beaten me so badly. After beating Enson, whose strengths were stand-up and ground, I knew that my understanding of the game was better than his. My strengths were the ground game and conditioning, and I bested Enson in both. I felt involved in the sport in a new way. I had so much new confidence in my conditioning. I felt like everything had connected for the first time.

I studied Kevin's game. It was obvious that he was an incredible wrestler. He had won the freestyle Olympic gold medal in 1992! But I also saw that because he was such a good wrestler he would do the same thing, over and over again, in every fight. He was going to get you down, and beat you as a wrestler. He beat everyone because he was such a good wrestler. He understood wrestling better than anyone. And everyone tried to fight that. Their strategy was to out-wrestle him, to push back against him, but no one could do it and they all ended up in bad positions after they lost the wrestling game, positions that they could not escape from.

But I realized that he used the same tactic every time. He takes you down, and then he gets you into a control position. What I noticed was a moment: when he was doing that, finishing the takedown and getting the control position, his arms were straight. You could go for an arm bar if you timed it right. I watched the tapes of his fights over and over, and I saw that moment. I became convinced that I could do this, that I could catch him in an arm bar. I went to the next training session with Eric to practice this split-second submission hold and to test my new theory and concept of flowing like water. I wasn't going to fight the takedown, I was going to accept that I was going to lose that part of the game, and try to get to the arm bar position while he was finishing the takedown.

So I went over to the gym and told Javier what I was going to do. He kind of laughed and patted me on the back, telling me, "Don't focus too hard on one thing." So the next day, I had Eric come to the gym and asked Javier to watch us wrestle. He immediately changed his tune and was 100 percent on board from that moment on. It was his idea to come out in a southpaw stance to force Kevin to reach across his own body. Later on, I told the press, "I think wrestlers need a lesson in submission, and I am the man who's going to teach it to them."

I could see Kevin was extremely arrogant about the whole thing. I knew he was going to do what he always did, because he had total confidence in it. But I had confidence, too. Part of that came from the fact that I had so little experience. Everyone else came from boxing or wrestling. They had all kinds of ideas. They had to undo something they had learned, and depended upon, in order to learn something new. I didn't have that. If something didn't work in one fight, it was gone. I had nothing to undo. I took a scholastic approach. I learned that a fireman's carry equals a leg choke, so I got rid of it. It was simple and linear. Things that I learned went from theory to application to law really quickly.

Kevin was five foot ten and 199 pounds. I was five foot ten and 193 pounds. He was wearing these red-white-and-blue American flag trunks. I was wearing regular black shorts. He was undefeated, and a three-time UFC champion. I was making my UFC debut. On paper, I wouldn't have bet on me at all.

The bell rang. We came out of our corners. The referee said, "Get it on!" We danced around. We exchanged a couple of blows. Then he did exactly what I knew he was going to do. He faked a punch and shot at my waist and tried to take me down. Driving my back to the cage, he scooped my legs out from under me and when he did he left his arm straight. I swung my legs up and caught his arm. I began to turn my hips, and I arm barred him.

And his arm was like butter. It was like an old lady's arm. I didn't have to break it. I had a perfect, perfect hold, and he knew it, and the referee knew it. He tapped. He had to. His arm was popping pretty good. Once I got my hips up, he was done. But when I turned my hips over, it was dangerous. The weight of my hips and legs was on his elbow—the backside of his elbow.

The fight lasted sixteen seconds. Sixteen seconds! It was over! I jumped up and started running around the cage with my hands in the air. The guys from my corner jumped in and grabbed me. Someone picked me up. Maurice was screaming. The crowd went nuts. I ran across the ring and jumped onto the cage and pumped my fists in the air, first on one side of the hall and then on the other. It was surreal. It shouldn't have been that easy. He shouldn't have left his arm there. I couldn't really believe it.

Neither could Kevin. He left the ring. I never talked to him. He was the only man not to shake my hand after a fight, ever. I don't know what that was about. It didn't seem very Olympic-caliber to me. Maybe he was just embarrassed. He should have been. I had only been brought into the fight because I had sort of a big name in Japan. I wasn't supposed to *win*. I didn't have strong stand-up skills. He had destroyed John Lober and John Lober had destroyed me. I was being paid to let him give me a butt-whomping. But it didn't go that way. He lost. I won.

In fact, I earned a Guinness World Record for it, too. I have a certificate at home that says, "The fastest UFC title fight to be won by submission was sixteen seconds, achieved by Frank Shamrock (USA) at UFC Japan, Yokohama, Japan on 21 December 1997." That record still stands today. My other Guinness record doesn't. I held the Guinness honor for the fastest knockout in a championship fight for a twenty-two-second victory that came a little later in my career. That record held for almost ten years, when it was broken in 2007 by Andrei Arlovski's victory over Paul Buentello (fifteen seconds).

I stood there waiting for the referee to announce the verdict, bouncing around on my feet like I was still fighting. I was on fire. I couldn't stand still. The announcer said, "Middleweight Champion of the World, Frank Shamrock!" I did a lap around the cage, and bowed to all four sides of the area.

A Japanese woman came over and interviewed me. She said, "So quick!" I said, "Ah, I got lucky. I was prepared, and everything worked out right." She asked me how I liked fighting in Japan. I said, "I love fighting in Japan! I love the Japanese. I love the fighting spirit. And I was just glad I could pull it off tonight." She translated my answers, and the fans went wild some more. She said, "And now you are the middleweight champion?" And I said, "Yes! And I'm going to be that way for a long time!"

I was paid $25,000, plus I got the title. That was huge. And it was also terribly, terribly disappointing. It had happened so fast! He was such an athlete, and I had built up in my mind this amazing battle we were going to have. I'd had a huge design for the fight. Plan A was my secret weapon, which was the weakness I had found in his style. Plan B was the knock-down battle that I was going to win because I was smarter and tougher and in better condition.

I'd had so much energy, and so much intention. Losing the fight to John Lober had really changed who I was and how I thought about myself. It made me very focused on not letting anyone ever kick my ass again. And now the Jackson fight was over. I thought, *That's it?*

I went to dinner with some of the UFC bigwigs. I wanted to celebrate and do something crazy. But I didn't. I had stopped drinking after the Lober fight, and I'd been sober for a couple of years. I was off everything. I have a very addictive personality, so this left with me a lot of extra energy. I took my obsessive nature and put it into fighting. For two years, I'd been doing nothing but fighting. So I experienced a letdown. Angelina had come to Japan for the fight. She was always there for my fights. After the meeting with the UFC guys I just went back to her at the hotel room.

My disappointment about the Jackson fight lasted a while. I had been so focused on the battle, and I thought it was going to be huge. Every moment of my life seemed to be about preparing for this huge fight to the death. After Lober, I never ever wanted to lose again. My whole mind had readjusted to that new reality—that I would never lose again. But the fight shouldn't have been that easy.

So I scheduled another fight right away. I agreed to fight Igor Zinoviev at the UFC 16: Battle in the Bayou, outside of New Orleans. I had less than three months to prepare.

After the Jackson fight, I was on fire. The Enson fight had been so important. That qualified me for Jackson, and that had been super-important too. Now I was at the next level. At that time there were two leagues, and two "best guys in the world." At the moment those two were Zinoviev and me. He was the Extreme Fighting champion. I was the Ultimate Fighting champion. He had fought John Lober to a draw. He had beaten Enson Inoue. So we were natural rivals. The winner of the fight was going to be, pound for pound, the best fighter in the world.

The fight was scheduled for the Ponchartrain Center. I went down there almost a month before the fight on my own dime, which was unheard of at the time. I had an idea about how I could beat him, and I needed to develop it. Zinoviev was a really good striker, and he had very good judo skills. He was better than almost anybody at striking. It was very hard to get him to submit. He could just stand there and be better than anyone.

He was a Russian guy from St. Petersburg. He had come up through a Russian sports academy, and he had trained in boxing, judo, and other fighting techniques. But I had seen a hole in his game. I was so deep in my game that I saw a nuance in his technique. I saw that in the midst of him standing there and beating people up, he made a mistake. When a guy would attempt to take him down by grabbing him around the hips or waist, he would grab the guy's head. He would *always* grab the guy's head. It was like I was having a dream, and I woke up, and said, *This is how I'm going to beat him.* I just knew that if I could pick him up and take him down, at that moment, and stun him, then I could beat him. I started telling the media I was going to knock him out and I started practicing this lift and slam move. My plan was to pick him up and throw him on his head. He'd be so damaged that I could just choke him out and win.

I practiced hard. I spent twenty days in Louisiana, in a hotel room, with no one supporting or sponsoring me. I trained at local gyms and I had people coming in every day to work out with me. We put the word out. "Frank says he will let anyone who shows up with gloves hit him in the head." I did that for an hour a day for twenty days. Sometimes I had fifty people lined up. They were driving in from thirty or forty miles around. I was preparing for a horrible brawl, and I wanted to be ready for it.

The fight was on March 13, 1998. The referee was John McCarthy, the same guy who had refereed my fight against Kevin Jackson. It was a big crowd, maybe a sellout one. John said, "Are you ready? Let's get it on!" We came out of our corners. We were both in black. I was really pumped. He had a military-style haircut that made him look like even more of a madman than he really was—and he was a madman already. I thought he was going to kill me. But I had a plan.

I tried three or four kicks. He moved in. I reached around his waist. He grabbed my head. I hoisted him up and dropped him hard. My plan went great, except that when I turned him upside down and stovepiped him, I broke his collarbone and exploded his shoulder and knocked him unconscious. I threw one more punch but it was unnecessary. I had broken some vertebrae in his neck. I heard the bones break. I will never forget the sound of it.

The fight lasted twenty-two seconds. Zinoviev was not getting up. The announcers were screaming. One of them said, "He's out cold! He's out cold! He dropped him on his head and he's out cold!" I ran around the cage a couple of times, but then I looked over and no one was moving. I got down close to Zinoviev to see how he was doing. He wasn't doing well. He was *out*. I thought, *It worked! I won! I am the greatest fighter in the world! And I have single-handedly destroyed the sport in a single night.*

In those days there was no padding under the canvas. The floor was made up of a piece of plywood on top of concrete. It was really, really hard.

After the fight, I had the same sense of letdown as after the Jackson fight, for the same reason. Igor hadn't even punched me. He never landed a blow. It was just like my dream, to a T. He felt like he weighed five pounds. He hit the mat and it all crunched. And the fight was over and he was done.

They gave me the belt. I thought, *It was really that easy?* I had barely expended a breath of energy.

He never fought again. I always felt bad about that. He was a good guy, a real, honest, look-you-in-the-eye kind of guy. A soldier of the fist and spirit. And he never fought again. I knew the minute the fight was over that he was really mashed up. I felt horrible. I knew what I did to him would change his life but I was not ready for how that feeling would stick in my heart and mind. I can't watch the fight even to this day. Yes, I was strutting around the cage flexing in celebration, but it was all an act—I felt sick inside. I had been determined to win the fight. Before, I had been afraid of hurting people. Now, I accepted that winning the fight meant hurting him and I understood that this was my job. I had to be willing to be hurt, and I had to be willing to hurt the other guy.

Years later, he was coaching some students in the International Fight League. I had a team in the IFL, too. I found myself sitting next to him at a team dinner. I said, "I just want to say that I'm really sorry I hurt you in that fight. I was just hoping to stun you. I didn't mean to hurt you so bad." He started laughing. He laughed so loud! He said, "Frank! It's a fight! That's what happens in a fight!"

Maybe he had hurt a lot of people, too. His style was to go hard and punch hard. I was relieved that he had no hard feelings, because I know he never recovered right. I ended his career as a fighter.

For me it was a great victory. In some ways, it was the fight I feared the most, and it was by far the toughest fight of my life. I thought Enson was going to beat me down and choke me out. I thought Kevin Jackson was going to outwrestle me. But Igor was the first hybrid striker guy I'd faced. I knew I didn't have that much stand-up skill yet. I couldn't just smash people. So when I beat Igor, I knew it was a big moment. I knew there was no one on the planet who could beat me.

But I was still figuring it all out. My boxing skills were terrible. My kicking was still off balance. I was still evolving. I wanted to be the best. That meant I still had to figure out the mechanics and make them right.

I got paid $30,000 for the Zinoviev fight. That was good money, but it wasn't money you could retire on. Besides, I'd spent twenty days in a hotel on my own dime. So my expenses were high. But I knew, after this fight, that this was my only chance of ever doing anything big. I knew with fighting I could go anywhere in the world.

9

AMERICAN CHAMPION

By this time my relationship with Bob Shamrock was completely zero. I had found that out on the Internet. I read an interview with Bob and Ken. They were saying all kinds of terrible things about me. The article said I had betrayed him, that I had screwed Ken over, and that I turned against the family.

I wasn't surprised that Ken was saying these things, but it hurt me to see Bob's name in there, so I called him. I told him I had read the article and that I was confused. He said he hadn't seen the article but that what I was saying didn't sound right. He said he was probably misquoted. He said he'd look at it, and I could call him back. When I did, a few days later, he said he'd seen the article and that everything in it was pretty much true. "It said everything I meant to say," he told me. "You're not part of the family anymore. You chose to leave. And you know what that means. If you're not part of the family, you're out. You're not with us. You're against us."

He made some more references to the family, and how the family is sacred, and how the family had secrets that could never be told. I didn't even know what he was talking about. What secrets? Were we some kind of Mafia organization? Maybe it was something to do with him and Ken. They had a very strong bond, a very deep relationship. But I didn't even know what there was to betray. I had no secrets and nothing to hide.

It had been less than a year since I'd left the Lion's Den and started training on my own, but it was obvious that Bob was finished with me. So I was surprised when I saw him at the Zinoviev fight. He and Ken had come down to Louisiana to support one of the Lion's Den guys, Jerry Bohlander, who was fighting Kevin Jackson on the same UFC 16 card. I just ran into him. I had just beaten Zinoviev. I was the champ. I was there with all my guys, with Maurice and Angie. Bob was by himself. He gave me a hug. He seemed happy to see me. I took him aside, and said, "What happened? What changed?" "I don't know," he said. "But you have to make it up with Ken."

I told him I didn't know how to do that. I didn't have anything to apologize for. Ken had basically thrown me out. I told him I had been forced to go my own way. "No," he said. "That isn't how it works. There's only one way, and it's our way. It's the family way. You chose to leave the family." I didn't want it to end like that. I said I wanted to have a relationship with him. He told me I couldn't. He told me again that no one would help me or talk with me. I had chosen to be on my own, and now I had to be on my own. "But congratulations on the championship," he said.

I was really hurt by this. And then I got mad. I felt more determined than ever to prove them wrong. It was obvious that the only future Ken and Bob could see for me was training Ken's guys in the Lion's Den. Maybe Ken had persuaded Bob to think that. Maybe he had made Bob choose. Ken's a very forceful guy, and he's a control freak. Everything is black or white, right or wrong. He has to have things his way. Bob is a little like that, too. But it killed me that they couldn't see it any differently. They *still* believed that I didn't have what it took, even after I'd beaten Enson, Kevin, and Igor. I was the champion! I had the belt! But they still thought my job should be serving Ken and training his guys. The only thing to do was prove them wrong and prove myself right. I had to become the greatest fighter in the world.

My next fight was a title match with Jeremy Horn in Mobile, Alabama. It was kind of a mess, and there were a lot of miscommunications. Our sport was having a really hard time. We were getting shut down and pinched off everywhere. We'd been thrown off Time Warner cable and some other outlets. The sport was really popular and it was growing, but we were being seen by a smaller and smaller audience.

Bob Meyrowitz, the first owner of the UFC, wanted to change that. He had worked in the music industry and understood how to create a public image. They asked me to come to New York to talk about how we could grow the sport. They had the idea to make me an MMA sports personality and commentator. They said for the next show they couldn't afford an entire pay-per-view card but wanted to do a show titled Night of Champions along with a never-before-seen fight with Frank Shamrock. The plan was to fight the first fight of the night (for the live crowd only) and then change into a suit and commentate the rest of the fights as if nothing had happened. Then we could sell a pay-per-view show without the cost of producing one.

I said that was OK with me. I had three weeks to get ready. I thought I could figure out how to be a commentator in three weeks. But I told the organizers to make sure to pick me someone to fight that I actually *could* fight and then still be OK to go and commentate for the rest of the night.

They put together a good group of fighters. They had Dan Henderson, Chuck Liddell, Pete Williams, Allan Goes, Tank Abbott, and a whole bunch of other guys. For me, they picked Jeremy Horn. Jeremy was a very tough up-and-coming UFC guy. He'd had ten or fifteen fights already, and he'd beaten almost everyone he'd gone up against. He had fought Dan Severn to a draw not long before—and Dan was a 250-pound fighter. This was not my idea of an easy fight. But they wanted a competitive match. That's what they got!

I hadn't been training very hard, and the moment I saw the picture of this tall, pasty, knock-kneed kid, I really let off the intensity. He looked like he couldn't fight his way out of a wet blanket. I thought I was getting ready to be a commentator. I didn't think I'd have to fight anybody serious. It was just supposed to be a warm-up bout. But he almost beat me. My whole style at that time was based on athletics and conditioning. It requires a huge amount of energy. If I'm out of condition, I lose energy fast. Well, this kid had my number. The fight was brutal. It was a sixteen-minute hug fest. Jeremy held me down and tried to control me, and I didn't have the energy to put him away. In the end, I got lucky. I just happened to knee bar him, and scraped away with a victory. I learned a good lesson. I couldn't mix my talents. I could be one thing or another thing. But being good at one thing required all of my focus. Luckily I was good on the microphone that night and the show was a huge success on pay-per-view.

My next fight—a revenge fight—was with John Lober. I hadn't forgotten the first one, in which I had taken an ass-whupping, and then taken that walk and had an epiphany about having a career. In that first fight, John had beaten me by controlling the striking and the stand-up position. I didn't want that to happen again. So I trained hard, mostly with Maurice. He got me tight on the striking. We did sessions three times a day. I ate and I took a nap in between—nothing else. We worked on striking and striking power because I really didn't have any. Maurice was working me up, making me strong. He had me running in water, swimming, running intervals. I was also doing resistance training for striking and kneeing and kicking. This would have been a tough training regimen for anyone.

For me, it was extra tough. I don't swim. I am terrible at it. I don't have a swimming body—I have a sinking body.

But it was really good training. I hadn't been taking care of my body because I didn't know how. I had no idea what effect the high-endurance sprinting was having on my spine, for example. I didn't know what the running was doing to my knees and hips. I was just beginning to understand the effects of all this damage to my body. When you're fighting, every blow does a little bit of damage. You kick a guy hard and bang him up a little, but the kick does some damage to *you*, too. When you're fighting, this is a big part of the fight. You're trying to do damage, but you're also trying to manage your body so you can stay in the fight. When you're training, too, you're trying to stay healthy so you can go to war.

Over the years, I had learned a lot about my own body. I had become a sort of gym doctor. Once, when I was in Japan, I got a cauliflower ear. Someone had grabbed my ears and banged them around. One of them got purple and swollen and felt like it was on fire. I couldn't touch that side of my head or sleep on it. So I went to see a doctor. All he did was stick a needle in my ear and drain off all the blood and pus. Then he iced it and sent me home.

Your ear is basically just some skin around some cartilage. When it gets abused, the skin gets irritated and separates from the cartilage. Your body responds by sending blood and gluey stuff up there to try and heal it. If you don't do anything, the ear will fill with gooey blood and turn purple. After Japan, I discovered I could do the work myself. When I was working at the Lion's Den and didn't have any money for doctors, I found out I could go visit the veterinarian and tell him I needed some needles to give injections to my dog, and he'd sell me 5 cc needles. When someone would get his ears all banged up, we'd take the needles and drain the blood and pus, then ice the ears, and send him on his way. I treated all the Lion's Den guys that way, and all the guys on all my IFC teams, too.

(The secret to avoiding this is to never let anyone grab your head. That's a golden rule in fighting. If your opponent tries, the defensive move is to rotate your shoulders very quickly and spin your head out of the hold. It's not that hard, because it's tough to hold onto a ball that's rotating. After my experience in Japan, I never let anyone grab my head again.)

I learned some other home medicine techniques. When I was still teaching at the Lion's Den, I worked with a guy named Haggar Chun Li. He was doing leg locks in training and he broke his leg—the little bone on the outside. You could hear it snap in the class. I had broken that same bone, so I knew what had happened. I took him to a chiropractor we knew and had him X-rayed. The chiropractor said, "Yep, it's broken. You've got to go to a doctor and get him in a cast."

I was living in Ken's guesthouse at the time. I didn't have any money. Chun Li didn't have any money. But I was his teacher. I was his mentor. I had to help him. So I went to the library and took out a book on broken bones. I studied up. I saw that it was just some plaster of paris and some fabric. So I went to the store and got the stuff and came home and casted his leg. It healed great. He went on to fight a Hawaiian guy who broke both his eye sockets. He left fighting after that. He's an FBI agent now.

I also learned how to use superglue to close a cut on a guy's face. I saw a doctor do it once. I asked him about it and he told me that superglue was invented for this, in Vietnam, as a way to close cuts in a hurry. I later found out that wasn't true at all, but it was good enough to get my attention. I started using superglue in the gym to close cuts when guys got injured.

If you are fighting or training and you get in close and take an elbow, you might get a one-inch gash on your forehead or eyebrow. That's very common. If you go to the emergency room, getting that gash tended to can be a five-hour procedure costing thousands of dollars. And if you don't get a doctor who really knows his stuff, you could wind up with a pretty ugly scar. Or there's superglue, which will close a cut immediately and perfectly. But you have to be careful. One time I saw a doctor who was nervous and shaky and he superglued my guy's left eye closed. It took about a gallon of Vaseline to get it open again.

By necessity, I got pretty good at emergency medical situations, to the point where I had my own doctor's bag, which I would constantly refill in emergency rooms and locker rooms around the world. I've popped fingers and wrists and elbows back into place. I've taped up broken toes. I've helped guys with broken noses. For a nose that is still straight you just lean the head back, put a lot of ice on it, and wait. And don't blow your nose. That's a massacre and your whole face will turn black and blue. When your nose is on the other side of your face, it's a quick crack with your thumbs to align it with your mouth.

The really horrible broken limbs you send to the doctor. I saw a guy get his whole forearm snapped in a telephone lock. That was an ambulance ride.

Otherwise, I learned a lot about active release and contusion relief massage. If you take a lot of kicks, or you get a lot of bone-on-bone damage, you have to do this, and you have to do it right away. The blood accumulates and everything gets stiff and hard, and if you don't massage it right away you can get into real trouble.

I remember when Brian Ebersole fought Cung Le; Cung kicked the shit out of Brian's leg. When it was over, he could hardly walk. I thought he had taken care of it, but I found out that after the fight he'd just had a few beers and gone to bed. Five days later, his leg was dark purple from his butt to his toes. He couldn't get out of bed. So we sat down with him and, for the next three days, massaged the dead blood out of his leg. We iced his leg from butt to foot so it wouldn't hurt. We froze water in Styrofoam cups, and used the cylindrical ice tubes to squeegee and massage the dead blood out of his leg, like squeezing sausage out of its skin. We could see the leg changing color as the dead blood drained out and the new blood flowed in. It's a very slow process, and horribly painful, but it works. It works better if you do it right away, and if you do it in public, immediately after the fight. Otherwise the guy's going to start crying and go home.

I knew a lot about pain—my own pain. Running had become hard and painful for me. Maurice understood that, so he got me into the water, which was a godsend. It took all the impact of training out of my knees and shoulders. But it also meant I had to train twice as hard because my swimming technique was so terrible. The training put me in a bad mood, especially the swimming. It was the only time I ever got mad at Maurice, and the only time he ever yelled at me. Maurice's biggest strength is that at forty he has the energy of an eight-year-old. He has this old man strength, and this old man knowledge, but he's enthusiastic like a kid. He brings all that to the training.

For the swimming, we were working with this Brazilian guy who'd been a water polo champion. We were swimming in competition, for conditioning. Maurice didn't think I was trying hard enough. He kept teasing me. He would say, "Come on, Frankie. Come *on*, Frankie." Finally I lost it. I screamed at him. I stormed out. It's the only time in my life that I've ever yelled at a coach, or walked out of a training session.

I sulked for a while and came back. We went back to training.

Maurice really helped make me strong and helped me stay healthy doing it. Part of my strength as an athlete was that I was always good at erasing everything in my mind, once I got going on something. Once I started training, my body would just go until it fell apart or broke. Maurice was very good at helping me go hard but not break down. I needed someone to stop or slow me down sometimes.

The training had been extremely effective. By the time the fight came around I was really ready. And I was mad, too. The fight was going to be held in Sao Paolo, Brazil. We flew down there—Maurice, Angelina, some of my guys, including the disc jockey Big Joe from 94.9 FM, the biggest morning radio show in the Bay Area. He was going to do a live broadcast of the fight during his show.

Right away, Lober started messing with me. He started doing stupid, childish things, like ordering me wake-up calls in my hotel room and ordering room service to my room at weird hours. He sent me dirty e-mails. He was being nasty. He said he was going "to strangle me like JonBenet Ramsey," the six-year-old girl from Boulder, Colorado, who'd been murdered a year or so earlier. I thought that was extremely crude. It really upset me, way more than it should have. As soon as the fight started, I found I had this heat in my head. I had almost never felt it before. It was as if my brain was on fire. So I decided to beat the shit out of him.

The fight started like the first one. He came out and got ready to go, standing up. He thought his strength would be controlling that. He thought he would be able to knock me down and get on top of me. But I had been training hard with Maurice. My stand-up game was strong. I'd figured out the striking thing, for the first time, and I was really making it work.

So he came out and got squared up and ready to strike. I kicked him in the leg. He threw a punch. I hit him with a punch-kick counter. I did that every time he threw a punch. Pretty soon I was making him fall down. I'd motion for him to stand up, and then I'd knock him down again. I did that quite a few times. I enjoyed it. I didn't want it to end. I was pissed off, and I wanted to hurt him.

It's not good to get that angry. That's why fighting on steroids is such a bad idea. When you're angry, you can't fight rationally. Your body chemistry is all messed up. Your energy goes to all the wrong places. You can't do anything well except get angrier. That's why I like fighting guys who are pumped up on steroids. Fighting is all about relaxing and releasing tension, so your body is flexible and fluid, able to bend and flex quickly, like water. I like fighting angry guys who are really tense. They can't think right, and they can't fight right.

I'm not sure any of the other popular medications are good for fighting, either. Except for ice, which should be the pain medication of choice in any situation, it's all bad for you. There was a time when all the pro wrestlers were taking the painkiller Nubain. There were guys using Percocet and Demerol. There were guys who ate Vicodin like it was candy. Then there was a wave of steroid use and then designer growth hormone use. If you get into any of that shit, you're done. You're finished.

Then there's weed. In the Brazilian MMA culture, particularly, that's the first drug of choice. There are guys who smoke pounds of weed and then go run twenty miles. The problem is that pain, in our sport, is important. Pain is what tells you that you're doing something wrong, something damaging. You need to know, in this sport, when you're doing something wrong. It's an important teacher.

Being angry didn't seem to hurt me with Lober. I just beat the hell out of him. After a little while, he didn't want any more of that. He started falling down, and falling into the cage to get out of the way, and holding onto me to catch his breath. I could have finished him, and I should have finished him. Two or three times I had him in a guillotine hold, and that could have ended it. But I let him go so I could beat him up some more. Because I wanted to beat him down. I kept making him stand back up.

Finally he'd had enough. I pinned him against the cage, and I was hitting him hard. His face was split open. He was fatigued from falling down and getting back up so much. He was done. He said, "OK, Frank. I'm done. You can stop."

No way. I said, "I'm not going to stop, you motherfucker. I'm going to beat you to death." Maurice had never seen me like that before. He loved it. I could hear him laughing his ass off in my corner.

I really wanted to knock him out. The fight ended. I won.

Right after that Angelina and I finally got married. We decided to get married in Hawaii, on the island of Kauai. We booked the wedding at a historic plantation, in the middle of a butterfly farm. The wedding ceremony included a butterfly release. It was a very small wedding. Angelina's mother and brother and stepfather were there. My son was there. He was living with his mom in Utah at the time, so I flew him out.

I didn't have much of a relationship with my family then. My mother was still with Joe. They had settled into the Morro Bay area. I had an on-and-off relationship with my sister Suzy. I had a minimal relationship with Robynn. I wasn't seeing my brother Perry at all and didn't even know where he was living at the time.

I didn't see much of anybody. I didn't have much of a social life at all. I was always getting ready for a fight, or fighting, or recovering from a fight. If you're really doing that, you don't have much room for anything else. It's a full-time job.

I don't think I realized that. And it put a strain on my relationship with Angie. She liked being a fighter's wife. She liked the fights. She loved all the noise and the crowd and the lights and the attention. She liked getting dolled up and being the beautiful woman with the champion. But she didn't like the lifestyle much. It wasn't as glamorous outside of the arena. My life consisted of training, mostly, and napping. I was working out two or three times a day. That meant I needed to eat three or four meals a day—big meals. I needed clean clothes, too, because I went through two or three sets of workout clothes a day. So for the person not training the day was about cooking food and doing laundry. She wasn't into that stuff. She wasn't interested in being a housewife.

I sat down with her and had some serious talks with her, which was very uncomfortable for both of us. It wasn't that important to me that she be a housewife, but that had been our lifestyle, and she had said she was OK with it. I had made all kinds of decisions and arrangements based on her being a part-time housewife. I depended on her to help me. But I was living on Costco frozen burritos and frozen orange juice. That was my training diet, because there was no food in the house.

She wasn't working outside the home. This *was* her job, or that's the way I saw it. We were married. She was my partner. I was training. She was supposed to help me. I was totally happy in my relationship, other than that. I thought she was, too. But there were things that bothered her. She didn't like my snoring, for example. I was always working on my stand-up game and my striking at that time, so I was getting hit in the face a lot. My nose was smashed in all the time. So when I went to bed, I snored.

Also, she was ambitious. She had dreams that she felt she wasn't able to pursue. She had always wanted to be a model, and I was all for that. I said, "Be a model! Go for it!" I put her into things when I could. If there was a photo shoot, I'd say, "Put her in the picture, too." I encouraged her to go up for jobs and auditions.

All these little issues came to a head when I fought Tito Ortiz. The fight was set for September 1999, in Lake Charles, Louisiana. It was UFC 22, and it was billed as "Only One Can Be Champion." I had been the *only* UFC middleweight champion, so I was there to defend my title and retain my belt. Also fighting that night were Chuck Liddell, Jeremy Horn, and a bunch of other fighters. The event was going to be broadcast over pay-per-view. It could have been the last of those for a long time, as the UFC was struggling to keep its finances in order.

Not long before the fight, I got a call from Bob Shamrock. From his tone it felt like he was just calling for no reason, just to say hello or something. But then he got to the bottom line. He didn't want me to fight Tito. He said he thought Tito was going to hurt me, and he didn't want me to take the fight. I was surprised. Tito was an up-and-coming guy, and he had fought a couple of people and won. But I was the champion.

Bob was serious. He said, "Ken says he's the wrong style for you. He's going to beat you. He's too big and he's too strong for you." I said I understood and I thanked him, but I didn't get it—at first. Then I realized that half the guys Tito had beaten were Ken's guys. He had fought these Lion's Den fighters, like Jerry Bohlander and Guy Mezger, and destroyed them. After his fights, he would do this thing where he flipped everyone off and act like he was digging graves around his defeated opponents. So he had disrespected Ken, and Ken didn't like it. He may not have wanted me to fight Tito and lose. But he didn't want me to fight Tito and win, either.

It made me more determined than ever to fight Tito. I couldn't see any reason not to take the fight. Everything in my life was working for me. I had been annihilating everyone I fought. I felt good about my chances. I trained hard. When I got to Louisiana, I was in great shape. And I had a plan.

Some years before, Angelina's stepdad, Al, had introduced me to an L.A. lawyer named Henry Holmes. Right from the start I thought he was the coolest guy. He took my call, and we met at his office. It was a big corporate office, but Henry had pictures of himself with every important person in sports, including Mike Tyson, Evander Holyfield, and George Foreman. I told him my plans. He gave me some advice on how to protect myself and plan for the future as an athlete and as a brand. I didn't think that much about it. But I started hitting him up for counsel every time I needed business guidance. Finally he asked me if I wanted to be his client. I said I did. But when he offered to negotiate a deal for me, and I found out how much it would cost, I couldn't afford him.

Later on, I needed him enough to afford him. I asked him to give me some direction and negotiate the Tito Ortiz fight. I had made a decision about my future. I really believe that MMA was going to make it and become the greatest sport in the world. But I was pretty sure it had to die first. The people making it happen had picked a horrible marketing tactic. The concept was "Eight men enter, and only one man leaves. And one of the men might die." It was very scary and very dangerous. Maybe it was good for pay-per-view; it drew a certain kind of audience. But it also drew the politicians, who were going to kill it. I saw the end was coming.

I wanted to get out and wait for it to be reborn. I wanted to fight Tito, to defend my title. But I didn't want to fight after that. My master plan was to retire, stop fighting, make some strategic moves, and in about five years be ready to come back as a fighter in a reconfigured sport. If I had to keep fighting those five years, while waiting for the sport to come around, I'd have to take the risks involved with all those fights. I could die waiting for my sport to mature. I wanted control of my own destiny, and I couldn't have that fighting for the UFC.

I took my problem to Henry. He said, "Fine. Put it in the contract." This sounded like an old pro-wrestling move. I didn't know I could do something like that. Henry showed me how it could be done. If I fought Tito and lost, I would continue with the UFC. If I fought him and I won, though, I could retire and get out of the contract. I would be a free agent.

That's all I needed. Now I was ready to fight Tito Ortiz.

Tito and I were similar in a lot of ways. We're both from California, and we're both from Mexican blood, and we're both tough. But Tito was much bigger than me—six foot two and well over two hundred pounds. He had a lot of height and a lot of reach. Also, we have really different styles. Tito is a wrestler who is willing to strike. He likes to stay on his feet and box and then take the fight to the ground to pound on you. I'm more of a shooter. I like to take you down and force you to submission on the floor. But at this point in my career I was turning into more of a striker. My ground game was so solid that I didn't care whether it went there or not, and I was happy to throw power, too. But when a guy has thirty pounds and four inches on you, that's not as easy as it sounds.

Because he was so much taller than me, I was going to have to punch *up* to hit him. And I was going to have to punch first. If he punched first, he was going to have weight and volume moving forward, and I was going to have to absorb some or all of it. So my plan was to punch first, then grab him and make him wrestle me. So instead of punching, staying inside his range, and giving him a shot to punch back, I was going to get in fast, punch first, and make him wrestle me until he got tired. And I knew he'd get tired before I did. I was at the top of my physical condition. I knew I could outlast him. The only issue was making sure he didn't hit me really hard in the first ten minutes. If I could do that, I knew I could beat him.

The referee was John McCarthy again. The crowd was huge—something like twenty thousand people, not counting the pay-per-view audience, which was the one of the biggest pay-per-view audiences in MMA history, and at the time it was the biggest money-earning fight in MMA history, too. Right before the fight, though, something weird happened with Angie. I was ready to go out. I was all pumped up. I had the towel around my head. I was going out in two minutes to fight the fight of my life. It was on. Angie was all dolled up, with the clothes and the hair and everything, the way she always was for the fights. But all of a sudden, she stepped in front of me. Her hand went out. She said, "Hold on, hon. Let me go first. Then everyone can see me." It really caught me off guard. I didn't know what to say. It was a bad idea, and it was a bad time to discuss it. So we didn't. She just strutted out ahead of me into the arena. I thought about it for two seconds, and then I remembered I was about to go and get my ass kicked. I decided to think about Angelina later.

Tito and I came out strong. We traded blows for three rounds. Somewhere in there Tito hit me hard. I started bleeding badly over my left eye. But I had the center of the ring and was pushing Tito around the edges, closing the distance, controlling the canvas. I was doing this by punching first. He wasn't able to hit back, which frustrated him, and the wrestling was tiring him. It was still brutal. He was still big, and he still had more than twenty pounds and four inches on me. It was a tough, tough fight.

It got tougher. In the third round Tito kneed me in the head and opened a cut that would later need sixteen stitches to close it. When we came back in the fourth, he actually grabbed at the cut and tried to tear it open. I could hear his corner yelling at him to tear it open! Who was his corner man? John Lober! He must have still been mad about that second fight.

After the third round, it became the longest fight Tito had ever fought. He had never gone more than fifteen minutes. Conditioning was starting to become a major factor. But he wasn't finished yet. I ducked under a big right hand and got in a couple of strong shots to his head—but then he took me down. He had me on the mat. I was on my back, with my legs locked around his waist, protecting my head with my arms. He had me around the neck.

The crowd seemed to get pissed off when he took me down. Maybe they wanted more stand-up. I couldn't tell. I also wasn't sure whether they were rooting for me or for Tito. I just heard them screaming. I could hear my coach Maurice Smith screaming, too. He kept telling me to get my feet inside, on Tito's stomach, and kick my way free. I was trying. But I was tired, too.

It wasn't a very effective hold. Tito had me down, but he couldn't do anything but hang onto me. He was trying to conserve his energy and get his wind back, but it cost him a lot. He was getting hurt. Every time he relaxed a little, I boxed his ears and the side of his head and moved to another position on my back so I could hit him more. He was paying a big price for maintaining the hold. He was getting really tired. I could feel the fight leaking out of him.

I guess he could feel it, too, because he got impatient. He loosened his hold and tried to finish me with a couple of wild punches and some elbow shots to the head. They all missed, and took a lot of energy, and that gave me the opening I needed. I flipped him over with a leg sweep, did my famous breakdancing turnaround, and then we were both on our feet. I got in several jabs and a knee before Tito shot me again and we were back on the floor. I got Tito in a one-armed guillotine choke and squeezed. He was hanging on, but it was almost over. He used everything he had left to wriggle free, but then I was standing over him and striking hard while he ducked and covered. Tito started tapping the mat. The ref waved me off and rolled Tito over. He was done. The fight ended about fifteen seconds before the end of the fourth round. The announcers were shouting themselves hoarse. I was the best under-two-hundred-pound fighter in the world, they said. I was still the best.

Tito went to his corner. I went to mine. The crowd was insane. My corner guys started plugging up my bloody forehead with Vaseline to stop the blood. Tito came out of his corner wearing a FRANK SHAMROCK T-shirt—a great show of respect. He always put on a T-shirt right after a fight, with a customized message on it. One time it said, RESPECT: I DON'T EARN IT, I JUST FUCKING TAKE IT. Another time, after he beat Ken Shamrock, it said, I KILLED KENNY.

This T-shirt had my name on it, and on the back it said, UFC MIDDLEWEIGHT CHAMPION. It was an old T-shirt, but it was the truth. I had defended the title and retained the belt. I was still the only man alive who had ever been the Middleweight Champion.

Later on, someone asked me how I was able to beat the bigger man. I said what I always say. I bring everything I have to the fight. I don't leave anything at home. When I fight, I'm fighting all the way.

I am absolutely willing to die, if that's what it takes to win. It's hard to beat a man who's willing to die. It took me my whole fighting career—and everything that came before it—to become that guy. It took a lifetime of abuse, neglect, mistreatment, and violence before I learned how to fight back and take care of myself. By the time I fought Tito, I was ready.

I was the champion, the undefeated champion. It seemed like a good time to retire. So I did retire, during a live pay-per-view event. I handed Bob Meyrowitz my belt and told him to let me know if he found anyone who could beat me.

10

GOING HOLLYWOOD

At that time, my master plan was to move to Los Angeles and become a TV and movie star. So right after the victory over Tito Ortiz, that's what I did. Angelina and I packed up our stuff and moved. We got a place in Los Angeles, in Marina Del Rey. I got my first acting job about two weeks later. It was a guest appearance on *Walker, Texas Ranger*.

I had met Chuck Norris at a social function, over lunch at a sushi restaurant. It turned out that Henry Holmes was Chuck's attorney, too. He said he had a script about cage fighting for his TV program *Walker, Texas Ranger*, which at the time was the top-rated show on CBS. There was a part in it that he thought would be perfect for me. So I followed up. Two weeks after I fought Tito Ortiz I was shooting an episode of Chuck's TV show in Los Angeles. I actually still had the stitches from the Tito fight in my forehead, which Angie took out on set.

We shot the scenes in Texas, in an abandoned Nabisco cracker factory. The episode was called "Fight or Die." I played a character named Hammer of D Block. In the episode, Walker finds out about an illegal cage-fighting ring at Copperhead Maximum Security Prison. Guards are staging fights to the death. I play a guy who was a Mafia enforcer but who's now in jail fighting for money and girls. In the first few scenes, I fight a guy inside a cage, inside the prison. I choke him out while an undercover cop is trying to expose the illegal cage fights going on inside the jail. When the guards find out he's a cop, they throw him in the ring and I kill him, too.

When Walker learns what's going on, he decides to go undercover as a convict, with one of his fellow Rangers going undercover as another convict and one going as a guard. Walker and I wind up in the ring together. I have some memorable lines. I say to one fighter, "You're gonna die *real* slow." When Walker pushes me in the chest and says, "Me first," I say, "You're gonna die even *slower.*" When we get into the cage together, I say, "I've been waiting for this." And Walker says, "Let's get it on."

Walker's sidekick calls for help. The inmates start to riot. The guards freak out. They decide to stop the fight by shooting Walker. One of them is about to blast him with a shotgun when one of the inmates grabs the gun. The guard shoots me instead.

It was fun. We shot eleven fight scenes over about ten days. The producers had brought together an amazing group. Chuck had been one of my childhood idols. He was really interested in martial arts and very connected to that world. He had trained in jujitsu with the Machado brothers. One of them was a stunt coordinator on the show.

The stunt coordinator had a general idea about each of the fights. He'd say, "What about something like this?" and the fighters would work out the details. I got a lot of good advice about doing stunt work from Vic Quintero, an amazing stunt guy who's been doing movie work since the 1980s. I thought it was so cool. I thought *I* was so cool. I was going to be on a TV show! Then the 5:30 A.M. call time came, and it didn't seem so cool anymore. Those TV guys work hard. The show was broadcast a month or so later.

The fight scenes had kung fu sound effects, like a Bruce Lee movie. It was great.

Everything went according to my plan, or even better than my plan. I got an agent right away. I got a manager right away. They got me auditions, and then I got every job I auditioned for. I got three commercials in a row. One of them was a national commercial for Burger King.

The whole experience for that was weird. I showed up horribly late for the audition, but they loved me. Two weeks later, I got the word that it was on. We set the date and I got all prepared. I showed up on time for the shoot—at 11:00 in the morning. The director came running over to me. He was a huge fight fan. He introduced me to everyone. He set me up in front of the cameras. I danced around. I punched a bag. I did some kicking, and some moves. Then suddenly the director said, "OK, Frank. That's good. We're going to break for lunch." So we went to lunch. The director took me around the facility. I think I ate once with him and once with the crew. Everyone wanted their picture taken with me, so I posed for photos. Then the director had me sign some papers, and he said, "OK. You're done."

I had been there about two hours. I had worked about forty-five minutes. I started getting checks, and in the end that commercial paid something like $25,000. I said, "Making commercials is good!" So easy! This is obviously the way to make money.

Things weren't going so well at home. Angelina and I fought a lot. When we lived in Los Altos, I was fighting or training all the time. She and I didn't spend very much time together. So it was easy for me to think things were OK, that we were compatible, that our relationship was a good one.

It wasn't a good one, and we weren't compatible. I found out a lot of things once we were able to spend more time together. I saw that she wasn't really interested in me as a person, that she was not really very loving or caring or honest. I don't know how I had missed that, but then I saw it clearly.

I knew she was tough and smart. She had these ideas about being an actress or a model. I knew she was ambitious. But I really didn't know *how* ambitious. Now I thought back to the night of the fight with Tito, and how she stepped out in front of me. I honestly didn't understand how badly she wanted to be famous—more famous, in that moment, than me. This was one of the biggest moments of my life, but she wanted it to be about her.

The moment stuck with me. Every time I thought about it, all I could see was how fake she seemed—fake hair, fake eyelashes, fake smile, fake everything. I couldn't get it out of my mind. It only lasted two seconds, but it completely changed the way I thought about her. I think she genuinely loved me. But I think she loved the idea of being famous more.

The timing was terrible. It was as if someone had pulled back the curtain and I could see her, really *see* her, for the first time. When we got to L.A. and things started not working out, I found it had stuck in my craw. It seemed like a really bad sign of things to come.

I was going to auditions, getting jobs, working out, and doing my thing. Angie was mostly shopping. She bought a lot of expensive furniture. She was always buying clothes. She liked money and she liked buying nice things with it. I tried to get her to slow down. I was making pretty good money with the acting jobs, but we weren't rich. I had worked really hard to put away some savings and I didn't want to go through it all at once. So we fought about money a lot. Pretty soon I was sleeping on the couch—an expensive designer couch that she'd insisted we buy for our place.

I was still getting a lot of work. I did an episode of *Oz*, the HBO series about life in a maximum-security prison. (A veteran stunt guy, Douglas Crosby, helped me get that gig.) That went well, so I did another. I loved the work and the people. I met Chuck Zito, and he became a friend. Chuck had been a badass dude in New York, a boxer, and a president of the New York chapter of the Hell's Angels. Then he'd become a professional bodyguard and parlayed that into an acting and stuntman career. He was my first celebrity friend. He was into MMA and really opened the door for me and brought me inside. He started introducing me to people. I was teaching a session in New Jersey and he said, "We're going to a boxing match." It was a prizefight at Madison Square Garden. He and the boxer Arturo Gatti snuck me in pretending I was their security guard. It was an extraordinary fight and an amazing night for me, and we had a lot of fun together. Then one day I got a call from my old friend Douglas Crosby who had Mickey Rourke on the line. Mickey just wanted to say hello! *Mickey Rourke*!

I also made my first motion picture. I got a job in a movie called *No Rules* (2005). It was supposed to be the world's first MMA picture. It was directed by Gerry Anderson, Pamela Anderson's brother. It was his first film, and it was kind of janky. All kinds of people were in it—Gary Busey, the fighter Randy Couture, and even Al Pacino's father. I thought that part was pretty cool. But the movie was terrible. I knew it from the start. I had been around cameras enough at that point to know this film was bad. I remembered all the continuity issues. I was always saying things like, "I wasn't wearing this watch in the last scene."

At the end of the day they didn't release it. The UFC threatened to sue them over the use of the octagon cage, which the UFC claimed they owned exclusively. (This was the new UFC era, when Dana White was running things.) The movie came out overseas. Later on it was released on video under a different title.

Then I made a mistake. I auditioned for a huge commercial, and I got offered the part—a national ad campaign for Old Spice aftershave. At around the same time, I got offered a commentating job for UFC. There was a scheduling conflict. The two jobs were happening right at the same time. I couldn't do both. So I asked my agent which one paid more. She said you never know about these commercial things. Straight money, the UFC gig paid more. So I booked that one. I didn't understand about residuals, I guess. The UFC gig was just a regular job. I got paid some money to do the gig, and that was that. But the Old Spice commercial was a national commercial, playing all over the country. It was on television *forever*. The actor who got that job is probably still getting checks.

One day Angelina and I were talking about something, and it turned into a fight, and the fight turned into a huge screaming match. I couldn't take it anymore. I was already sleeping on the couch. We weren't getting along at all. So I said, "You know what? This is uncomfortable. I'm unhappy. I don't want to do this anymore." My sister was living in Redondo Beach. I said I'd go stay with her for a while. Angie was very calm about it. She said that was OK with her. I put my gym bag together and went to work out.

But I couldn't work out. I was fuming. I felt miserable. So I went home. Angie wasn't there. But two hours later she came home. She was dressed real sharp, in a business suit. She said, "Guess what? I just finished emptying your bank account. I'll see you in court." I lost it. I told her she had to leave. I threw her out. Then I packed my stuff and left, and moved in with my sister.

Angelina had, in fact, taken all my money. I had saved about $180,000 from fighting. That was my entire fortune. It was going to be the money that financed my movie career. Well, that was gone. She had taken every penny. I had two retirement accounts that she didn't know about, that I'd set up before meeting her. I cashed those out. That's what I lived on while I stayed with my sister.

We wound up in divorce court. By then, the money was almost all gone. Angelina told the judge she had spent $160,000. She couldn't say how. But she wanted more money to live on. That

The Juarez clan of four, circa 1981: Robynn on top, and, left to right, Perry, Suzy, and me.

Mom was a great cook and always had a garden with fresh fruit and vegetables.

Flexing with my brother Perry when I was twelve.

In 1989, Christy's parents brought her and Frankie to visit me while I was in juvenile hall for the casino brawl. This was the second time I got to see my son.

In Jamestown Prison with my cellie and weight-lifting partner, Butch, in 1992.

Defeating Kevin Jackson, the 1992 Olympic gold medalist for wrestling, in just sixteen seconds at UFC Japan. SUSUMU NAGAO

The band Biohazard attended our Pancrase fights and afterward invited us to their show—onstage.

Pumping iron in the old Lion's Den in Lodi, California, 1996.

Walking down the ramp at NK Hall to face Enson Inoue, the Shooto heavyweight champion, in 1997. Those are my Adidas running shoes and the kimono robe I bought at the gift shop—one of my early costumes.

SUSUMU NAGAO

My adoptive dad Bob Shamrock and I traveling to the UFC to support my brother Ken, 1996.

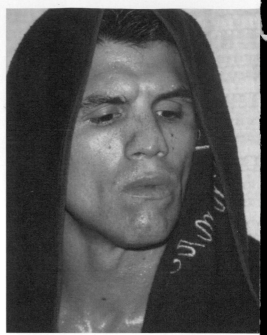

After a wild slugfest with Enson Inoue that ended when I put him to sleep with a knee, I was calling out everyone.

Preparing for my first kickboxing bout in Las Vegas, 2001, which I won in fifty-six seconds.

The Alliance: Frank Shamrock, Maurice Smith, and Tsyoshi Kosaka.

After beating the hell out of John Lober in Saõ Paulo, I was pissed and let Jeff Blatnick have an earful. But my sponsors were very happy.

Macho Man and I on the set of *Walker, Texas Ranger,* in 1999. He was the nicest and most professional performer I ever met and one of my idols. R.I.P. MMASTARS.COM

On the same set with my hero Chuck Norris. This was one of the best days of my life. MMASTARS.COM

Slipping Phil Baroni's jab in June 2007 and countering with a hard jab. TOM CASINO

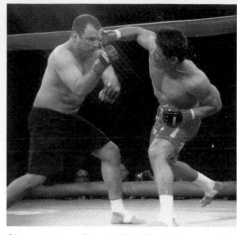

Shamrock vs. Gracie (2006) sold a record-setting 18,265 seats and launched the Strikeforce brand in twenty-one seconds with this punch. PEARCI F. BASTIANI

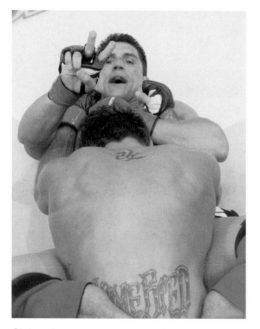

Giving the peace sign to my favorite photographer, Tom, during the Baroni fight. TOM CASINO

The final seconds of the third round with Cung Le, 2008. I knew my arm was broken and had to use my face to block the kicks. TOM CASINO

When Cung Le broke my arm it was a huge eye-opener and a blessing in disguise. I found out that I was not invincible and that I wanted to get out of fighting. This photo was taken after the titanium plate was removed.

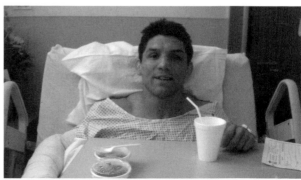

Sparring with Shamrock MMA youth students after teaching.

Shamrock MMA student Anita putting on the battle demo for National Autism Month at the Cinnabar Golf Course in San Jose.

Having dinner at Mastro's with my super lawyer, mentor, and new father figure, Henry Holmes.

Introduction on the senate floor in Albany, New York, where I was campaigning to legalize MMA.

My little boy with my UFC championship belt when he was nine years old.

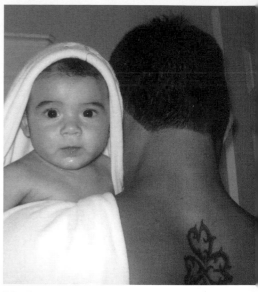

My little angel Nicolette. She softened my heart and my fists.

Enjoying retirement with Amy in Saint Tropez, France, on our cruise aboard the *Christina O*.

pissed the judge off. He told her to get a job and to come back in two weeks and be ready to account for all the money she had spent. The following day, she offered to settle. She told me, "I'm sorry. I don't know what I was doing." She said she didn't have any money left, not even to pay her attorney, who ditched her after the judge's demand. She asked me to forgive her, and said she would come back to me if I wanted.

I didn't. Paying her attorney fees and mine cost me my last $7,000.

A couple of years before, at a wedding in Hawaii in 1998, I had met a really nice woman named Amy. I knew her brother-in-law, a chiropractor in San Jose. For the past three years he had been giving me treatments for my bad back. Amy was married at the time, and so was I. But by the time we met again, both our marriages had fallen apart. Now, suddenly, we were both living in California, both living with our sisters. I was still seeing her brother-in-law regularly for treatment. I would go up to Los Altos to work or to train and to see him. He took appointments at his house. I'd go over there to let him work on me. Amy was living in his guesthouse. We started hanging out. I was back and forth between L.A., Japan, and San Jose. I was training and trying to get acting jobs.

Over the next six months, I started getting really serious about Amy. Things with Angie were over. I told Amy, "We need to be hanging out more." I had some work in L.A. that was going to last a few months. I asked her if she wanted to come live with me down there. She had a high-paying marketing job, but she quit to come to L.A. and be with me.

I saw Angelina once more after that. I was in San Jose. She called me and said, "I need to see you. Can you meet me?" We arranged to meet in a park. She showed up, looking all dolled up and hot. She said, "I'll do whatever you want if you'll take me back." I told her, "No. I'm sorry. I'm not interested. You're not pretty to me anymore." She wasn't. I had seen what she looked like on the inside.

I had always kept in contact with my son. I tried to call him once a week no matter what. I tried to maintain a relationship with him. He was a flighty kid; his mother was a flighty person and I am his dad. I never got to see what she was like as a mom; I was in prison at first, and then we were separated. And I never really got to be a dad. My son was four when I got out of prison, but during the time after that I was working a lot, or running around and being irresponsible.

I had changed, but my ex-wife hadn't. She and little Frankie were living in Salt Lake City. I didn't know at the time, but she was addicted to meth. She was always disappearing. The phone or the lights were always getting turned off because she hadn't paid the bill. I never knew what was going on, but every once in a while I'd have to send them $200 to get the phone turned on just so I could talk to my son.

By the time little Frank was seven or eight years old, he could travel by himself. So I would fly him out to meet me. It was important for me to spend time with him, and I thought it was important for him to have a healthy role model in his life. His mom always had men around. There was usually a guy living with them. She had a couple of husbands after me. She had children with four or five men. My son has half-brothers whose names he doesn't even know.

It was hard for him and hard for me. On paper I was not very fit to be his father, with my record and history. I always figured he was better off with his mom. I worried about him a lot. By the time he was twelve, I was able to get him a debit card and his own phone. Before that, I'd send him money and it would just disappear. Now I could send money to his account and be pretty sure he was using it for himself, for the things he needed. We had a rule: you always call home on Sunday. I started hearing from him more regularly.

Things were going well with Amy. For the first time in my life, I was with someone who was a really good person. She had had a normal childhood, with a mother and father who were truly pre-

sent. She had a real family—very tight and loving. So she's very normal, stable, and together. She's caring, in a way that I had never
experienced. She's honest, and she's fair. I'd never had that in a relationship. It made a huge difference in my life and in how I felt about
myself.

I had some business ventures that didn't do as well as I'd planned.
My acting career wasn't taking off the way I'd wanted it to. I got
invited to do some MMA training seminars, and that was cool. Amy
and I went to Japan and Denmark to do some fight training work-
shops. That was good, but it wasn't going to sustain me as a career.

So I decided to return to fighting. I went to work for the Japanese Yakuza. K-1 is a powerful Japanese combat sports organization, and at that time it was the top kickboxing organizer in the
world. But everybody knew it was controlled by the Yakuza, or the
Japanese Mafia. All the big combat shows in Japan were financed by
the Yazuka. It was common knowledge in the underworld who provided the money for the shows. In Japan the Yakuza touches nearly
every corner of normal business. Right out of a cheesy foreign film,
they all dressed in black leather trench coats and drove black AMG
Mercedes. I knew that, too. But I went to work for them. I agreed
to fight Elvis Sinosic in December 2000 in Tokyo.

Kickboxing rules were similar to MMA rules. You couldn't strike
your opponent with your head or your elbow, and you couldn't use
choke holds or submission holds, and you couldn't attack when the
other guy was on the ground. Pretty much everything else was OK.

I trained hard. I got ready. I studied Elvis Sinosic. He was known
as "the King of Rock 'n' Rumble." He was big—six foot three, 205
pounds—and he'd had a lot of success in his own country, Australia.
He was the first MMA champ there and had beaten pretty much
everyone in that part of the world. The fight in Tokyo was going to
be his first fight against an American champion. He wasn't expected
to do very well. I didn't think he'd last more than one round. I knew

he was tough, but I knew he had a breaking point, too. I thought I could get him to that point quickly, and I thought I could break his spirit.

I had watched his fights. I had watched his reactions to adversity. You can learn a lot, watching that, if you know what to look for. Some guys, when faced with real adversity, don't wilt. A real tough guy automatically steps it up. A so-so tough guy ramps it up, but there is a sort of dip before he ramps it up. A not-so-tough guy, it goes flat. It bottoms out. It may ramp up after that, or it may not, but you can see it go flat.

I had seen Elvis get into a bad spot during a fight, with some real adversity, and then question himself and experience that dip—and then recover. I thought if I pushed him further I could push through that dip and beat him. So I wasn't too worried about beating him. But three weeks before the fight, while I was training, I got a SLAP tear in my shoulder. I was training in San Jose, boxing with a lightweight guy, and after a few frustrating rounds had finally trapped him in the corner. When I went to smack him, he stepped out of the way and my arm just kept going. I was wearing eighteen-ounce gloves, and the ligaments and tendons in my shoulder just snapped.

I told the doctors I had to fight in three weeks. They told me to forget it. I went to see my chiropractor. He said no go. Then my coach, Javier Mendez, took me to see this dude named Calderon, who ran a tire shop on the east side of San Jose. Javier had taken me there once before to get treatment on my neck. Calderon was about seventy years old, and he had this back room at his tire shop. He took me in there and put me on the table and moved some stuff around. It didn't seem to do anything. Javier said, "Give him twenty bucks." I didn't think I'd ever see him again. But the shoulder injury was serious, and I didn't know what else to do. So when Javier said, "We'd better go see Calderon," I went.

Calderon took me into the back room again, and put me on the table, and moved some stuff around. He told me to boil a pot with the herb arnica in it and soak a rag in the mix. I had to put it on my shoulder for a half hour, several times a day. He told me not to punch anything for a while. I gave him another twenty bucks.

I wasn't able to do any more boxing training before the fight. I did the ice thing and the arnica thing. I wore a sling until a week before the fight and then took it off so no one would know I was hurt. When it was time to go to Japan, Amy went with me.

The fight was a big deal. It was the very first MMA-style fight ever broadcast on Tokyo TV, which is like the CBS or NBC of Japan. The Tokyo Dome was full. There were sixteen fighters on the bill for the night. Ours was billed as the "Superfight." The reigning K-1 champion, Ernesto Hoost, kept his title. Elvis and I were going to go for five three-minute rounds.

This was probably one of the largest martial arts events in history. There were eighty thousand fans in the arena waiting for MMA action. But it turned out they weren't ready for it. They'd never seen anything like American-style MMA. I came into the ring and the fight started, and I foot-kicked this guy in the face and I could hear that they didn't like it. I could actually *hear* it. All eighty thousand of them seemed to get really quiet, like . . . this was *bad*.

The fight went my way right from the start, except that my shoulder hurt. I thought Elvis was going to give up. But I didn't know he wasn't going to give up until the end. I found out later that he went to his corner after the first round and told them he was done. He told me so, himself. But his corner guys screamed at him and called him names and made him mad. So he came back out. We had to go the full five rounds. I won by decision. I thought it was a good fight, even though I could hardly lift my arm and was not very effective on one side. But it was still a real battle. I came out and stomped his head and kicked his face and won the fight. But it was the last one I ever fought in Japan. People weren't ready for it. The sport was still too new.

When it was over, I went back to California and saw the surgeons again. They opened my shoulder up, cleaned it and sewed it and reattached it. I don't know if I made things worse fighting Elvis with an injured shoulder or not.

One of the main reasons I fought Elvis was that I'd made a deal with the K-1 guys. They were going to use that fight to launch a huge MMA league—*our* MMA league. They were going to give me a bunch of money for that. They were going to use my name and image to brand it, and we were going to build an MMA empire in Japan and come back to the US to compete against the UFC.

But I hung around for a year after the Elvis fight while they tried to get things going. I went to endless meetings at which there was a lot of talk and never any decisions. I learned about the Japanese way of doing business. Finally it became clear that they didn't know what they were doing in MMA, and they didn't have any money. Before that, I'd always gotten paid in cash. After a fight, the promoter would invite you to his suite where he would sit at a table with two leather-clad guards behind him and enormous stacks of money in front of him. He was always smoking a cigarette, and he always handed you a tiny paper bag filled with cash. It was always clean, fresh, sequential one hundred dollar bills. He'd always present me with the bag and ask me if I wanted to count it.

It didn't matter how much I was getting paid. I always got paid the same way. Sometimes it was $10,000. One time it was $80,000. In *cash*. That was a big bag. But now there were money problems. No more gobs of cash. I told them it was time for a change—they were using my name and they weren't paying me! Luckily, when I first began studying Japanese business methods I learned about a common business practice to help guide a business decision or dispute. It's called the Naniwambashi strategy. It's the melodramatic story of how you have sacrificed so much for the company and without this decision in your favor, you and possibly your whole family will be on the streets. The more drama the better!

Now it was time to tell my story to Master Ishi and the heads of K-1. Then the checks started coming, and it was good money, but after another year or so it was obvious they weren't going to be able to make it happen. I was very serious about branding, and about moving my brand forward. I had giant hopes for my sport. I knew it was going to be huge. But I couldn't be tied up with people who weren't able to make it happen. So in 2002 I told them I was out, and they let me go do my own thing.

I realized that I would have to get the money myself. I would need to study financing, and understand distribution. I had been relying on them to do that. I would have to rely on myself. So I started studying business.

Some time before that I had started talking to gyms. Partly on Angie's advice, because she was so into fitness, we looked at expanding the MMA idea into gyms. We started pitching Gold's Gym, which had been the original sponsor for the UFC. The Gold's Gym people told us to come on down to Venice Beach. Angie and I met them and started training with them. They were wonderful to work with. They sponsored me for a few years with clothes and equipment, and I'd get to pose for pictures next to Arnold Schwarzenegger.

Nothing came of the Gold's conversations but some great friendships, and they eventually sold out to another company. But I started thinking about teaching and ended up doing a huge amount of it. This wasn't new for me. I had taught a lot of Ken's guys in the original Lion's Den in Lodi. I had opened Ken's gym, Lion's Den Submission Academy, in 1997. In San Jose, I started teaching at the American Kickboxing Academy. Any time I wasn't fighting, I was teaching. I taught the judo students at San Jose State. I taught the tae kwon do guys. In 1998 I started going overseas, teaching in Japan, teaching in Denmark. I was expanding my brand and increasing my teaching ability. I started doing seminars in Europe.

I did one pro wrestling match in Japan, too. It was what I call "stiff" pro wrestling. In Japan, the line between fighting and wrestling is very thin. It's a kind of soft fighting. There are kicks, and you can use your knees, and you can use all the submission moves. It's just like a real fight. You do all the moves. You just don't finish them. And you know who the winner is before you start. It's not exactly staged fighting. It's like *real* staged fighting. They took real fighting, which is dangerous and unpredictable, and gave it an ending. The winner is determined ahead of time. But everything else, 90 percent of the fighting, is real fighting. You decide ahead of time who's going to win and how. For example, I'm going to finish with a leg lock. For the next ten minutes, you beat the hell out of each other. Then you do your leg lock and it's over.

I fought a guy named Daisuke Nakamura. It was my last pro wrestling match. I didn't fight again for another couple of years, but I was busy. I always had a fighting team that I managed and traveled with. (That was how it always was with me. When I left Ken and the Lion's Den, I had started a team of guys almost at once. We trained together every day, ate together every day. That was how I always worked with fighters. We became family.) We fought all over. One time we got a contract to do a fight in Wenatchee, Washington. That's an apple-growing area, out in the middle of nowhere. We arrived to find everything all messed up. Everyone at the hotel had been drinking. My guys and I tried to go to bed, but we all kept getting woken up. There were fighters running in the hall, knocking on doors, acting like idiots. Someone set up a bucket over my door so that when I opened it I'd get soaked.

I chased two guys down to their room. When they ran inside and locked the door, I said, "If you don't open up, I'm gonna kick this door in." They were laughing their asses off. So I kicked the door in, just in time to see them jump out the window. I threw all their training gear into a bedsheet and used that to soak up all the water in my room.

The next morning I got a call. "Can we get our clothes?" They were the people we were supposed to fight. They didn't have anything to train or fight in.

Then we found out the venue had changed, less than forty-eight hours before the event, and no one seemed to be in charge. I hunted down the promoter and made him give me the cash box. I told him, "I'm going to fix this show, but you have to sit down and shut up." We resurrected the show, renegotiated the pay, and had the fight. Everything seemed to be fixed up. But then the next day when we arrived at the airport to fly home we found out the organizers had only gotten us one-way tickets. I was so mad that I went and found the promoter and threatened him. I took away his wallet. I took all his money, and we flew home.

I'm not saying *this* was the face of MMA, but the MMA business was not a professional one. This was the kind of thing that happened in our industry. This was what I was determined to change. So I dabbled in the business of MMA. I believed that the basic problem with our sport was presentation. At the time, the whole concept of the cage was too much. We needed something softer and more mainstream. I had a vision of an arena, something less scary and threatening.

But it wasn't a shared vision. I used to go out on these money-raising excursions, and people would laugh at me. The idea of a mainstream MMA was so far-fetched. No one got it. It was *cage* fighting. The view of the sport was 100 percent negative. Society just was not ready for it at all. People would say, "Look at them. They're animals. There are no rules. You can't kick a man when he's *down*. It's not cool." That's what I was facing. So I got busy trying to come up with something new. I became a promoter for a while.

I got a call one day from a woman in Arizona. She was an American Indian, and she had some sort of nonprofit organization behind her, and she was interested in MMA. I had been working with the idea of promoting and about the concept of Bushido, which is a Japanese expression, from the samurai days, that means "way of the warrior." She introduced me to a graphic designer who created a really cool Bushido logo.

So I put the two ideas together, and we went into business in early 2001. For the first time, here was an MMA event that said, "Frank Shamrock Presents . . ." on it. I pulled together some really good fighters, and we staged our first fight. We had Yves Edwards, Pete Spratt, Trevor Prangley, Shannon Ritch, Josh Thomson, and Bobby Southworth. It was a great show, with everyone representing his respective martial art. I thought I knew everything, and I thought it was going to be huge.

It wasn't huge. We lost our asses. I made peanuts. It was a disaster. I was a fighter and didn't know about being a promoter and neither did my partner. I had never had to attend to the finer details, like administrative tasks. So I decided to get out of the promotion business. But then three months later, in 2001, we did Bushido II. It was another disaster.

I kept thinking about how to do something different in my industry, about different ways to get MMA across, different types of presentations. I was very aware of the limitations and the barriers. MMA was too bloody. There weren't enough regulations. It was too scary. The ropes and the cage made everything too cold and unpleasant.

I came up with an idea for something called Shootbox. I spent months polling people, studying arenas, and designing a combination of new ideas and old ideas. I designed a presentation that included a sunken, four-sided box. Around it were elevated seats, and above it was an elevated, four-sided TV screen, like they have at hockey matches. There would be nothing between the fan and the fight. Everything would be open and visible. The storyline wouldn't be the fight to the death. It would be about the art of fighting and it would be seen like never before. Our tagline was "NO Ring, NO Ropes, NO Cage—No Limits."

Soon we had our first investor, from Arizona. He had seen advertising for the Bushido shows. He and his father were working with a public company and they wanted to get into MMA. They asked me to create a concept for network TV, so I showed them the Shootbox concept. They loved it, and we worked out a deal. I sold them the rights to Shootbox. They got 100 percent of the company and my services. I got ten million shares in their company and a big salary.

I was back in the promotion business. I thought I was really taking off. I started driving a BMW! I was a promoter and a presenter. I was the president of sports and marketing for a major multimedia company! We organized our first show for August 2003, in Orlando, Florida.

In order to get approved by the Florida boxing commission, we had to build an actual Shootbox. So my friend Crazy Bob and the boys built one. On his front lawn. It was a huge wooden box, thirty-six feet square. When it was done, we shipped it to Florida.

We debuted on a Saturday night. The event was sold out. The fighters were Dave Velasquez, Alex Kababian, Erik Wray, Jason DeLucia, Mike Swick, Butch Bacon, Matt Rogers, Jeff Ford, Jerome Smith, Chad Washburn, Daniel Wade, and more. The fights were being filmed so we could show the footage to the networks. We had some press there, and a lot of MMA people in the audience. Bas Rutten and Dan Severn were there watching and Don Frye and Jeff Blatnick commentated the action.

It was a great event. The fighting was good. Mike Swick knocked out Butch Bacon with a punch that required the paramedics, so that created a lot of scary drama.

The idea was to film the event and present it to the networks and to investors. But the two backers ran out of money before they even got that far. The night before the fights happened, one of the principals knocked on my door and said, "Do you know what's going on?" Our company had been sold to another company. The money was funky. Something weird was going on. My partners didn't know where the next round of financing was coming from, or if it was coming at all. It turned out it wasn't.

My plan had been to hold ShootBox 2 in Las Vegas, and to fight Cesar Gracie myself. There was never a ShootBox 2. I never even got a VHS tape of the first show. I had shares in a worthless company. I got rid of the BMW. But my belief that I could take MMA more mainstream didn't change.

11

FEUDS AND THE FIGHT BUSINESS

I continued to have a very distant relationship with my brother Ken. I wasn't in communication with our dad at all. Sometimes I would see them at an event. Sometimes Ken would say something in the media about me. It was all kind of painful.

Ken was famous for his feuds. He and the Brazilian jujitsu fighter Royce Gracie were in each other's face for decades. Royce beat Ken after a controversial decision in the very first UFC fight, UFC 1, in 1993. Ken was determined to avenge this loss and trained for a 1994 rematch, but he broke his hand while training and had to bow out. So he entered a tournament later that year and fought his way through several opponents in order to face Royce again and reclaim his dignity. When he found out Royce had dropped out of the tournament, Ken refused to come out for the finals. If he couldn't fight Royce for the championship, he didn't want to fight at all.

The following year Ken had another chance. He and Royce were going to meet in the first-ever UFC singles fight, a "Super Fight." But there was more controversy. Right before the fight, the promoters changed the rules and instituted thirty-minute rounds because the television distributor needed an end time for the show. This wrecked Ken's strategy and threw both of them off balance. The fight was boring, ended in a draw, and did nothing to end the feud.

Ken had also been feuding for years with Tito Ortiz. Tito had dissed him after a fight and then started coming to fights wearing provocative T-shirts. (Tito beat Lion's Den fighter Guy Mezger, then flipped off Ken and put on a shirt that said GAY MEZGER IS MY BITCH. Later on, Tito showed up to fight Ken wearing a shirt that said PUNISHING HIM INTO RETIREMENT.)

I got into the middle of one of Ken's feuds when we were all in Mobile, Alabama, for a fight in 1996. Tank Abbott was a self-described street fighter from Huntington Beach, California. He traveled with a tough posse, including a guy named Big Al who used to shadow Tank. For some reason they hated the Lion's Den guys. One night we all got back to the hotel at the same time. Our cabs pulled up to the lobby doors. Big Al got out of his cab and for some reason threw a hamburger at me. It was 4:00 AM and he was obviously drunk. Suddenly he starts making a move on me. He's six foot eight and heavy, but he didn't look or move like a fighter. So I said to his crew, guys I had hung out with before, who were sort of egging him on, "This guy is drunk. You better get him out of here." But they didn't. Big Al grabbed my chest and started pulling my shirt. That wasn't cool, so I hit him with a right, and then I hit him a bunch more. He got really short all of a sudden, so I kicked him in the face a few times. Then I said, "Take your guy out of here. I'm going to bed."

The next day he came up to me with his face all bandaged up and said, "I'm sorry, man. I was really drunk." So I thought we were all cool. But a few months later we were all in Buffalo, New York, for another fight. Tank and all his guys were there. Everybody had been drinking. I was with my girlfriend. Tank came over to me and put an arm around my shoulder. He said, "Hey, cowboy. If she doesn't go down on you tonight, I'll take you home and suck your dick." Security broke us up before I could hurt him. I guess that's a good thing.

I remembered what Bob Shamrock had told me all those years before about never getting into a street fight. I rarely did. I was afraid of street fights. They seemed really dangerous to me. What if the guy had a knife? What if he had a gun? What if he had ten friends in the room?

Twice, though, I got caught up in something and wound up fighting that way. The first time was when I was still with the Lion's Den. We were attending a UFC bar party. Some bar out near Modesto was showing the fight on pay-per-view. We went as a team to watch. They had a VIP section for us. We spent the evening hanging out and drinking and watching the fight.

It was really smoky inside, and after a while I went outside to get some fresh air. Out of nowhere this guy came up and started hassling me, bumping me in the chest and sort of challenging me. He was obviously wasted. I was dressed really nicely, and he was drunk, so I just ignored him and started to walk away. But he said, "Hey! Where are you going?" and came up to me. He looked like he was going to hit me. So I shot in on him, grabbed him around the waist, and pulled him to the ground. Somehow, just like a move right out of the movies, he fell into position for a rear naked choke. It was the most natural thing in the world. So I took advantage of the hold, choked him out, and put him to sleep in about two seconds.

I got up, angry because my nice clothes were all messed up. I started brushing myself off when suddenly I realize that the guy had woken up, stood up, and lunged at me. So I grabbed him as he came at me and snapped another choke hold on him. It was another movie moment. I felt like Bruce Lee! He walked right into it, and I snapped it on him. I held the choke and put him back to sleep.

I didn't think I should just drop the guy, unconscious, onto the asphalt. So I lowered him to the ground and we sort of sat down together. When he started to wake up again, I choked him out a third time and tied his shoestrings together. Right then some security guys from the bar came out. I told them everything was cool. I brushed my butt off and untucked my shirt and went back inside as if nothing had happened.

My second street fight was many years later, when I was living in Los Angeles with Angelina. I had to go to Home Depot for just one little thing—one of those plates that covers a light switch. It was hot, so I was wearing a tank top and shorts and sandals. I got my light switch cover and went to stand in line. It was a long line with twenty-plus people. When I finally got to the front of the line and was almost at the cash register, this little Mexican dude slides up and parks his cart in front of me. I said, "Excuse me, but we're all in line here." He ignored me. I thought that was pretty rude. But I didn't want to make a big deal out of it. So I said again, "Hey, buddy. All these people here are in line, and the end of the line is back there."

He turned to me and said, "Fuck off." I couldn't believe it. He was a little fat guy, and I'm there all pumped up in my gym clothes. So I said again, "Buddy, you got to get in line." And he said, "I told you to fuck off." I got really angry! I started talking to myself. I started talking to the other people in line. Can you believe this guy? Who does this guy think he is? What the hell is wrong with this guy?

He ignored me. So I decided I was going to take him outside and beat the living shit out of him. He paid for his giant shopping cart full of items. I was next. I paid for my one little light switch cover. I walked out. I found him, and started walking behind him. I followed him to his truck.

I composed myself. I changed my mind about killing him. When I got to his truck, I said, "Hey, man." He turned around. I was in my interview position, hands up and palms open, very relaxed. I was just going to talk to him. I said, "What's your problem? Why would you treat another human being like that?" And he said, one last time, "I thought I told you to fuck off." I literally screamed, like a crazy man, and attacked him. I front-kicked him in the stomach. When his head fell forward, I grabbed his hair and kneed him in the face. Then when his head came up, I punched him in the face, really hard, with my right hand.

He went down bleeding, making these moaning noises. I figured he was done. In the time it took to look around the parking lot to see whether anyone had seen me, he got to his feet and came up with a huge eight-inch hunting knife. He said, "I'm going to kill you."

He looked serious. So I ran. I was in my sandals, but he was fat. I figured I had a chance. I also figured he wasn't crazy enough to chase me around the Home Depot parking lot with a bloody face and an eight-inch hunting knife, but I was wrong. He *was* crazy enough. I ran and he chased me. I got near my car. I was thinking I'd jump in and lock the doors and drive away. But then I remembered I was driving my Camaro—and it was a convertible. He'd cut my throat. So I kept running.

We did two or three laps around the parking lot. He kept coming, with his bloody face and his knife in one hand and his cell phone in the other. Was he calling for backup? I don't know, but he wouldn't give up. Finally I ran back into the Home Depot itself and lost him somewhere. I made my exit through the garden shop. I got into my car and then, because I couldn't help it, drove around until I saw him. I beeped and yelled, "Hey! I just kicked your ass! There's nothing you can do about it!" Then I drove home.

I remembered Bob Shamrock telling me not to street fight. He was right.

Periodically someone would ask me about Ken, whether the two of us ever planned on fighting each other. They wanted to talk about our "relationship." I tried to explain that I had never had a relationship with Ken that was about anything except fighting. We've never had a serious conversation about anything else. He was my mentor. I owe my life in martial arts to him. I will always honor that. But that's pretty much it. I've never received a Christmas card from Ken. He didn't come to my wedding, or send me congratulatory notes when my children were born. We would see each other every six months or so, usually at a fight. "Hey, bro, how's it going?" I know my next-door neighbor better than I know Ken Shamrock. That's just the way it is.

By 2003, I had been away from fighting for almost three years. In March, I was scheduled to meet Bryan Pardoe at a fight in California, organized by World Extreme Cagefighting, that was billed as "Return of a Legend." I was already a legend. We were going to fight for the WEC light heavyweight title.

Bryan Pardoe was a big heavy dude who was known as "Pain Inducer" Pardoe. He weighed about 220 pounds. I had bulked up from my usual 185 and weighed in at 205. (In truth, I weighed in wearing slacks, covering my legs, because I had three-pound leg weights on. I am not sure if this was cheating; I was trying to weigh more so that I could fight someone who was bigger than I was. I knew that the WEC 205 title was vacant and would look great on my resume. Our fight was on an Indian reservation, so I knew the commission would be lax. No one said a word about the Hugo Boss slacks I was wearing. But it boosted my weight up; I only really weighed about 194.) But Bryan was tall. He had four or five inches on me. When we met in the ring, he looked down on me—but I noticed he couldn't look me in the eyes. I felt like I had him beat before we even started. The announcer said, "We've waited years to see this. The return of Frank Shamrock . . . starts now."

And it was on. I threw a kick or two. He threw a punch—and landed one, hard, that rang my bell. When I blinked my eyes to recover he rushed me into the cage and ripped my legs out from under me so he could get on top. He held me there and tried to hit my face for a full minute, but it cost him a lot. I was hitting him hard in the side of the head, boxing his ears, and he had to spend a huge amount of energy just keeping me down and staying out of the way.

When he got tired, I was able to swing my legs up and over him, flip him over, and trap his arm in a straight arm bar—an upside-down version of the arm bar hold I had used to beat Kevin Jackson. The fight was stopped at 1:46 in the first round.

Bryan was cool about it. He congratulated me and we hugged. The announcer said, "He's ba-a-a-ack."

By accident, I acquired a nickname. Everywhere I went, people would say, "Hey, what's up, Legend?" The title of the event, the pay-per-view title, and the title of the DVD from it was now my nickname. Before that, I was just the guy who came out, kicked your ass, and sauntered off. I didn't take a nickname out of pride; I wanted the fans to give me one, and they did after the Pardoe fight. I became Frank "Legend" Shamrock, or Frank "the Legend" Shamrock, and it stuck. It would be a while before I fought again after that win. But I was busy. For one thing, I got married.

Amy and I had put ourselves on a five-year plan. She wanted to get married and have children right away. But I was just coming off a tough marriage and bad breakup. I didn't feel ready. I was traveling the world, fighting and teaching, and I dragged her along with me. It was great, but I was still stung from my last marriage. So I suggested a five-year plan. We went into the hanging-out phase. The theory was in five years we'd get ourselves together and be ready to get married.

I knew right away that I loved her and wanted to be with her. (Here's one way I knew: at night, when I stayed over at her house, after I was already asleep, she would put toothpaste on my toothbrush for me so I wouldn't have to do it when I woke up.) I knew we were going to be together. After five years, I was ready.

It was a very private event. Amy had come from a Jehovah's Witnesses background, just like me. She had a lot of issues with the church and religion. So we didn't want to have a church wedding. Because of that, her family wasn't going to attend. My family was scattered all over the place. So we decided to save our money and have a dream wedding and honeymoon all in one. We went to Jamaica. The wedding was attended by a preacher, some singers, a guy playing a ukulele, and a girl with flowers. No guests, just us. It was August 12, 2005, and it was incredibly beautiful.

I think we got our groove going even better once we got married. We started thinking about raising a family. We bought a house in south San Jose. I was training and fighting. I was ready for the whole thing. I could see the future. I could see the industry was finally turning around.

I was still working to bring MMA up to the level I thought it could reach. I became a coach with the International Fight League. The IFL was the brainchild of two investors who were huge fight fans. They raised $150 million to start a company that they thought could challenge the UFC for MMA dominance. The theory was to create a league of fight camps and bring them together for face-offs. They got the best people in the business as coaches, and the coaches pulled together the best fighters.

They had all the top names. Ken Shamrock's Lion's Den became the Nevada Lions, based in Reno where Ken and Bob were living. Maurice Smith was coach of the Seattle Tiger Sharks. Igor Zinoviev was coach of the Chicago Red Bears. Renzo Gracie was coach of the New York Pitbulls. And I was coach of the San Jose Razorclaws.

We had a lot of trouble setting the whole thing up. The UFC sued. IFL countersued. Threats and counter-threats flew around. It took a couple of years for IFL to get a TV contract, on Fox Sport Network's My Network TV. When the first fight was televised, the IFL became the first MMA show to have a regularly scheduled time slot on broadcast TV.

The promoters took advantage of my relationship, or lack thereof, with Ken. They advertised my camp versus his camp, brother versus brother. "Two brothers! Two legends! Too bad they hate each other!" They quoted Ken saying, "I would have no bones with punching him in the face." They quoted me saying, "I equate it to going out to war." They billed it as a fight "for family honor."

We didn't meet in the ring, but our teams did. I had Josh Odom, Donny Liles, Jeff Quinlan, Brian Ebersole, Vince Lucero, Raphael Davis, Brent Beauparlant, and Ray Steinbeiss on my side. But Ken's guys beat us three fights out of five.

For a long time, people had talked about matching me up against Ken as fighters. With the two of us faced off as coaches, that talk got a little louder. The IFL produced a promo spot, in fact, advertising the fight as if it were already happening. The ad was mostly Ken talking. "Frank has been talking about fighting me for years," he said, looking serious. "But every time I tried to make it happen, he's disappeared. Well, I made sure it's in the contract this time, so there is no disappearing. On *his* part."

There were pieces of video cut into it, including some of me. But Ken kept talking. "I don't dislike my brother. He's my brother, and I love him and I wish the best for him. This fight is about Frank coming of age. And Ken Shamrock putting his little brother back where he belongs."

He didn't dislike me. He just wanted to kill me. But in a loving way. "I've fought many, many guys," he continued. "I mean, I've fought everyone in the world. I've made a lot of people a lot of money, fighting with me. Why not, I make my brother money? I beat him up *anyways*. For free! So why not put him in the ring and let's do a brother-on-brother thing. It's never been done before."

So it was just about him trying to make me some money.

"Fighting is not a dirty thing," he said. "Brothers fighting is not a dirty thing. It happens every day in this world. They just don't get paid for it. So now I'm gonna bring my brother into the ring. I'm gonna beat him up. And I'm gonna pay him for it."

I never made an ad to say what *I* thought about it.

Over the years there were many attempts made to get us into the ring together. At one point, we actually got really close to doing it. I had met some Silicon Valley finance guys. They were really excited about MMA and a "blood brothers" concept. We were going to tell the story of MMA, using the stories of Ken and me, and then finish with us fighting each other.

But Ken kept signing all these other contracts that got in the way. He was fighting this person and that person. Then he had a weird encounter with Kimbo Slice. Ken had signed to fight Kimbo at an October 2008 EliteXC event. It was a big fight and was going to be broadcast on CBS. But the day of the fight, while Ken was training with a sparring partner, he took a head butt and got cut above his eye. It took six stitches to close it. The examining doctor said Ken couldn't fight.

I don't know what really happened. What I believe is that he found out right before the fight that Kimbo was being paid a whole lot more money than he was making and that he went a little nuts. He demanded more money. He made some threats. I think he lost control of himself and got injured—not on purpose, exactly, but the way a guy who has lost control is bound to.

Ken became a bit of a black sheep after that. No one wanted to invest in a fight that involved him, or him and me. The Silicon Valley deal went away. But a weird rumor got started. Someone started saying that I had offered to fight Kimbo myself—and offered to take a fall.

What is true about that is that I was part of the group that had organized Ken's fight with Kimbo. I was involved with ProElite and EliteXC. So I was one of about twenty-five guys in the room trying to figure out what the hell to do when Ken couldn't fight, and trying to come up with some way to save a multimillion-dollar production that was a very big deal in our sport.

So I did volunteer to fight Kimbo myself. We made the offer to Kimbo's people, and I was actually waiting to get cleared by the commission to take the fight. Up until the evening of the fight itself, up until about an hour before the live TV event started, I thought I was going to do it. But then the word came from Kimbo's camp— "absolutely not." It was a question of skill level. I had about ten times Kimbo's experience and ability. But he was a bigger guy. If I went out there and smashed him, it wouldn't look very good on his record.

I was disappointed. I thought it would make a great sports story—Frank comes off the bench for his brother, defends the family honor, and beats the big guy. But I was also a little relieved. My back was in bad shape. It was hurting me a lot. I hadn't been training for a fight. It would have been a tough fight for me. But I would have done it, for the story.

In the end, Kimbo went up against a fighter named Seth Petruzelli—who beat him by TKO fourteen seconds into the first round. Petruzelli said after the fight that the EliteXC promoters had offered him more money to stand up and punch it out with Kimbo rather than take him to the ground. He later retracted that, but the Florida sports commission convened an investigation anyway. They didn't come up with anything.

Years later, a former Elite guy named Jared Shaw started telling people that I had secretly offered to do the fight and throw it in Kimbo's favor. He said he was shocked and disgusted, but that he thought I was serious—because he thought I had worked the fight against Cung, too. Why else would I have stood up for that fight and not gone to the ground unless the promoters had paid me to do it? It was a ridiculous charge, and I don't think anyone took it seriously. Why would I do such a thing? My career was doing fine. I had no reason to throw a fight. They couldn't have possibly had enough money to induce me to do that, even if I'd been willing.

As for the guy making the charge, I think he was just a little confused. I actually think Jared Shaw is just a guy who smokes too much weed and was upset not to be more involved in MMA than he was. This was his attempt to use the popularity of my brand to create a little heat for himself. He hinted that he was writing some sort of tell-all book about the MMA world. Maybe he was trying to get people excited about that, but it didn't work. It made him look like an idiot.

But one of the beautiful things about MMA is that it's still so small that any idiot with the gumption can get up and make a fuss about something. I don't know what the guy's problem was. My lawyers said I could sue him, but he didn't seem worth bothering about. I told his people to tell him to shut up, and he did, and it was over.

Back in 2006, I had another family feud on my hands. I had started having conversations with Scott Coker about something new he was putting together called Strikeforce MMA. Scott was a local guy, a kickboxer and kickboxing promoter. We had known each other since way back in the K-1 days, and I had a lot of respect for him. He had organized a new fight company and he asked me to be in its premier fight—against Cesar Gracie.

The Gracie family was perceived to be the number one enemy of the Shamrock family. The feud went way back to the early Lion's Den days. The Gracies are a huge family and they had already had a giant influence on the world of martial arts. Cesar's great-uncles Carlos and Helio invented Brazilian jujitsu. Between the two of them and Cesar's uncle Carlos Robson Gracie, they became a dominant force in California MMA. A bunch of them opened gyms that were in direct competition with Ken's Lion's Den.

Ken had lost his first matchup against another Gracie, Royce, back in 1993. They'd had their rematch in 1995 and fought to a draw.

(If you see the pictures from that fight, you'd think Ken had won. He's smiling, and Royce looks like he's been hit by a bus. But it was still a draw because we had no judges back then; if you didn't lose in thirty minutes, it was a draw.)

Even though Ken and I were hardly even speaking by then, the fight between Cesar and me was hyped as a superfight between bitter rivals. The fight was set for March 10, 2006, and scheduled for the new HP Pavilion in San Jose. It was going to be the first sanctioned MMA fight in the state of California. And it was a huge success for Strikeforce. The fight was a sellout, and it set a new record for paid attendance at just over eighteen thousand.

It had taken almost two years to put together. The Gracies started it; Cesar cropped up on the Internet, talking crap and making outlandish statements. He said he could beat me easily, once I was retired. Someone brought that to my attention, and I said, "Hey, this is money!" I was on the beach in Hawaii, vacationing with Amy, when I first heard about it. When I got back, I started talking to Scott Coker about setting it up. I wrote a note to Cesar, accepting his challenge and posting it online. But the sport wasn't legal in California. Scott had no TV deal. There was no money for a fight like this outside the local San Jose community. But we rallied the state. We kept the heat alive. A commission was appointed. Scott went to them and said he was the most experienced fight promoter in the state. The commission did their thing, and we got our shot.

Cesar had kept up his line of talk. He was going to kill me. He was 10 and 0 in his fights in Brazil. But there were no videos of any of them. Going in, we couldn't find any actual records either. We did not think he was 10 and 0. They do these challenge matches in Brazil, where someone just shows up at a gym and challenges you. Maybe he had ten of those. But there was no evidence that he had actually *fought* anyone. We thought maybe he was making up stuff about his experience. But I still trained really hard. I trained my ass off. I got into fantastic shape. I had Maurice working with me, and all my guys. I knew he was a jujitsu guy and a grappler. I didn't think he was a striker. I believed I could beat him in striking. But he was an unknown in a lot of ways. I knew the fight was going to be one of those pivotal moments, where I suddenly saw my opening and got my shot, or one of those "oh shit" moments where I suddenly realize I'm in trouble. But I didn't think he could beat me.

The undercard was impressive. A relatively new guy named Gilbert Melendez was fighting Harris Sarmiento. A new guy named Nick Diaz was fighting Tony Juares. Gilbert and Nick were both Gracie camp fighters. It was also the MMA debut of a new fighter named Cung Le, another local San Jose guy who'd already been a kickboxing champion. I wasn't paying too much attention to all that. I was the headliner. I was busy thinking about my fight. I came out in red shorts, ready to go.

I had fought in front of a larger crowd before. But that was in Japan, where everyone is polite and quiet. This was nearly eighteen thousand fans and they were insane. I'm not sure what they were expecting. At the time, I wasn't sure whether they knew it was Cesar and me, or thought it was Ken and Royce, or what. They wanted to see a Shamrock and a Gracie kick each other's asses. They were super-excited, and loud. I had never felt anything like the energy in that arena. I got really fired up.

I was bouncing around on the balls of my feet—very energized. I was watching Cesar. He actually looked a little out of shape. We were about the same weight. I was a little taller. Then he took off his shirt and I saw he had a little roll. He had a little cheese around the middle. I knew he hadn't trained very hard. We had met at the photo shoot. He had a very, very strong grip, which made me a little nervous. My question was about his stamina. I always expect the worst. I expect long, hard fights. I train for long, hard fights. For this one, I didn't think he was going to strike a lot, and I didn't think he was going to have the stamina to fight fast and hard for very long. So that's what I was planning on. When he took his shirt off, I got a little more confident.

We faced off in the center of the ring. I got in close to him and stared in his eyes. He didn't flinch. He looked tough. We went back to our corners. I came out the way I always do, with a lot of intensity. I threw a punch and followed it with a kick. I took the center of the ring. I pushed him around a little. We exchanged some blows. He hit me hard once. I landed a hard kick to his ribs. We swapped some more punches. Then I came around with an overhand hard right and caught him on the side of his head. He went down like a bag of sand. I hit him with another left and then a right as he went over. Then I got on top of him and hit him two or three more times, really hard. But the towel from his corner was already flying through the air.

Then it was over. Only twenty-one seconds had passed. I did a little victory lap and then went over to his corner to make sure he was OK. He was. The Gracies did their usual thing. They said the fight shouldn't have been stopped, or that it was stopped too early. They said the fight was fake. But there wasn't anything to say about that. They had thrown in the towel; the ref had stopped the fight. It ended too fast, but it ended on their terms.

For me, it was a huge victory. I broke my hand, but otherwise it was a giant moment. San Jose, my hometown, became the mecca of mixed martial arts in California. I was an immediate superstar. The opportunities for MMA fighters exploded.

Doing ringside commentary was Phil Baroni. He sounded excited about the fight, at the start, because he was hoping to fight one of us himself. "I might be fighting the winner real soon," he said. But then the fight was over. He said, "They say he's the best there is, the best there was, the best there ever will be." It sounded like a compliment. But then he added, "I don't believe it." He was eager to fight *me* now. So that was the beginning of another feud.

But first I had to fight another Gracie.

It took a while to set up. After the Cesar Gracie fight, there was a lot of heat, but we still couldn't get a TV deal. We knew that TV was where the money was. It didn't make sense to keep fighting live shows in small markets, even when it was my hometown. The industry was obviously going to television. So for a year, I tried to make a TV deal, and Scott tried to make a TV deal, and we sort of languished. I had been contacted several times already by Dana White and the UFC. Now they contacted me again, and flew me in for a meeting. But it was the same pitch I'd already heard, and it was bullshit. Their deal was they'd give you a bunch of money and you'd fight exclusively for the UFC. You had to sign everything over. You had no rights. And when you were done, you would leave and that would be it, you're done forever. It was a crap deal. I had bigger things in mind for my brand. I wanted to build the sport. My interest was in promoting the martial artists, in telling their stories, in expanding the brand beyond just two guys fighting.

The UFC was interested in applying the WWE model to the sport. I didn't like it, and they took offense. Dana White is *still* pissed at me, and he never misses an opportunity to say something bad about me. That's how that feud started.

A new suitor came along then, a company called World Fighter. They said they had a lot of money. They said they had a deal with Showtime to put fights on TV. So I said, "Let's do a contract." They offered me a huge deal, with massive guarantees. The first year was $2 million, the second year was $3 million. No one was doing that kind of money. The biggest deal I knew of was $350,000. So this deal made huge news in the MMA business.

Scott Coker, my contact at Strikeforce, didn't object to my signing with them. I figured they might or might not make it, but if they did, I would take Scott with me. So we agreed to do it. We liked these guys a lot. But they couldn't produce the Showtime deal after all. They had no TV deal. Five months later, around the end of 2006, we got a call from another company. *They* had Showtime. I called the guys we had our deal with and said, "What's up?" They told me it was true, that they couldn't produce Showtime. I said, "We don't have a deal if you don't have Showtime." They agreed. We called the other guys and made a deal, and signed a contract to fight Renzo Gracie.

The other guys were ProElite, with their EliteXC MMA series. We were scheduled to fight the first Showtime fight. We went and met with the Elite guys. They were amazing. They were the nicest guys in the world, and they didn't know a thing about MMA. They had all kinds of money—$30 million from their original IPO. They had gobs of cash but no information about fighting. I went in and did my spiel and expressed my concerns. I said, "I like you guys, but you don't know what you're doing." They were very nice. They listened. We were all friends when it was over. I picked up my stuff and left.

But when I got home I found out I'd left with someone else's notebook. Inside were all the numbers for the executive compensation packages. It was insane. I took that to the president of the company and asked him what it was all about. He went to his executives and said, "He's onto us, guys. He knows we don't know what we're doing!" So I made a new pitch. I told them how to run the business, where the real costs were and what the industry standards were for pay and percentages. They seemed interested, but we had a fight scheduled already, for Showtime. There was no getting around it. It was promoted as a big fight. Showtime was happy. Elite was happy. But ProElite and I immediately starting butting heads. Legal letters started going back and forth. It started to get ugly. I had all kinds of concerns. Elite's attitude was, "Yeah, whatever. We gotta get you fighting." I was distracted by the lawsuits and negative media about the Elite deal. The fans didn't know what was going on and thought I had screwed over my partner Scott Coker, but I started training.

I knew a few things about Renzo. I knew he was tough on the ground and that he understood striking but that he didn't have any power. I knew he had limited cardio and didn't have a good chin. He didn't have the whiskers—the ability to take a punch to the chin. Some guys do and some guys don't. They can't take a hit on what I call the lever or the handle. It's the ladle that shakes the Jell-O. A sharp strike to the chin really shakes your brain up. Some guys take that and take it again. You can just plow them and they don't seem bothered. Other guys shy away, or run away. Those guys don't have a good chin.

So I had that going in. I also knew Renzo was an older guy, and wealthy. He was very successful. He was tough, but I didn't think he was going to go in there and take a terrible beating just for the money, or just for the win. With that information in my mind, I decided I wanted to make it a fast and dangerous fight that would force him to fatigue. I was going to try to add striking inside the grappling. He understood striking enough to get away from me but not enough to hurt me. I though if I could try to hurt him for ten minutes, I could take him. I didn't think he could go fast for longer than ten minutes. He would get tired and go flat, and I could knock him out.

I had cut weight seriously for the first time. I was down by about seven pounds. Mentally and physically I went in feeling fantastic. I was weirded out by the lawsuits and negative media, but when I walked in there I was 100 percent sure I was going to kick this guy's ass.

The fight was called EliteXC Destiny and was held at the DeSoto Civic Center in Southaven, Mississippi. The main card aired on Showtime. The undercard was streamed over the ProElite website.

The main card was strong. Gina Carano fought Julie Kedzie. Wesley Corriera fought Antonio Silva. Charles Bennett knocked out K. J. Koons. Joey Villasenor beat David Loiseau. And then it was time for me to fight Renzo.

The fight started just like I wanted it to. I forced him to strike and wrestle with me at a very fast pace. He got me into a side mount early on, against the side of the cage. He was hanging on and I was banging him on the head and in the sides, and dropping a lot of knees into his ribs. He spent a huge amount of energy just holding me down, but he didn't get anywhere with it. I told him so. I started talking to him. I said, "I feel you! You're getting tired! I can hear you breathing!" He didn't answer.

Elite had instituted something new in MMA. They had a stand-up rule. After two guys had been on the ground a while, they had to break apart and stand up. After Renzo had me in the side mount hold, the whistle blew and the ref told us to get to our feet. I got up and did a quick half-lap, with one fist in the air. I felt great!

I took control of the round. I took the center of the ring and started pushing Renzo back. He ducked a punch, into a sharp kick. He tried to land a punch and got a knee to the chin. It wasn't going his way at all. I kept advancing and moving in on him. He was retreating, backpedaling the whole way.

We went down again. Renzo got another side mount. I almost got the knee bar. The fight might have ended right there. He was holding me down but paying a huge price for it, taking knees to his ribs and unable to do anything but hang on. He dropped one punch on me, but then the buzzer sounded and the round was over.

Round two started. We came out and touched gloves, and it was back on. We sparred around. I pushed him back. I landed a sharp right, and he looked a little stunned. I felt a little heavy in the calves because I was really trying to stay on my toes and keep pushing him. There were several exchanges, and I could really felt myself landing on him. I knew this was going to work. Everything was going perfectly according to plan.

Then we went down again, and he got that side mount going. I started dropping knees into his ribs again. I could feel the life leaking out of him. He was exhausted. I didn't think it was going to take very long to finish him.

Then I saw how. Renzo was using his arms to hold me down, and he was completely exposed. I slammed a knee into his shoulder and the back of his head, which landed perfectly. So I did it again. It felt perfect. I felt Renzo go slack. He seemed totally stunned. Then the ref said, "Stop!" Renzo rolled off me, clutching his head. He started groaning. I didn't know what was going on. The announcers didn't either. They were asking, "Wait, what do we have going here?" Then we all found out. I had thrown an illegal knee. Apparently it was illegal to knee someone in the back of the head.

I didn't know what to do. There had been a rules meeting before the fight. I hadn't attended it but sent Maurice in my stead so I could sleep. I thought that I knew the rules of MMA—I had helped create them. I had asked the EliteXC guys about rules changes. They said, "Mr. Shamrock, you can do whatever you want."

Renzo was on his knees. The ringside doctor got in there and checked for a concussion. The ref took my arm and raised it and turned me around the arena. I think the crowd thought I had won. They started cheering. Then it became clear the ref was taking a point off or something, and the crowd started booing. I looked at my corner. I put my hands up, pretending to pray, and said, "Do something!"

In Mississippi, there wasn't a real fight commission. There was just one guy. This was the first fight in the state. They didn't know what they were doing. *I* certainly didn't know what they were doing. I had been fighting for ten years without losing, and now it looked like I was going to lose this fight on a technicality.

Renzo stayed on his knees. It still wasn't clear what was going to happen. The ref told Renzo, "You have five minutes to recover. You have five minutes before you have to make a decision." So we were going to keep fighting! Renzo was wobbling on one knee, trying to get up—or pretending to try to get up.

Then the announcer came out and said that Renzo had won due to disqualification, due to "an intentional foul." There was some booing from the crowd. I clapped for Renzo, along with everyone else, but the look on my face—"Are you kidding me?"—said it all.

Renzo was doing the drunk dance, acting all hurt. I didn't believe it. I don't believe it now. He wasn't hurt; he quit. He was tired, and he quit.

So when the ring announcer asked me what I was thinking, I said, "I thought we came here to *fight*. That's what I was doing. I don't know what happened. . . . Apparently I kneed him in the head on the ground. I guess I'm old school. I come to *fight*. We do what we gotta do to be a winner. I'm sorry I hurt the guy. I would have liked to stand up and knock him out. I was telling him the whole time, 'I'm gonna stand you up and knock you out,' and I think he starting believing it. That knee kind of convinced him to leave."

The ring announcer asked if, at the time, I had known what was happening.

"No!" I said. "I was just fighting! . . . I popped him with the left knee and then I popped him again. I mean, I barely hit the guy! God bless him, but, obviously he took the foul and he got the win. Like I said, I'm old school. We're here to fight!"

The ref explained that he was required to take a point off me, due to the illegal blow. Then, because Renzo said he was unable to continue, he had to call the fight in his favor.

Renzo wouldn't come out. Cesar came out, instead—Cesar, whose ass I had kicked in my last fight. "We have rules in these fights," he said. "These aren't bar fights. . . . You can't kick to the back of the head in the United States. That's just the rule, and everybody's aware of the rule." He said Renzo had been taken to the hospital with a concussion.

When the announcer asked me if I'd like a rematch, I said, "Are you kidding me? I wasn't even sweating! I was telling Renzo I was going to tire him out and knock him out. . . . But . . . my bad. I'm sorry. I'll take the loss. It's not my first, but it's my first in ten years."

Cesar observed that Renzo had won the first round and was on his way to winning the second. The crowd started booing. When the announcer asked me what was next, I said, "Apparently I gotta go to the rules meeting." I repeated that I had come to fight, that I'd had a good strategy for beating Renzo, and that it had been working perfectly. "I guess I broke the new rules! . . . I hate to lose like this, and to disappoint the fans. I know they would have wanted me to knock him out. . . . The family rivalry goes on, and I'll be glad to fight *any* of them."

Hours later, someone interviewed Renzo. He said he was fine. He said he had been nauseated and had blurry vision. He had felt dizzy, trying to get up. But he hadn't blacked out. He said that I'd felt he was dominating the fight and was looking for a way out. He said the fight was easy. "It was mine—all the way," he said. "It was a walk in the park!"

I knew that wasn't true. It hadn't been true at the beginning of the fight. I *knew* he was going to break. His spirit wasn't ready to fight my spirit. He was game, and he was in shape, but he wasn't ready to go to war. As we exchanged energies, I could feel I was stronger than he was and that he was going to crumble. I could feel his fear, all the way through the first round. I knew he couldn't sprint and keep up with me for more than a few minutes. At the end of the first round he was tired. Halfway through the second, he was done.

ProElite was done, too. They wanted me to fight someone else right away, but I felt like I'd been screwed on the Renzo fight. I asked them to appeal, or support me, but they said they wouldn't do that.

I should have known the rules. That makes it my fault. It was demoralizing. I was very upset with the Elite people who told me I could do whatever I want, but mostly I was mad at myself. I should have attended the rules meeting. I should have known the rules. I knew the Elite people didn't know what they were doing. I had *told* them they didn't know what they were doing. I shouldn't have trusted them.

I realized that I had gotten so disconnected from the fighting. I was spending my time being a businessman and a producer and a promoter. I wasn't a fighter any more. I wasn't thinking like a fighter. What kind of fighter doesn't even know the rules?

But on the other hand the "illegal" knee was a very common strike before that. I had used it in many previous fights. I remember *teaching* that move. I remember Maurice Smith beating Mark Coleman with exactly that move. I had taught him how to do it! You hold the head down, and when they lift up—knee them in the back of the head. It's a very effective strike. And now, apparently, illegal.

I do understand it. The back of the neck is fragile. The spine is not well protected. There's stuff back there that's not designed to get hit. In the front we have this thick plate called the glabella bone and many layers of tissue. In the back, there's just the spine and the brain. That's why it's natural to want to clutch and wrestle instead of standing up and fighting. It's organic to get inside and grapple, where you don't have all those big bones swinging at your melon.

But honestly I didn't know it was illegal. Now I know.

ProElite went bankrupt after about eighteen months. They lost $55 million in a combination of overpaying for talent, bad purchases, lawsuits, and executive compensation. This had been their big debut show, and it ended with a technicality. They had a decision to make, right away. I think they made the wrong decision. It made them look bad and it turned me against them. I put my reputation and ten years of being undefeated on the line and they wouldn't stand up to the commission on my behalf.

It made me look bad, too. It wasn't a big financial hit. I had a guarantee, so I got my money. But the public opinion was pretty bad. The view seemed to be that I was a cheater. That damaged my brand.

The fans were very vocal. They knew me. I was a leader in their industry. I was a hero. I was supposed to be this martial arts do-gooder guy—one of the guys whose moral principles are supposed to be the foundation of the whole sport. I had never had a rule violation in my entire career. But now I was a rule-breaking dick.

A lot of the younger fans had been brought up as fighters in the Gracie camp. They had trained in the Gracie gyms. They had been taught that the Shamrocks were the bad guys. Ken was dealing with accusations about steroid use. Now, this fit right in with the image of me that the Gracies were trying to promote.

In those days I was already a big participant on the Internet. I was on the message boards all the time. I knew we had a million fans out there, actively consuming our product. At least 20 percent of them seem to be saying something negative about me. Martial arts, Shamrock style, was supposed to be about honor and respect. Now I was going all street fighter. So when I was asked to fight Phil Baroni, it was essential that I say yes. And it was essential that I fight hard and win. I had to bring honor back to my brand.

12

FIGHTING BARONI, ORTIZ, AND CUNG LE

The Phil Baroni fight was set for June 2007, just five months after the Renzo Gracie fight. It was set for my hometown, San Jose. I had never fought Phil before, but I knew him and his situation pretty well. He was a former wrestler with a lot of stand-up boxing ability. We were about the same size at the time, although naturally I was ten pounds heavier. He was originally from New York, but we both lived in San Jose. He was a longtime UFC guy and had fought for PRIDE, which was the premier Japanese MMA organization for a long time.

But UFC had just bought PRIDE a couple of months before, and they had cut Baroni from their roster. He had lost his last fight, on New Year's Eve. He needed a big fight, and he needed a win.

So did I. The fans had to see me fight a tough fight and win clean. They had to see me show up and defend my title. If I didn't show up and fight well, I was finished. They would think I had cheated, that I was old, that it had all been smoke and mirrors the whole time. My brand would be toast.

There was another reason I had to show up and win. Baroni had called me out—literally, called me out—in public. It turned into one of the ugliest feuds in MMA history. In fact, Phil Baroni didn't start it. Josh Thomson did.

Josh Thomson had been one of my young boys when I started training fighters for the Shamrock team at the American Kickboxing Academy. But he was a spoiled white kid who couldn't take it. He was a quitter. He always quit when things got tough. He was a loudmouth and full of big talk, but he was a quitter when it came time to back it up in the gym. So I rode him pretty hard. I used to beat on him and try to make him stronger. But he was a punk, and I didn't like him. Ultimately, I threw him off the team.

But then I stopped training the team. They were still my guys, but I wasn't personally around as much. I was in Los Angeles. I was going around the world, doing trainings and seminars. While I was away, Josh came back and started training with the team again. I still didn't like him, and he was still a punk, but he was training with my guys.

While we were trying hard to get the Gracie fight set up, the MMA scene was starting to take off on the Internet. There was a lot of new media. People were using YouTube and message boards in really aggressive ways. Josh saw an opportunity to go after me. He started commenting online, and saying nasty things about me, as a way to build his own brand. He was smart to do it. My brand was high, my name recognition was strong, and he was a nobody. So it was a clever way for him to get some attention.

But then it started to get even more public. I was commentating at one of his fights, and he wore a T-shirt that said, FRANK GLAMROCK IS MY BITCH. Now, this was an old gimmick. Tito Ortiz had done it forever.

Then it got a little more intense, because Josh Thomson's roommate and training partner was Phil Baroni. Baroni's not the sharpest tool in the shed, and he got all caught up in this feud, and he started posting things, too. He saw an opportunity to advance his name and maybe get a fight with me. And that created an opportunity for *me*. I knew I could never fight Josh. He was too little—a lightweight, about 155 pounds. But I could definitely fight Phil. So when he started posting things, I didn't brush him off like I had Josh. I saw a chance to get something going. I started antagonizing him back.

His early online comments were mean. I always spoke professionally as a martial artist in those days. I'd say things like "Here is the lesson" and "This is what I believe about fighting . . ." His comments were all along the lines of "He's a total pussy" and "He's a douchebag" and "I'm going to bounce his head off the cage."

These were draw-the-line statements. I took the bait. I started putting out my own little videos. They were great. I called him Phil Baloney, and Phil Steroni. I taunted him. I wanted him to get mad enough to fight me. It worked. We came to an agreement for a fight. I took it to Scott Coker as part of my Strikeforce arrangement with him. Everybody was in.

We put together a December 2005 date for the Baroni fight. I started building it up on the Internet. I shot more videos. But then a problem came up: Baroni was trying to get to 185 pounds to fight me, and he took steroids to do it. He's a natural 170, but suddenly he was huge. That was going to be a problem. This was a championship fight. The California fight commission told Baroni he'd have to pass a drug test. He'd failed one once before. They told him he'd have to take another test thirty or sixty days before the fight.

He couldn't do it. He advised Scott Coker that he wasn't going to make it. Suddenly the fight was postponed. His drug test became a contractual roadblock. I took advantage of that. As soon as there were scheduling problems, I started making fun of him. I went public. I saw a way to capitalize. I made another movie. In it, I'm sitting in my backyard, wearing a T-shirt and a cap, smoking a fat cigar.

"I got breaking news," I said. "I'm smoking a cigar, which means I'm not training 100 percent. Phil Baroni has backed out of a December eighth pay-per-view event. Apparently Phil Baroni had some 'personal' issues that will not allow me to knock him out for American pay-per-view. Don't know why. Don't know why the guy called me out. But if those issues are going to prevent him from being a man, then they must be very, very personal. My personal opinion is he's a steroided miniature idiot who should have never challenged me. Look, here's the deal: If you guys want to challenge me, you want to be a player, if your name is Gracie, give me a call. I can put the fight together. I'll be more than happy to knock you out on pay-per-view. If you're an idiot named Phil Steroni, don't call me back. You're wasting my time."

The barbs went back and forth. Baroni said, "Frank Shamrock is a punk. He's going to stand with me and knock me out? I'm a fuck-ing knockout *artist*. I'm gonna break this dude's jaw. I'm gonna hit him and forget him. He can't hurt me. He wants to go punch for punch? He can't hurt me. *I'm* gonna hurt *him*." I got on camera and said, with a sort of amused smile, "I don't know if Phil is aware of how stupid he is. He's a complete meathead. Phil? You're a complete idiot." He came back, very angry, with "You ready? You better be ready. 'Cause I'm coming for you, bro. I'm coming to get you."

The feud was both good and bad for me. It was good because it built up expectation for the fight. But Showtime really wanted to move forward. When we couldn't make the Baroni fight happen, suddenly the Renzo Gracie fight was on. The buildup for the Baroni fight brought a lot of extra heat to the Renzo fight. But I lost that, I looked like an asshole, and my brand took a huge hit. It became essential that I get the Baroni fight going and that I win.

The fight was finally scheduled, and it looked like it was really going to happen. I may have been smoking that cigar in the video, but I took this one very seriously. I left home for a training camp, which I'd never really done before. I moved down to Temecula, California, to train with Dan Henderson at his place down there. I moved in with my friend Bryan Foster. He had a sort of farm out there, with sheep and horses and pigs. It was a good place to concentrate on training. They had a little empty room, and I put my air mattress and books in it. That was my training camp. It reminded me of prison.

It was a good plan, but it didn't work out. On the very first day of training, I was working out with a judo champion who was going to show me some stuff. We were boxing and sparring. I knew that I was going to have beat Phil Baroni standing up. There was no other way to do it, and it was what the fans were going to demand. I was going to have to knock him out or get killed trying. There were huge expectations going into that fight. Nothing else would be acceptable.

So I was training with the judo guy. He threw a jab, then he just exploded with a huge judo leg chop, and my knee collapsed. My leg was planted and it just stayed there. The knee took the whole blow. Then the rest of me went down. It blew out my ACL completely.

I was screaming with pain. I screamed like a little baby. It was the worst pain I'd ever experienced in my life, except maybe for the day I did the initiation with Ken at the Lion's Den. It was horrible. Somehow I managed to get to Whole Foods. I bought a bag of vegetables to make soup and a bag of ice to put on my knee. I didn't see a doctor right away, and I didn't tell anybody what had happened. I was hoping it wasn't as bad as I thought it was.

It was only three weeks until the fight. There was no way I could back out. I *had* to show up. If I told the truth about what happened and said I wanted to reschedule it, the fans wouldn't believe it. Baroni would make me look like a fool. I had to find some way to show up.

For a while, all I did was meditate and read. I couldn't run. I couldn't even walk. I tried to do some training that didn't include anything on the ground. I got into a swimming pool with my legs tied together with a bungee cord, to see how that would work. It didn't work that well.

I finally went to see a doctor. He said, "You have literally got *no* ACL." He told me the only treatment for it was surgery. I told him I had to fight a championship fight in two weeks. He told me there was no way I could be ready for that.

It was not good. We had settled everything. ProElite was in. Strikeforce was in. We were making our deal with Showtime. And then we got word that CBS was coming to town. Everybody at CBS was going to be at the Shamrock-Baroni fight to see if it was time for CBS to take a chance on MMA. This fight was going to be the test case, the one that could qualify us.

So there was no way I could back out. Instead, the fight was going to be a really heavy mental test. I was going to have to bypass this really huge physical liability. I was going to have to go in with a new attitude: if you get knocked out, and you get killed, so what? Who gives a shit? That outcome was going to have to be OK.

I trained what I could train. By the time of the weigh-in, I could walk with two knee braces on and not look like I was in pain. No one outside my camp knew what had happened. Usually I'm very vocal about my injuries and my problems. Most fighters hide that stuff. Not me. I tell everyone who will listen what is wrong with me: the fighters, the media, everyone. I don't know why I started doing it, no one else does. But once I started talking about my injuries I noticed that some fighters believed it and other didn't, so I kept telling everyone to confuse them. It worked because the fighters thought I was trying to mislead them with false information about injuries, because no one talked about getting hurt. Normally, I just laid it out there. But this was different. I started putting out rumors about my *other* knee.

My wife and my son, who flew out for most of my fights in the United States, and my trainers knew what was going on. I said, "This is really bad. You guys should know." So they knew. It was clear that since I hadn't been able to do my training, and since my leg was hurt, I wasn't going to be able to do my basic thing, which was wrestling. I was going to have to stand up and strike. I had a lot of confidence in my striking, but I didn't have much experience. I had no idea whether I could beat Baroni that way.

I was scared. The Phil Baroni I was about to face was a scary guy. A lot of that was an act. I know that because, way back when, Phil came to me when I was teaching and approached me in a very humble, very normal way. He was outside his persona, and he said, "Would you teach me some of that stuff?" He was very personable.

But this was a different guy. He was angry, and he was taking steroids. He wanted to kill me. He was a guy who hit really hard and who was able to take a serious beating himself. I had never really been knocked out cold, like when your brain really turns off. I had been knocked unconscious, when I had my bell rung and went away for a second. But I had never been knocked out to the point where someone had to wake me up. That is very, very bad for your brain, and I really didn't want anyone to do that to me.

Phil Baroni looked like the guy who could do that. And the guy who really *wanted* to do that.

I spent two weeks sitting on that mattress in Temecula, meditating, pumping my soul up for the fight that was coming. I wasn't worried about performing. I had always performed, no matter what kind of injury I went in with. But I worried about concealing the knee injury, and about not having to back out.

The night of the fight came. We had fourteen thousand paid admissions. It was a huge fight. I was ready. I was still in very bad shape, but I had a plan. The fighters are supposed to be in their dressing rooms an hour before the match. I was planning on getting a big shot of lidocaine in my knee right before I went out. The shot lasts about an hour. I made them wait with the shot, and just sat there in pain, until the very last minute. When they came and knocked on my door, I said, "Doc, give me the shot."

I went out. I was scared. I had limited gas, and I knew it was limited. I knew I was at 65 percent or less. It wasn't good.

Phil Baroni was scared, too. He had to have been. He was stepping into a fight that was way bigger than anything he'd ever done, on a stage that was way bigger. He had come to California despite the drug test threat. He probably knew he wasn't going to pass. If he won the fight and got the championship, they'd probably take it away from him. But I had challenged his manhood. I had called him out. He was physically ready to kill me.

For him, it was a career maker. For me, it was going to be really good or really bad. When it was over, either my career was going to be finished or I was going to be a superstar. I couldn't have said one way or the other which way it was going to go.

We came out. I wore white shorts. He was in red. I had on two red knee braces, one on each leg. I looked OK if you didn't know why I was wearing them. Some sort of prefight online poll showed that most of the fans thought Baroni was going to win. For a while, at the beginning of the fight, it looked like they were right.

He got me pinned against the cage, just like he said he was going to, and he bounced my head off it a few times. He was hitting fast and hard. This wasn't necessarily a bad thing. He wasn't doing any real damage, and he was using up a lot of energy. This is something that happens to guys on steroids. Enson Inoue fought me like that. He came out on steroids and was brutal for a few minutes, and then he ran out of gas. I thought maybe Baroni would do that.

We went down. We got up. We danced around. His initial burst of energy didn't come back. I got the center of the ring. I hit him really hard on the chin. Nothing happened, but it felt really good. I moved him around the ring a little. I started to think maybe this was going to be OK.

So I taunted him a little. I took my fists away from my face and sort of waved him in—*come on and get me!* Then I took my hands and did a little "nighty-night" move, like I was going to sleep, and then pointed at him—like I was going to put *him* to sleep.

Two seconds later I hit him with a left jab and huge right, and he went down. I was on top of him fast, and hit him a bunch more times. He turned his head and I hit him in the back of the neck without thinking, just like during the Renzo fight. I couldn't believe what I was doing. I am totally kicking his ass and for whatever reason I start fouling him. I got a warning and a point against me. Then I got him in a front choke. The announcers actually called it. One of them said, "He's going for the choke!" and then, "It's over!"

But it wasn't over. It was only two minutes into the first round. And I was fighting Phil Baroni. Some guys might have tapped. But Baroni didn't tap. He broke free. We were on our feet again. Then we were on the ground again. He was on top. He was hanging on, but he was absorbing a lot of blows doing it. I hit him again and again in the head.

We were up again. I pushed him around to the edge of the mat, and got him hard with a knee to the face. He went over, and I got another choke hold on him. He slipped out of that, but he was on the ground and I hit him again and again to the head.

He escaped. He was up. I hit him again, with a really hard right, and then followed up with a knee. He looked a little stunned, but he didn't fall over. So I did that some more. I was having fun. I was smiling. I taunted him some more—*come on!* I got inside and hit him with another really hard right and knee combination.

The round was nearly over. I hit him again several times. His face looked terrible. He was staggering around. I got him to the edge of the cage, then we were on the floor. He was holding me down. It was all he could do. I saw Tom Casino, the Showtime photographer, shooting cageside and instinctively flashed him a peace sign. Baroni was too hurt and didn't have the energy to do anything else. He managed to hang on until the end of the round.

In the next round, he came back strong. He was boxing again. He hit me a couple of times, pretty hard, and I was tired. I couldn't see the punches coming. He was bouncing around like he was fresh and ready to go. But it didn't last. I hit him hard a couple of times, and then he was just swinging. He threw his arm around trying to land something. A couple of them landed. But I hit him again and again. I hit him *hard*. I had almost never hit anyone as hard as I hit Phil Baroni, and I hit him again and again. He was taking the most amazing amount of punishment.

At two minutes left in the second round, I caught him by the edge of the cage with a combination of rights and lefts. He took me down as he fell. He tried for an arm bar. I tried for a guillotine. We grappled around. I got a rear naked choke on him. But he wasn't going to go quietly. He was struggling. He was trying to hit me. He was getting weaker. But he wasn't tapping. For the longest time, he wasn't tapping.

I put everything I had into that choke. I was losing steam, too. Every second we fought, every second I held onto him, I was losing steam. I could feel him slipping away, but I was thinking, "If he gets out of this, he is going to kill me." But he didn't tap. With forty-two seconds left in the second round, the ref called it. He waved the fight over.

Baroni was out. He was actually unconscious. I couldn't get out from under him. I pushed him with my arm, and then sort of kicked him off me with my foot. I had defended my title. I had won. I had defeated a terrible opponent, but it came at a cost. My hands had never hurt so much after a fight. I thought they were both broken. They hurt for days from beating on Baroni's head so much. And my face was mush—I spent days falling in and out of naps on the couch with ice packs on my face. But it was also incredibly liberating. I had fought an almost entirely stand-up match. It ended with a choke, but the whole fight had been standing up, against a guy who specialized in that kind of fighting. I felt unbeatable.

Baroni later said he wasn't ready to tap, wasn't ready for the fight to end. But he ended up failing the drug test anyway. He tested positive for stanozolol and boldenone. He was fined $2,500 and given a one-year suspension from fighting. He got that reduced, but it was still his second bust for steroids.

I learned so much from the Baroni fight. I learned a lot about being tough, and what kind of tough, and what to do with it. Baroni was the kind of fighter who could take an amazing amount of abuse. He has this amazing chin. You can hit him forever and he still keeps coming. But when we were fighting, when I got close to him, I could feel the strength oozing out of him. I could feel he was losing power faster than I was. He was angry, and he was tense. Fighting is all about relaxing. You can't be angry and tense and keep going for very long. It tires you out.

I can usually get close to a guy and see his spirit, see if it's strong. It doesn't have to be my fight. I was watching the Marquez-Lopez fight in Las Vegas. In the eighth round, Marquez went to his corner and I could see he wasn't coming back. I said, "I guarantee you he's going to sit on that stool and not get back up." And he didn't. He is an amazing warrior, but I could see in his spirit that he wasn't going to make it.

Fighters fall into different categories of tough. There's really tough, so-so tough, and not so tough. Tito Ortiz is a middle guy. He's so-so tough. You can break him. At his core, he is not a real believer. You see that if you study his antics and his outward persona. The persona he puts out isn't who he really is. Inside, he's a regular nice guy. Outside, he's this killer dude. The difference between those two, the use of that persona, made me see there was a weakness in him. In his fighting style, just like in his public persona, he's a big bully. But if you take that away—just like with all bullies—he turns passive and starts wheeling backward. So I knew, before I ever fought him, that I could break him. I knew it would take a little time, maybe fifteen minutes, but then he would get tired and I could break him.

Renzo Gracie was the same way. He put out a lot of bluster and bravado, but I knew his spirit was weak in our fight. I knew he was game, but as soon as we started fighting and exchanged energies, I knew he was going to fold. I know, with a guy like Renzo, that he's forty years old, that these are his last fights, that this is his body, and that this is his limit. I knew I could sprint, balls to the wall, for ten minutes and take him. As it was, he took that knee to the back of the head and saw a way out.

Cung Le, who I would fight later, was in the not-so-tough category. He was dangerous but not lethal. I love him and he's a fighter, but at the end of the day he doesn't actually *want* to get into a fight. He wants to get into a gentlemen's sparring contest, not a fistfight. Now, I don't really want to either, but it's my job. I know with guys who don't really want to fight, or don't really want to get hit, that if I can lure them into a fistfight they will crumble. I thought Cung was in that category. He was never going to kick my ass technically, or knock me out. He wasn't going to kill me. I knew that if I fought him hard, and fought him dirty, and made it more like a street fight, it would take him out of his comfort zone, which is the martial arts zone. And then I could take him into the getting-your-ass-kicked zone.

Ken Shamrock was the toughest guy I ever met, back when I met him. He was mentally tougher, and physically tougher, than anyone else. He got the nickname "the World's Most Dangerous Man" for a reason. But things change. Ken changed. His ego got involved. His weakness is his ego. That is what has made him vulnerable. In

2000, his career record was 24 wins to 5 losses and 2 draws. That's an incredible record. He had fought and beaten everyone in the world. The only guys who'd beaten him were the Pancrase masters Funaki and Suzuki, Royce Gracie, and Dan Severn. No one else could touch him.

Ten years later, his record was 27-14-2. He had won three more fights, but he lost nine. He'd had his ass handed to him by everybody. Tito Ortiz beat him three times—twice in one year! His ego made him fight all these stupid fights, and maybe made him lose. So Ken, I think, went from the super-tough to the not-so-tough category.

Phil Baroni is super-tough. When we fought, he didn't know he wasn't good enough to beat me. That made him dangerous. He didn't know he didn't have the skills. That and the steroids made him dangerous. He was overconfident. He was ready for the fist-fight. He wasn't afraid to get hurt or get knocked out. He wasn't worried about getting an ass-kicking. He was very, very ready to go all the way. And he did. He never tapped out. I had to choke him into unconsciousness to win the fight. That's tough.

I would put myself into the super-tough category, too. That doesn't sound very good or very humble, but it's true. When I came to my fights, I came expecting to be hurt really bad, even killed. I accepted that. I understood it, and I accepted the possibility that I was going into the cage to face my death. I learned to do that even though I was afraid, and later I learned not to be afraid. That made me very hard to beat. A man who is not afraid to die is very hard to beat in a fight. After the tryout initiation routine with Ken, the first day at the Lion's Den, I never tapped out, except in Pancrase. That's how we ended a lot of the fights, so I tapped a few times. But I never once tapped out of a professional MMA or no-holds-barred fight—never. Not many fighters can say that. I never quit. I was never submitted. I was never knocked unconscious. I never asked to have a fight stopped. I got beat fair and square a few times, and I got cheated out of winning a few times, and I complained about that. But I never tapped out.

Part of that is heart. Part of it is spirit. But part of it is the conditioning factor. During my fighting heyday, I was at the very cutting edge of athleticism in the sport. I had conquered cardio like no one else. No one else trained like I trained. That made me extra hard to beat because I didn't get tired. I didn't lose a lot of energy just keeping up with the other guy. So I wasn't breathing hard, or trying to catch my breath, or running out of gas early in the fight. I was a sprinter, and I could sprint harder than anyone else.

So, because of the conditioning factor, if I could just not get knocked out, or tagged really hard in a way that broke something, I could outlast almost anyone. I could make the fight into a war of attrition. I could just keep coming back at you, round after round, and outlast you. With guys like Tito Ortiz or Renzo Gracie, I knew all I needed was ten or fifteen minutes. Same with someone like Cung Le. His style is all about evasion. It's very physical. It takes a lot of energy to dance around like that. I knew I could grind him down and finish him off.

But that was then. These days, almost everyone in the business is an incredible athlete. You can't just run a guy into the ground anymore like I used to do. The conditioning has become so important. Even the young guys who are wild and partying half the time, guys like Nick Diaz, are in incredible shape. They are super athletes, and that makes them super-hard to beat, the same way it made me super-hard to beat.

With the victory over Phil Baroni, I was Strikeforce's first middleweight champion. I added that belt to my collection. My fight record was 23-8-2. I wasn't sure who to fight next. There weren't that many guys. I was only willing to fight championship fights. I didn't want to fight little local fights. I wanted to do big Showtime pay-per-view fights that would continue to build my brand and advance the sport.

Lots of names got thrown around. Later on, people would add even more names. People would ask me why I didn't fight Randy Couture, or Chuck Liddell, or Rich Franklin. There was actually never a chance of my fighting any of those guys. First of all, they were always a weight class ahead of me, or even two weight classes. I was always a middleweight or light heavyweight. All those guys were light heavyweight at one time, but never when I was. They're giants, and I'm a little guy. (Check it out: Chuck is six foot two and 205. Randy is six foot one and 205. That's why they fought each other instead of fighting me.) Besides that, when those guys came into their prime, I was almost always in the competing organization. Once I left the UFC, I never got a shot at any of the UFC guys. So I might have fought someone like Anderson Silva, who's really tall but not as heavy as Chuck or Randy, but he was a UFC guy. So he was out, too.

But when people started talking about Cung Le, I got interested. When I started thinking about going head to head in a stand-up fight, I got really interested. Cung Le is a great guy. I would say he is a friend. I trained with him for years when I was younger as a sparring partner. He and I are about the same age. He was born in Vietnam but moved to the United States when he was three years old, escaping Saigon in 1975, just three days before the city fell to the North Vietnamese. He started training in tae kwon do when he was really little, and then got really into wrestling. He was a college wrestling star. Then he took up martial arts, studying san shou, which is a Chinese free-fighting discipline. He excelled in that and was undefeated, with a 16-0 record.

He made his MMA debut on the night I fought Cesar Gracie. Cung went up against Mike Altman and knocked him out in the first round. He went on to beat Brian Warren, Jason Von Flue, Tony

Fryklund, and Sammy Morgan. He was undefeated in his MMA career when we set up our match. In his kickboxing career, including his san shou fights, he was 17-0, with 12 knockouts to his credit.

It was a good match. He was five foot ten and 185, which meant we were the same size. It was going to be a good fight. But I thought it wasn't exactly a fair fight. I knew all about Cung and his fighting style. I knew his skill set. He was very fast. He was able to lean his center quickly in all four directions and avoid strikes. This was important, because it was going to be hard to damage him. I knew he was very good with his feet. He had kicked me in the head a few times over the years.

But I had a game plan. I knew two things about Cung that gave me an edge. First, I knew he didn't have the conditioning. He has never made it, and remained strong, past fifteen minutes. Most of his wins had been in the first round. So I knew he couldn't fight a long fight. I knew if I could keep him fighting and get to the third round, he'd be toast. I also knew that he is afraid to get hit. He hates getting hit. That's one of his dirty little secrets. He doesn't want to have a fistfight.

I also knew that Cung fought way better standing up than on the ground. He was trained as a wrestler, but his ground game is actually not that strong. He is a good wrestler but not a great one. He is not dangerous on the ground. So I knew the odds were that he would not go there. If we got to the ground, I knew I would destroy him.

But that would make for a less interesting fight. I would win, but it would be boring. So I made a decision. I decided to stand up. I decided to fight him at *his* game, not at mine. I knew how to beat him. I knew how to challenge him in a game of martial arts, just like I knew how to beat other guys in a street fight. I had a great camp. I was trained to perfection. I was going into the fight without any injuries of any kind—which was unusual for me. Usually I am distracted by having to manage some injury or other. I went in without any superstitions. I didn't feel hesitant on any level. I wasn't afraid to be hurt. I wasn't afraid to lose. I was looking forward to the challenge. It was exciting.

The fight was a Strikeforce/EliteXC event, held again at HP Pavilion, the Shark Tank, in San Jose. It was being broadcast on Showtime and pay-per-view, and we had a huge live crowd. It was a middleweight championship fight, and there were big expectations. We were both local, and we were both popular fighters. It was hard to know which way the energy was going, but the energy was enormous. I could feel it when I came into the arena.

We faced each other in the ring. I stared at Cung with my death stare, like I always do before a fight. Cung didn't look at me. He watched the ref and paid me no attention. Then we tapped gloves and it was on.

He stood southpaw style, with his right leg forward. I stood with my left leg forward. I was wearing shorts. He was wearing trunks. We looked very well matched in size and strength.

We had both done some of the same kind of training. During that time in the sport there was a wave of training techniques coursing through MMA. One of them was an oxygen reduction training, or oxygen deprivation training. Both Cung and I were doing it. The idea was to use this special oxygen mask while doing your cardio. As you do your workout, the oxygen supply diminishes, just as if you were training at higher and higher altitudes. We worked it up to something like twenty thousand feet. This was supposed to teach your body to produce at that level, when the oxygen is depleted, so that when they raise the oxygen back to normal your body will be that much stronger. I believed in it, but I didn't like it as much as simply exhausting myself doing an old-fashioned workout. I believed that if I ran as fast as I possibly could for twenty-five minutes then I was going to be just fine during the fight. The oxygen deprivation theory seemed to be that you could run at medium speed for twenty-five minutes while they just tweaked the science. For whatever reason, I didn't believe in that 100 percent.

I didn't go quite as far as some guys. I heard people were sleeping in hyperbaric chambers, trying to really force their bodies to do something different. I heard Cung did that, but I never tried it myself.

It turned out that training was going to be the issue. We were both extremely prepared. We were going to have a good old-fashioned fight.

The fight started fast. Within the first minute we exchanged some blows. He had some very sharp high kicks, right at my ears. He threw a wide roundhouse kick that surprised me a little. He got a crack at my chin, early in the first round, that rang my bell a little. But I stuck with it. I was determined to stand up. I had said in all the prefight interviews that I was not going to make it a grappling fight, that I was going to fight him on his own level. I wanted people to see, in the first round, that I was serious about that.

But I found myself getting tired, trying to hit him when he wasn't there. He was really fast, and he moved in very unusual ways. He used angles that were not traditional fighting angles and were not the usual modern fighting style. You never lean back and drop your hands in boxing. You never lean forward and drop your hands in kickboxing. But he was doing that kind of thing. It took me a while to figure out how to hurt him, and it took me a while to figure out how to not let him hurt *me*.

He had some interesting moves. One of them was a right-left jab and right side kick combination that was very effective. He got me with that two or three times before I started to see it coming. He got me with a right hook to the side of the head that was kind of interesting. I had the center of the canvas, most of the time, but he was hitting me effectively.

The fight started to feel good. I could feel everything that he had, and what he had didn't feel super-strong. He didn't feel sturdy.

With 1:25 left in the first round there was this amazing moment. Cung threw a huge kick at me, a wide spinning heel kick. I ducked it and came inside and socked him hard with a left, right on the button. He went down, and I almost got him in a guillotine choke hold, and then shot him a knee. He got loose but looked very dazed. Like I said before, he does *not* like a fistfight, and he suddenly looked like he was having a very bad time.

But a minute later he shot a foot jab at my left leg, and I reached down to block it with my right arm. Right after, he came with another kick to the body, and I blocked that with the same arm. This time I really put some weight behind it. That was a mistake. I felt my arm crack. I actually felt it, and thought I could hear my bones snap. It was a weird feeling, like someone had stabbed a knife in my arm. I shook my hand. It didn't feel that bad. I knew it was injured, but it didn't seem like that big a deal.

I knew the time was short. Cung and I exchanged a few more shots. I did my sleepytime act, like I was going to take a nap, and then pointing at Cung. *I'm going to put you to sleep.* He didn't seem that impressed.

The first round ended. I went to my corner feeling really good. I had this great big smile on my face, even though my face was a little mashed up. This was a good fight, and the fans knew it, and I felt great about being in it.

I felt composed. Maurice Smith was giving me directions, scolding me for holding back and playing Cung's game. But I was waiting. I had a plan and I was sticking to it. My arm was pounding a little bit. It hurt. But the pain was not disabling or even that distracting. It was just some information, like that arm isn't feeling as good as the other one.

The commentators had talked in the early part of the first round about Cung's kicks and how dangerous they were. One of the commentators had even said that I might wind up with a broken arm defending myself. But he recognized I was doing what I said I would do: "Shamrock's true to his word," he said. "He stood with Baroni, and he's standing with Le."

The second round started. I got more comfortable. I was smiling and laughing. But then he kicked me in the side of the head with a roundhouse and knocked my mouthpiece out. He hit me with his shinbone, and I didn't see it coming. We stopped and he let me pick up my mouthpiece, and we grinned at each other. But it made me nervous. I didn't even see the kick. It was that fast. I didn't like being hit by something I hadn't even seen.

I got knocked over about halfway through the round. I sat on my butt and said, "Come on!" I was only kidding. I knew he wouldn't come down to the ground after me. He'd get killed if he did that, and he knew it. So I popped back up. We were going to fight his fight. No problem.

I was still walking him down the canvas. He was still using the right side kick effectively—in the leg, in the side, in the body—but it wasn't hurting me much anymore. It was more distracting than anything else. He did land a right jab that caught me by surprise. I nodded my head a few times, as if to say, "Yeah, that was a good one."

I got a good one into him, too. I hit him really hard a few times, once in the throat. I felt my fist go in and squish, and I thought, "Wow, that's going to hurt." I had blocked a few more kicks with my right arm, which still felt weird. When I hit with it, I could feel it vibrating. But it didn't seem all that important. It just hurt.

The third round started. Cung came with a couple of high kicks that got me on the side of the head. I started to wonder if he was going for a decision, just trying to outlast me and score some points and win that way. I was starting to get tired. I could see he was starting to get tired, too. I could hear him gasp, a few times, on our exchanges. I was glad about that. Maybe my cardio was better than his. Our rhythms were similar. We were moving at about the same speed.

But I also noticed he was starting to look really relaxed. He was finding a range. He was getting comfortable with the kicks. I didn't like that. I needed to overcome that. He could see his range, and I needed to correct that. I remember feeling a sort of urgency about it—like I had to stop that *now*.

It's a little like dancing. One guy is usually leading. If the other guy controls the distance and controls the space between the two of you, then he gets the confidence and the timing for where and when the strikes are. If you control the area, you dictate. Most fighters dictate with the strike—with the jab or the punch. Cung was dictating with the side kick, or the fast round kick. He understood that was happening before I did. He had the range, and I couldn't take it away from him. He got more confident, and his kicks increased in power and combination. He kicked me in the body a few times and it really hurt. He got a heel into my face, and that hurt pretty good, too. Then I hit him really hard, super-hard, with a left hook. It didn't seem to do anything at all.

He swept me with a leg kick and knocked me on my butt. I got up, nodding my head—*that* was a good one. But I got back into it. At about a minute left in the third round, I landed a very sharp right, and followed it with several really successful strikes. It looked like the fight was going to turn. The crowd went insane. I pushed Cung around pretty hard, and got him up against the side of the cage. We clinched, and then pushed off.

I felt really good. I was sort of bobbing and bouncing as I walked him across the cage, with my hands down. I thought I might be able to finish him. Then he got me with another kick, a left kick to the right side of my head. That hurt. When he threw the next one, I blocked it. The pain was horrible. I felt the bone separate, and then I thought I was going to actually crap myself getting to my corner. The pain was unbelievable. I had never felt anything like it. The horn went and the round was over.

The crowd went insane. They were on their feet. But I didn't even make it to my corner. I fell down halfway there, and they had to pick me up and carry me to the stool. I felt like I was going to *die*. The pain was worse than anything I could ever remember feeling. When the bell rang, I couldn't answer it. I was lying on my back, moaning. They called the fight for Cung. It was over.

Cung strutted around the ring. He yelled that he loved his girlfriend. He crossed himself. He hugged people. He mugged for the cameras. I was lying on my back, crying and whimpering. I was begging for pain medication. I was begging for morphine. I don't think I'd ever done that before.

They brought out the belt. They ruled the fight a technical knockout. They crowned the new middleweight champion.

I knew Cung couldn't go past fifteen minutes. I knew I could outlast him. I knew he was afraid to get hit, and he didn't have the conditioning. But I had made a mistake, a technical mistake. I didn't anticipate his kicks would come that fast or have that much power. Fast kicks aren't usually very powerful kicks, and I didn't see that a fast kick could hurt that much. So when I blocked the kicks, I blocked with one arm. I had trained that way. I had practiced that. But I should have been using two for those big kicks. That's what Maurice had said, but I was too arrogant to think that Cung could break my arm. If I'd done that, I would have KO-ed him in the third or fourth round.

That's the reason I stood up with him. I knew he would be toast by the end of the third round, and I could do what I wanted. But I was losing the fight. I had stood up and fought the way I wanted, but he was winning in points. I was doing some damage. I could see his eyes cross a couple of times. He was almost knocked out a couple of times. I was banging him up bad, in the third round, even while he was scoring more points.

But his kicks were awesome. He really rang my bell hard with that last set of kicks to the side of the head. I never thought he was going to knock me out. He never hit me and made me see stars—although I think I did see two Cung Les, side by side, for a second, after one of those kicks that I didn't see coming, probably the one that opened a cut that required eight staples to close.

I hadn't been aware how badly my arm was hurt. The rush is so high when you're fighting. There is very little fear. You don't feel much. You're just flooring it. If you feel like you're winning, there is this enormous rush of energy. If your opponent is whacking on you, and you feel like you're losing, the opposite is true. Every time you try something and it doesn't work, you can feel yourself wilt a little.

But otherwise you find yourself in this weird zone. You feel bolts of energy flying off you, and into you. You don't really hear the crowd. You don't really hear your corner. There's almost no time for that. If you stop to listen or think, it becomes too late to act or react fast enough. You're in a very heightened state of awareness, in a very narrow tunnel. When you break away from that energy, you lose momentum. You can't do that. You have to keep going.

I felt like I was still going. I felt very conscious of what was going on. I saw Cung breathing hard. I saw he was getting tired. I thought, *perfect. We're right on time.* Until that last kick, if you had stopped the fight and asked me how I was doing, I would have told you I was going to knock him out and finish the fight and retain my title.

But at the end of the third round, I knew I was done. I told Maurice, "I think my arm is broken," and then the pain was just too much. I am Mr. Pain Tolerance. I can take a lot of abuse. But this was amazing. I was screaming for morphine.

They took me to the hospital. I underwent surgery the next morning. I got a big metal plate and a bunch of metal screws in my arm. I was afraid I might not be able to fight again. I was afraid I was finished.

13

FATHERHOOD

Something wonderful happened to me right after the Cung fight. My wife, Amy, gave birth to our daughter, Nicolette, on April 24, 2008.

It hadn't been easy. We had been trying for a while. Maybe we were trying too hard. I noticed an ad in *Baby Magazine* for a watch called the Ov-Watch. It was a brand-new, patent-pending, FDA-cleared ovulation tracking system that only required her to wear a silly watch; my kind of program. All the pee sticks and schedule sex were wearing us out. It cost a hundred bucks, but we were getting anxious, so we got the watch and went to Kauai for vacation. That's where Amy got pregnant.

I had not been around when my son was born. I was locked up. I had not been much of a father to him, either, when he was young. I was determined to be a different kind of dad this time around. It was a difficult birth. I spent five days and nights at the hospital with Amy. I read every book I could find about babies and about being a father. I must have read fifty books. I didn't want to miss a single thing. I *didn't* miss a single thing. I was 100 percent there for the arrival of my daughter.

That cost me a movie role. About three or four months before Nicolette was born, I had told Amy that I was not going to let anything interfere with my job as a father. I was going to cancel everything and be there when the baby was born, no matter what. Then a package arrived from 20th Century Fox. It looked very official, and marked CONFIDENTIAL, and it was a script for a movie version of the video game Max Payne. Mark Wahlberg was going to star, and the director wanted me to play the part of the evil bad guy. It was all set up. All I had to do was sign. But I also would have to go to Toronto for the shoot and be gone for a week or two.

I read the script. I took a day. Amy looked at me as if to say, "Yeah, you're going to do it." She tried to pretend she was excited for me. But I knew it wasn't right. I had said I was going to be there. I had to be there. So I called the production office. I said I was really flattered, and thought the project was awesome, and that I'd love to do it if they could postpone things for a few months.

The woman at the production office was very, very polite. She said, "I'll run that by the director and see what he says." As if that would ever happen! Someone else got the part. I never saw the movie. I think I made the right decision. But the timing could have been better.

Over the years I had maintained as close a relationship as I could with my son. We had been through some crazy stuff. One time, he decided he really wanted to become a sword swallower. Being an overcompensating father, I said, "OK, I'll help you." I told him to start training for it and after three months I bought the best sword-swallowing sword that money can buy.

He's always been a little eccentric, and a little adventurous, like me. He was really a daredevil. He would always say, "Is it going to kill me?" If it wasn't, he'd go and try it. I thought I was being a thoughtful and supportive father. But he got into trouble. One night I got a call. My son was performing in a show in a church, doing his sword-swallowing act, when he nicked something in his stomach and started bleeding. He bled for thirteen hours. He was in the emergency room and he was dying.

Just before that I had been forced to take him out of his home. His mother's drug use had gotten really bad. He was having trouble, too. He had a breakdown of some kind at school. So I sent him to Utah to live with his grandparents, Christy's mom and dad. They helped raise him, and even though they had kept her drug issues a secret from me, they were the best parents for him. I really wanted him to live with Amy and me, but we were always on the road and I was perpetually in a fight camp. So he was kind of on his own, even though he was only sixteen years old.

It was a Memorial Day weekend when he injured himself. I got up to Salt Lake City as fast as I could and rented a car and drove to the hospital. He was in surgery. They had to slice him open to do it, but they stopped the bleeding in his stomach and saved his life. He was going to be OK. For some reason they gave me the sword. I ended up stopping in a gas station and giving the sword to the attendant. It was a $200 sword, but I just gave it to the guy. He must have thought I was nuts.

It was a life-changing event for me. I thought I was invincible. I thought my son was invincible, too. But he had almost died. It freaked me out.

I had not kept in very close touch with anyone from my family for a long time. My brother, Perry, had taken off when he was still a teenager. He had joined the navy at age eighteen and run off to see the world. He got a girl pregnant on the East Coast, where he was stationed. Then he came home on a visit and got another girl pregnant on the West Coast. My mother told me he was bipolar. She had always said he was "special." She said she did a lot of drugs when she was pregnant with him. I think she blamed herself for his condition.

Suzy lived in Colorado, Robynn somewhere in California. We weren't close as adults. Suzy had been so traumatized by much of her childhood that she was always cutting herself off, always closing off contact because she got angry about something or upset with someone.

I didn't stay close to my mom. She had stayed with Joe despite everything. They were together for more than twenty-five years, until Joe died.

Joe smoked Camel nonfilters. He smoked so much, I used to imagine him smoking in the shower. My mom smoked with him. But they both quit when Joe got lung cancer. The doctors diagnosed him with mesothelioma, a kind of lung cancer that people usually get from asbestos. Joe had worked for the military on ships, scraping asbestos off things, breathing that stuff into his lungs. Then he was a smoker all his life. So it wasn't really surprising. The doctors said he had stage four cancer and gave him six months to live. He died about two years later.

Perry came home from wherever he was living to be with my mom. He was supposed to move in with her and take care of her, help her handle her affairs after Joe died. Instead, I think he moved in with her and spent all her money getting high and hanging out.

Somewhere in there, someone hatched a scheme. My mother had bought a jungle house in Belize. She and her new boyfriend, Barry, along with Perry and his son, Matthew, were all moving there. They bought a motor home, and the plan was to drive that motor home across the United States and Mexico to Belize.

I don't know whose plan it was. They got slowed down in Texas and were stuck for a while, all four of them, in two motor homes, in Galveston. I didn't think they'd ever get out of there. I certainly didn't think they'd ever get to Belize.

My sister Robynn visited me in San Jose in the spring of 2011. She had come up to San Francisco to attend some seminars relating to her business. We hung out together, just the two of us. It was the first time we had done that since we were little kids, since before I got sent away to juvenile hall the first time—the first time in almost thirty years.

We talked a while. When we were alone, I asked her if she remembered how the family moved from Lancaster to Redding. She remembered. She remembered a *lot*. She told me that our mother left Lancaster because she was leaving my father. "She got fed up with him," Robynn said. "She couldn't take it anymore." So she left Frank and ran off with another man. First my mother left the whole gang of us kids with an aunt of ours, who we called Aunt Dolly. Later, she and the guy came back for the family. Somehow they found their way to Redding.

I only remember him from pictures. He was a white dude, with long hair and a beard. He was a few inches taller than my mom and looked like a typical hippie guy from the 1970s. The pictures included some from a wedding album. I know my mom and this White Hippie Guy got married somewhere in the woods—a hippie wedding—and then went on a camping honeymoon. I don't think it lasted long, maybe a year or so, before White Hippie Guy was out and Joe arrived on the scene.

I always imagined that life before Joe was more normal. That's not what Robynn said. She told me that my mother left my father and ran off with White Hippie Guy because she had found out that he and my father were lovers, that they were both pedophiles, and that they were doing things together. They were best friends and deviant sexual partners. My mom found out something, or got freaked out by something, and decided to take off. In her mind she was getting back at Frank, somehow, by stealing his best friend and running off with him.

Then she left him, Robynn told me, when he started molesting Robynn and Suzy. I was shocked but not entirely surprised. I knew that my father, Frank Juarez, had been incarcerated for many years for some sort of sex crimes. In about 2008 I had been contacted by a representative of the California prison system, asking me if I'd be willing to sponsor my father out of jail.

I got the letter out of the blue. I hadn't heard anything from my dad and I hadn't seen him, physically, since the few months that I lived with him in Lancaster when I was a little boy. I knew he had been with other families. I heard he had disappeared. What I learned later was that he had gone to prison for ten years for child molestation. He was a violent offender. When you are a violent sex offender, you don't just do your time and get released. You do your time, and then you go for some kind of psychological evaluation, and then you have to find someone to sponsor you back into society. That's why they were contacting me. He had become eligible for some kind of parole or release. He put me on a list. I was on there with my grandfather. My dad's attorney or his public defender initiated it. The letter didn't say outright what the deal was. It said the state of California believed I had specific or important information about this individual. Please contact the district attorney's office.

I saw the name on top. I saw that it was Frank Juarez. At first I thought *Oh no, someone has stolen my identity!* In the last ten years, I have had a bunch of attempts at accessing my identity under my old name, Frank Alicio Juarez. I always assumed it might have been my dad, trying to use my credit or get some of my money. So I thought this was another one of those attempts. So I followed up and contacted the district attorney's office. I discovered that they wanted to find someone to vouch for him so he could get out of prison.

I was shocked. I was a little scared. But I didn't feel responsible. I wasn't tempted to do what the state was asking me to do. That was very clear to me. So I said, "I don't want anything to do with the guy." I had a young daughter at home. I didn't want a violent sex offender living with me. I didn't even want him to know where my house was. I was sorry about him being locked up, and sorry that he had no one to vouch for him, but I did not feel responsible for him. I hadn't seen him or heard from him in over twenty years. He had never been a father to me. I didn't even remember him from my childhood. I didn't want to have him in my life—at least, not this way.

The guy from the prison board told me that I could say no, and that probably what would happen is that my father would remain in custody. Then, every two years or so, I'd be contacted again when he came up for reevaluation. I'd get the call. I'd be asked again if I wanted to vouch for him.

I asked the guy to take me off the list. I told him, "I'm a public figure. I'm easy to find. This isn't something I want to be involved in—ever. I don't want to be contacted anymore." The guy said he'd take me off the list. I didn't hear anything else about it. I felt really weird for about two weeks. My dad had been so removed from my life for so long. I never heard from him, or heard anything about him, so I hardly ever thought about him. Now he was on my mind, and it disturbed me. Then time passed, and I went back to not thinking about him.

But then Robynn gave me this new information. I was shocked, like I said. But I wasn't totally surprised. It made sense. It even made sense that my mom knew about it, and maybe even accepted it for a while. She had told me once that her own mother had engaged in some sort of deviant sexual stuff. She kind of hinted that was why her mother had left her father and gone off to live with an alcoholic guy in a trailer park. It had something to do with sexual behavior, and my mom was exposed to that, somehow, when she was a little girl. So for her, maybe, it was almost normal to be around that kind of thing. Maybe she was also molested; maybe I was, too.

I didn't know and hadn't even considered it until now. Was that one of the reasons that I could not control my actions when I was a little boy? Did something happen to me that I was too small to process and purposely forgot? I began searching my memories and past for clues or feelings. I was really freaked out with all this new information about the past. Thankfully there was so much good in my life at that moment that I decided to put the spirit of healing out into the universe. Whatever "it" was, I was going to face it. The universe answered, via Facebook.

Shortly after I started writing this book, and months before Robynn came to visit, I posted a childhood photo on my Facebook fan page. I was around six years old in the picture. It looks like an elementary school photo, and I have on a yellow shirt, a huge frown, a bowl cut, and a chubby belly. Within days of posting it I received a lengthy Facebook message from a woman calling herself my aunt Jewell. She said she was married to my mom's brother, Mike. She had helped raise me when I was a little boy. She had lost track of me some thirty years ago when their family moved away to Colorado. I was her favorite baby boy, Frankie, and she wanted to talk.

She was so proud that I was successful and had worried herself sick about me all these years. She said I was shy and overweight, everyone teased me, and my mom was always locking me in the closet. This felt like a kick in the gut. I was hurt, angry, sad. I remember Joe putting me in the closet and I hated him for it, but I don't remember Mom authorizing it or putting me in there herself. Robynn kind of remembered Aunt Jewell, mostly from stories that Mom told us, but nothing solid or concrete, nothing that I could use to bolster my courage to contact her back. But I finally did, and we set up a phone call, or tried to. I was really busy, and sometimes I would just lose courage. I was also writing this book at the time and the emotional toll was exhausting—I didn't know if I could handle any more. Aunt Jewell wouldn't let it go, though. She kept resched-uling every time that I got "busy"; it was obvious that she needed to talk. Jewell had just survived a bout with breast cancer. She was tough like that, but I began to realize that she had things that were weighing on her spirit that needed to be released. I called her. She started bawling and talking at the same time, gushing out her story.

She and Mike had married when she was a virgin. When she met Lydia, my mom, Lydia already had four kids, her own house, and her own car. Jewell really looked up to her. The two families grew up together. Mike didn't work but insisted that Jewell have a job. He would stay home and do whatever—smoke pot, screw around. He was a total loser, and she picked up the slack. That's around the time that Mom met her soon-to-be-next husband. He immediately moved in. He was a loser, too, with the same work ethic Mike had. They hung out all day while Jewell went to work. One day when she came over to Mom's door to see if White Hippie Guy was there, she heard a child's muffled screaming coming from the living-room coat closet. Jewell quickly opened the door to find me hanging upside down by my knees over the hanger rod, screaming. I was two or three. She sobbed out that she had wanted to save me, run away with me, that she knew what was going on was so wrong. But she was just a young girl. She said she was so sorry that she could not save me.

Listening to her words and hearing the emotion melted my heart. I told her it was OK, I was OK. Everything worked out. I was happy, healthy, successful, famous. It was OK now. I asked questions. She told me that Lydia and Mike were not affectionate people at all. The kids learned to work very young, cooking and cleaning. Aunt Jewell confirmed that White Hippie Guy was a real creep and deviant, and she was terrified to be alone with him. After a few years in Redding, she and Mike had more financial troubles and one day picked a place on the map and moved. Mike told her to never speak to my mom or her family again and never to contact us. I am glad she defied him. We talk often now, and our families are back together. It's time for the secrets of the past to die and for everyone to start living, right now.

By early 2009 I was healed enough from the Cung fight to think about fighting again. I still had the plate in my arm, and breaking it again would be a bad thing, but the doctors said I was strong enough. So we started looking around.

I had a deal with Scott Coker, and we were basically partners. I had signed a deal for six fights with ProElite earlier, but then Pro-Elite had fallen apart. Scott and Strikeforce had bought their assets and renegotiated their deal with Showtime. Scott said to me, "We need a barn burner. We need you to fight someone incredibly relevant and tough." We started talking about who the other fighter would be. We talked about a rematch with Cung Le, but he was making a movie and he wanted too much money. We talked about a rematch with Renzo Gracie, but he was with the UFC and he wanted too much money, too. We talked about Tito Ortiz, but he was with UFC, too. That was sort of the problem. Strikeforce had a roster of about seventy fighters, but only four or five of them were big names. Everyone else was with the UFC. We needed a big name to move everything forward.

Nick Diaz seemed like a logical choice. He was another tough Mexican kid, like me. He came from Stockton, California, which is a pretty tough place, and went to high school for one year in Lodi. He got into MMA, he said, because he was bullied by bigger kids when he was a teenager. He became a swimmer first, then began studying martial arts. He found his way to the Gracie organization and, along with his little brother Nate, became part of the Gracie camp. That made us natural enemies, and it gave the fight a hook. It was Shamrock versus Gracie again.

He was already one of the top contenders in his weight class. He was the up-and-coming guy. I was the old guy. It was clear that Strikeforce and Showtime were looking for me to step up and fight the young guy. It was going to be a good story, and it would make a statement about the brand. Either I'd beat him and we'd have this bad-ass competition that could play out for a few years, or he'd beat me and the story would be more about the changing of the guard.

I wasn't too worried going into the fight. Nick seemed like a loudmouth punk. He was always saying rude things about his opponents. He was a big trash-talker. He didn't look like he was in good shape. He also seemed like a big stoner. He made no secret of his fondness for weed. He joked about it. I thought he might have a hard time passing a drug test. But I knew he was a serious opponent. He had a good record, 18-7. He was taller than me at six foot one. He wasn't heavy or burly, but he had really long arms and legs and was a good striker. He was also eleven years younger than me. But I was eleven years wiser and more experienced than him. It seemed like a good match, but balanced in my favor.

It was an evening of strong fighters. Brandon Michaels went up against Raul Castillo. Scott Smith fought Benji Radach. Brett Rogers fought Abongo Humphrey. A Japanese woman fighter named Akira Hitomi got beat by Cristiane Santos. Gilbert Melendez, another Gracie guy, beat up Rodrigo Damm. (Rodrigo had been brought in at the last minute. Melendez was supposed to fight Josh Thomson, but Thomson broke his leg sparring and couldn't compete.)

I was pretty amped up for the fight. I felt bad about the way things had gone with Cung. I had shown up ready to fight and had given the fans a tremendous battle. If my arm hadn't gotten broken, I think I would have won the fight and retained my middleweight title. Now I was fighting a catchweight fight against this kid. I was confident that I'd beat him. I was already thinking about a rematch with Cung. I was looking ahead. But I wasn't in top shape. I had torn some muscles in my abdomen in training. Every time I turned my torso, I felt a horrible burning pain. I was a little worried about that.

The event was held in my hometown, in my home arena, the HP Pavilion "Shark Tank" in downtown San Jose. We were broadcasting on Showtime. We were almost sold out, with something like fourteen thousand tickets sold. I don't know how many people were there to see me, or to see Nick Diaz, or to see another Shamrock-Gracie fight. This was where the first fight happened, when I kicked Cesar's ass in front of eighteen thousand fans. Some of them might have come back to see the next installment.

The night opened with a moment of silence for an old friend, Charles Lewis, known as Mask. He was a founder of the TapouT clothing company and a big personality in the MMA world. He had been killed in a drunk-driving, drag-racing accident in Newport Beach less than a month earlier. People were really fond of him, and they were feeling the loss.

The crowd was into it. The fight celebrities were there. Mickey Rourke, with whom I had started to become friends, was in the house. So were Cung Le and Gina Carano. Then the fighting started. Brett Rogers came out and gave Abongo Humphrey a terrible beating—knees to the face and some brutal shots before Abongo went down hard. Then Cristiane Santos, known as Cyborg, came out and gave the Japanese fighter an ass-whipping. Scott Smith came out and for a couple of rounds looked like toast. Then he turned it around and knocked Benji Radach out.

Gilbert Melendez took the cage and gave the Brazilian Damm a bad beating. Melendez knocked him out, and it took the trainers a full two minutes to bring him back to consciousness.

It was time for me to work. The announcer called the fight "a grudge match of the generations." The fans got to their feet as we came down to the cage. Half of them seemed to be cheering for me.

Half of them seemed to be booing Nick Diaz. We had already had a couple of press conferences. Nick had made his feelings known; he never missed an opportunity to give me the finger, to give the fans the finger, to show his bad-ass attitude. We exchanged some words at the weigh-in. We traded some more smack in prefight interviews. He said, "I'm gonna put him down in the first round." I said, "I don't think he's prepared for me. I don't have any doubt in my mind that I'll smash him. I think he's making a huge mistake."

We had some nice dialogue at a press conference in Los Angeles. We came out to meet the reporters. I stuck my hand out to shake. He gave me the finger. I was smiling and laughing. He had an evil frown on his face. He took the microphone and said, "I feel confident. Frank's too small for this weight class. He's got a little-guy complex."

I gave some back. "My son's five years younger than Nick," I said. "If he acted like this, I'd send him to his room and take away his allowance."

"Where's he at right now?" Diaz asked. "I'll fight him, too."

"He's in college," I answered. "You wouldn't know."

Later, I said, "I just hope Nick has his friends there, so they can catch his head when I knock it into the second row." I don't think he answered that one except to flip me off again.

I was asked whether we had any difficulty getting the fight set up. I said the only problem was Nick having to take the drug test. I asked him how that had gone. He said, "I think they're gonna let me fight no matter what."

I said, "Well, there's your answer to that one."

What he didn't know, because nobody knew, was that I was not feeling 100 percent. Certain things had not gone well leading up to the fight. I had popped a few ribs during practice; I was wrestling, doing some grappling training. I had been having some rib issues. I didn't think they were serious. What even I didn't know was that my C7 disc had compressed. This was a bad combination. So I went to do this giant bridge while training, and I tore my abdominal muscles several levels deep. The pain was extreme. I screamed. I actually screamed. I hadn't felt pain like that since Cung Le broke my arm. It was horrible.

It passed, but then it didn't seem to get better right away. I was told I would have to rest for a while. My ribs still felt messed up going in. I hadn't been able to train the way I like to train. I couldn't do any kind of grappling for about two weeks before the fight. But I still went in there 100 percent convinced I was going to beat him. Like a man whose faith is unshakeable, I once again picked up the metaphorical sword, and I believed the sword would strike him down.

The ref, as usual, was Big John McCarthy. He said, "Let's get it on!" and we did. I knew pretty early in the fight that I was in trouble. I saw that he got my range. He knew where to stand and how to hit me. I knew he was going to box me around until I got tired and then, bam! He kept his hands down a lot, asking me to hit him. He actually stuck his jaw out for me to smack it. But when I moved closer, bam! I was really surprised, also, at how *hard* he hit. His punches were very powerful.

I could tell really early in the first round that I wasn't fast enough. I wasn't strong, either, like I normally was. In the first couple of exchanges, when we connected, I didn't feel the energy and intention that I usually feel in the first part of the fight. Usually, no matter who I'm fighting, I'm not conscious of the other person's strength. That comes later, sometimes, but in the first part of the first round I never feel it.

This time I felt it. My stuff wasn't connecting; his stuff was. I started getting punched in the head a lot. It didn't hurt that much, but it started to back me up, mentally. He got me down and on my back, and he held me there a while. He hit me a couple of times.

Then I slipped out from under him and hit him a couple of times getting up. He threw a foot into my face.

Mostly he stuck his long right arm out and measured the range. He looked like a gorilla with those arms—waving them around, waving me in, and taunting me the whole time. I threw a couple of punches that landed and a couple that didn't. He didn't seem too worried about it. I didn't think I was hurting him any. Then he got me down and starting throwing punches, lefts and rights, that weren't hurting me any.

I didn't think I was going to lose. But I saw it was going to be harder to win than I thought. Midway through the first round I started running out of ideas. I tried one thing, and it didn't work. I tried something else, and that didn't work. That was a new feeling. It felt like I was climbing a hill that kept getting steeper. I didn't know if I was going to make it. Then I realized I wasn't making it. This was a brand-new feeling for me. I had never had anybody run over me in a fight. I get hit, and I back up, and I come at you again. But this was like I was getting run over.

Nick had started talking to me right away, right from the beginning. He taunted me, telling me to throw the right hand. He was angry, and he was emotional. He cursed me. He stuck his face out and told me to throw the right. I did, and hit him hard, and he responded, "Oh yeah!"

I've got a lot of power in my right hand. It's my go-to punch. But it takes a lot of energy. He knew that, and he was trying to get me to whittle myself down. Throwing the right tired me out. He'd stick his face out at me, and I'd throw the right. Then he'd punch me in the head a few times. With a few of them, I missed. That takes about three times as much energy. You throw the punch and then you have to bring it back. It's exhausting.

I could hear the fans. They sounded restless. Some of them were chanting, "Dee-az! Dee-az!" Then some others started chanting back, "Sham-rock! Sham-rock!" I couldn't tell who was the favorite anymore. I could hear my corner yelling at me, too. But I wasn't really hearing them. I wasn't doing what they were telling me to do. I wasn't listening. I was just really tired. When we got to the end of the round, and I sat down, I wasn't really aware of what they were saying.

And when I went out for the second round, I wasn't listening. Whatever they were saying did not sink in. I just remember thinking that I was really tired, and that I had tried these nine different gear shifts, and that nothing was working. I needed to find another strategy. But I still thought I was going to win. I just thought it was going to take a lot longer than I wanted it to, and that it was going to take a lot more out of me.

Then with about three minutes left he punched me in the ribs. My body hadn't been working right. I was tired. I was getting hit. But I was still going. I was bleeding a lot. But I wasn't really hurting. I was just beat up and tired. But that punch in the ribs felt like someone stabbed me in the spine, like an electrical jolt to the spinal cord. It took all the juice out of me. It was like I had been Tasered. And I thought, *Oh my God, I'm going to* lose.

I had honestly thought the rib thing wouldn't have a big impact on the fight. I didn't think it was that big a deal. But I was really struggling. I could feel that I couldn't get any power into my shots. I had to keep the fight standing, and take the beating, because I didn't think I would have any power on the ground.

It was a weird, unpleasant experience. Usually I can take three rounds of *anything* and be fine. But it felt like my body started shutting down after the first round. Then came that shot in the ribs and I just went down. I couldn't defend myself. The ref let it go on a little, and then waved the fight stopped.

Diaz reached down and tried to pull me up. He had been talking shit the whole fight. Now he yelled at me. He said, "You're a legend!

Get up! Don't lay there!" He got me on my feet. He raised my hand over my head, and put his arm around my neck, and said, "The legend! The legend!"

Then we were in our corners. I was breathing hard and bleeding from everywhere—even the back of my head. I had hit it on something. When we stood up to shake hands, Nick bowed to me, like I was his *sensei*. He gave me some respect. He said, "I've been watching Frank Shamrock fight since the beginning. . . . It's hard to hate that guy. He's been doing what I want to do and saying what I want to say for a long time." Then it was my turn. I said, "I give everything to Nick Diaz. I trained for him 100 percent. I didn't take him lightly. . . . I always step it up. . . . I always come to entertain. But Nick kicked my ass tonight, no two ways about it. He beat me."

They replayed the moment when he hit me in the stomach. It was brutal. I said, "It doubled me over. And then he put a whuppin' on me."

The announcer asked me about the future. I said, "I'm gonna keep coming back here. This is my hometown. This is my arena! I brought the sport here. I'm gonna keep representing. . . . I'll be back here—don't even worry about it. . . . Nick got the better of me tonight, but there's always tomorrow. That's the martial way."

At the press conference after the fight, he said, "I just wanna say I had to get that one done for my boy." He had wanted to beat me to avenge my knockout fight with Cesar Gracie three years earlier. Cesar had been in his corner. He won the fight for his coach.

After the fight, I went with some friends to an Italian restaurant around the corner from the arena. I tried to celebrate. When someone asked me what happened, I didn't pretend. I said, "I got hit! He was like a monkey, with that reach. He kicked my ass!"

I was happy not to be in the hospital. Usually I'm in the hospital after a fight, even when I win. One of my friends said, "It's a victory!" I said, "Yeah. I came in second!"

But actually I hate to lose. It *hurts* to lose. Especially in my home-town, it was hard to lose. For the fighter, it's *always* about winning. It's always about facing the challenge and meeting the challenge. This was the only time in my whole career that I flipped the switch and the lights didn't come on. I went out to perform, and the cur-tain came down before I got to do my bit. That had never, ever hap-pened to me before.

Because of our contracts, Nick got $39,000 for beating me. I got $400,000 for being beat. The story of the fight was that the baton was passed. It was a big fight for Showtime. So the event was very successful all the way around, except for me getting my ass kicked. Everything else worked out exactly as it should have. Diaz has proven that he was worthy of the win. Since then he has demol-ished everyone else. His career went up to the next level after he fought me.

But I don't think he's a good representative of our sport. Lots of the new, younger guys aren't. The beauty of their experience is that they didn't have to fight for ten years to figure it all out. We did that for them. So they could start from what we had already learned and move forward from that. Guys like me started from zero. We had to invent the whole thing.

Besides being light-years ahead of us physically, though, they are bad representatives of the sport. They are professional martial art-ists, but what do they represent? If you're out gangbanging, smok-ing weed, and street fighting, you are not a good representative of our sport. You are *hurting* our sport. You're not acting like a leader. You are not taking a leadership role. Most of these younger fighters are clueless about that. They feel no sense of responsibility for their sport or their art. They are fighters, but they are not martial artists. They are not warriors.

14

RETIREMENT

Getting married to Amy had made me more serious about life in some way. I was committed. Having a second chance with another baby made it more real. Amy and I had been keeping house for a while, since we got married. When Nicolette was born, we felt more together than ever. We were a family.

Somehow being a new dad made me even more ambitious, more determined to do the things I had set out to do. With my son, I had always worked hard and made money and supported him. But he wasn't there every day, living with me, growing up with me. Nicolette was *here*. She wasn't going anywhere. She wasn't going to leave, and I wasn't going to leave. I had a new understanding about responsibility—that I had to protect her and take care of her and make a place for her in the world that was healthy and happy and safe.

I felt an overwhelming sense of love, too. Being a dad made me feel more settled. I felt needed, and necessary, in a completely new way.

I had not had any kind of relationship with Bob Shamrock since he had called and told me not to fight Tito Ortiz. He just wasn't in the picture that much. It was uncomfortable for me. I didn't feel good about it. My trainer, Maurice Smith, told me, "Make up with your dad. Find a way to make up with him." But I couldn't find the right way to do that. At first, I tried to do it through Ken, to patch it up that way. But that obviously didn't work. Ken was my mentor, but I realized that whatever his demons were, they weren't mine. I had to go my own way.

Then I heard that Bob had had a heart attack, so I went up to see him. He had actually had two or three heart attacks. He was in pretty bad shape. He was in the hospital, but he was hardly there. He was conked out.

I knew he hadn't been in good health. I wasn't surprised. He had stopped doing anything like caring for himself years before, when he was in his mid-forties. He went from working out and eating right and living clean to just sort of closing the door on his physical health and never opening it again. He had been a bodybuilder. He worked out obsessively. He was really buff. He wore custom-made shirts and lived like a celebrity. I heard him talk about those days, and saw the photographs from those days. But that had all ended around the time I first came to his boys' home. I always thought it had to do with losing his wife. That changed everything about him. Something left when she ran off. He gave up.

He had been living with Ken for several years. He'd been out of the group-home business for a while and wasn't working anywhere. Bob told me that he had lost his last group home *because* of Ken. Bob said Ken was always making trouble of some kind, and that one day Ken drove his car to Bob's house and laid a two-hundred-foot stretch of rubber down the road. The people in the neighborhood complained one more time and Bob lost his license to run the home.

After that, I heard he had bad money problems. He was always a big spender. He was not a saver. But he had Ken to take care of him. After he lost the last home, he was always with Ken. They moved to Reno.

I spent some time at Ken's house with him and all his crazy family. It was all very strange and sad. Bob lay there looking half-dead. Ken walked around looking really traumatized by the whole thing. I didn't stay long. I had to leave the next day. I thought it might be the last time I ever saw Bob. I thought he wouldn't make it. But he woke up the next day, or a few days later, feeling all right, and went home.

But he wasn't all right. He wasn't able to take care of himself, so he moved into an assisted-living facility. Not long after that, he had another heart attack, maybe his third or fourth. He was such a tough guy, so stubborn. He drove himself to the hospital instead of calling 911 or asking for help. He checked himself in, and then he checked himself out. Then he had another heart attack.

Ken's wife called me and said, "Bob's had another one. We think he's going to go." And he went. We had been on alert. He had been in a nursing home. It didn't seem like he was going to make it. Ken and his wife, Tonya, brought Bob home so he could be surrounded by the people he loved. He died several days later on January 14, 2010. He was sixty-eight years old. I heard about it on the Internet. People started sending me condolences. I was really sad, but I had had to bury him many years before, unfortunately, because he had stopped being my dad. I was used to letting people go. I was used to moving on, emotionally. I had made my peace with him. It was still sad, though.

I struggled with the question of whether I should go to the funeral. It was my last chance to do something for him. I wanted to go. Bob was my family. He was the only father I ever knew, and the only one who ever really loved me.

But Ken was not my family. Besides training me and being a mentor to me, Ken was never a brother to me. Bob chose me to be his son. Ken didn't choose me to be his brother.

I thought that going to the funeral would have been the right thing for me, but not the right thing for anyone else. It wouldn't have been right for Ken and his family. So I chose to stay away. That felt like the best way for me to show respect to Bob, to Ken, to everyone.

It had been hard for me to make peace in my mind. All the things Ken and Bob said I couldn't do, that I wasn't going to do—I went and did them. And because they had said I couldn't do those things, for a long time I didn't give them any credit for helping me. I gave credit to the people who were standing with me when it happened. When people asked me how I'd done what I'd done, how I got where I was, I gave credit to other people—the ones who were helping me when I did it.

I think they took offense at that. They hated it. It didn't sit well that I was accomplishing all the things that they said I couldn't do, *and* all the things that Ken hadn't been able to do. I got the championships and the world records. I beat a lot of the people who had beaten him. It must have been difficult, from their perspective.

But I had felt abandoned and betrayed by them. I couldn't do it any other way. When I think of Bob now, I don't think of betrayal. I admire Bob for how much he loved, for what he did, for what he believed in. This is what being a human being is all about. He was passionate. His whole life, he stepped up and said, "This is how we're going to do this thing," and then did it. I have a great admiration for that. I even admire him, in a weird way, for loving Ken so much that he carved me out of his life. He had to choose, and he chose what was the most important thing to him, and he didn't waver.

My mother met Bob once or twice, very casually. She never understood the relationship. She thought he was just some strange guy who adopted me. Where she came from, it didn't make sense. But I see him as my father. He *is* my father. He will always hold the top position of respect. I am proud and happy to be a Shamrock. I chose that, and I'm happy with that choice. My Juarez father experience wasn't that good. In the end, I *am* a Shamrock.

Over the years I had become closer and closer to Henry Holmes. He started as my lawyer and adviser. After a while he had become a father figure. When I fought Tito Ortiz and won, I gave Henry my championship belt. It went into his trophy collection at his house, right next to the Mike Tyson gloves and the George Foreman gloves.

But the friendship part happened really slowly and very organically. We just sort of grew into each other. We're both focused and neurotic and super-honest. But for a long time it was just a business friendship. What brought us closer was his having a son. Henry was on his fifth marriage, but he'd never had children. Now along came his son, Ben. Henry was winding down a crazy career. He had been this total shark in business. Now his world was becoming more and more about Ben.

For years I had been the one calling him and asking questions, trying to take advantage of his wisdom. It was mostly professional. But slowly I had started to talk to him about personal things, and he started talking back. Now we were talking and he was the one asking *me* questions.

I was teaching kids mixed martial arts. I understood children and had some experience with them. So he started coming to me for advice as a father. Because he had come to know me and love me and trust me, he listened to what I had to say.

I knew a lot about being a father, even though I had not always been around when little Frank was little. I had, between all my "dads," maybe one good father. I understood what worked and what didn't. You don't scream at your child in anger. You don't lock your child in the closet. You don't do these things because they don't work. I knew that because of what had been done to me as a child.

As my own son had grown older, I had been faced with some interesting challenges as a father. Little Frank had met a woman from Arkansas. He was planning to move there and marry her.

We had a lot going on. My wife's father had fallen ill and died. That was a huge event. Bob Shamrock had died. That was a huge event. Now my son was moving away to Arkansas to marry an older woman and start some kind of life there.

I wanted to put a stop to it. Amy and I thought it was a mistake. But it was his mistake. In the end, we couldn't do anything about it. And, in the end, it didn't matter. He married her and moved to Arkansas. The relationship didn't last. Within a year they were separated, and I started trying to unwind that for him. But at the same time he lucked into this job in Arkansas and began training as a flyman—a person who works in the wings of a theater, manipulating the wheels and pulleys that lower and raise the scenery and the curtains and all that. It's a highly specialized occupation, and he got an apprenticeship in Arkansas. By the time his marriage was ending, he had learned how to do that and had gotten himself a job in Long Island, working as a flyman for a theater production company there.

My relationship with him became more normal. We got back on the calling-every-Sunday plan. He came home for my retirement and hung out. He came for Christmas and hung out. I got to have the new experience of being a father to an older son.

Henry was having the opposite experience, being an older father to a younger son. Because he's an older guy, and because he's been so successful in his business, he's very set in his thinking. I could see he was doing everything for the right reasons, but he didn't have a lot of experience. So he'd call me and say, "Am I completely wrong about this?" He had been so honest with me about my decisions over the years; now I was able to return the favor. I was able to bring him the dad stuff. Out of all that, we connected in a new way. He turned into my dad.

Not long after Bob died, I got a call from my mom. She lived in a weird commune situation in Texas. She had been there a year—she and her boyfriend, Barry, and my brother Perry, all living in this trailer park. They were still on their way to Belize to take possession of the piece of land my mother had bought on the Internet, in cash, from some stranger.

Things weren't going too well. Barry had a lot of legal problems, including child support liens against him. He couldn't get a passport. Perry had gotten out of control, too. He'd had some sort of breakdown. He was on disability, and he was supposed to be contributing some of the disability money to the mission to Belize, but he wasn't. So he and my mom had a falling out over that. He moved into a different trailer and brought in this woman he'd met from Canada. But one day the police had to be called because he'd tied the Canadian woman to the bed or something. That was it. Perry was out.

The family was blown apart. No one was talking to anyone. Suzy was living in Colorado. She was married and had two kids. But I wasn't talking to her. I couldn't. It wasn't possible to have a normal conversation with her. The talk could start anywhere, but then it would always turn to childhood trauma and about my career or money—all subjects that I did not want to share with anyone. For a long time Amy and I tried to avert, divert, change direction, whatever. After a while we just stopped answering the phone when we saw it was Suzy.

Robynn was still the most normal of us all. She had married a wonderful man named David, and she also had two kids. She had a job and a normal life and I liked talking to her.

But it didn't look like my mom was depending on them to help out with the Belize issue. That was going to be me.

It turned out there was some problem with the house, too. The lady who owned the house, or the real estate agent who had sold her the house, had been murdered. The house was for sale. My mother had to go down there and sort it all out. So she called me and asked me for help. She said, "I need you to go to Belize and help me get my house."

This was my mom, who never calls me and never, ever asks for help.

I was really busy. I didn't have time to go to Belize. I asked Henry for his counsel. In his infinite wisdom, he said, "If there is ever anything you can do for your mom, you should do it right away, or you'll regret it for the rest of your life." So I went to Belize. It took five days. It was a mess. My mom had very little information. She had never seen the house and didn't even know where it was. We started driving around the town of San Ignacio, asking people what they knew about the house, the owner, the lady who had been murdered. It was insane. Word had gotten around that my *mother* was the one who'd been murdered. It was assumed the house was free and clear. Now someone was living in it, and someone else was trying to sell it.

I put the Frank Shamrock business mind to work on the problem. We got it all sorted out. We got a new deed. The house was all hers. But she still couldn't fulfill her dream of moving to Belize because her boyfriend was stuck in Texas. I wasn't going to spend the $50,000 to pay his back child support. I wasn't going to break the law to solve his problem. I needed another solution. So I worked out an exit strategy for that, too.

I hired an escort to drive my mother down through Mexico, all the way to Belize in her motor home. And with my big brain I figured out a way to get the boyfriend out, too. There is a loophole in the passport laws. If you're a US citizen and you're leaving from a US port and returning to a US port, you can get on a cruise ship without a passport. No one expects you to take a cruise ship and just leave. But that's what Barry did. He got on the cruise ship in Texas, and on the fourth or fifth day, he got off the cruise ship in Belize, walked away, and never came back. He can't ever come back to the United States. But he wasn't contributing anything up here anyway, and he doesn't want to come back. He wants to be with my mom in Belize.

Hanging out with my mom on that trip was extremely strange. It was the longest time we'd spent alone together since I was a little boy. We were busy most of the time with all the house problems. But we had a little hang time, too, in our shared jungle hotel room. I finally asked her what had been going on when I was a little boy. I asked her why she had let me go, and why she hadn't tried to get me back. She said, "I was just trying to survive." She said, "I missed you. I wanted you back." That's all she said. It was a lot for her to say. I had to wait a long time to hear it. I held her hand and cried and told her I had missed her, too. It felt good.

In the end, she realized her dream. She made it to Belize. She was happy.

For a while after the Diaz fight, I had some plans for setting up something else. I talked to some people. I had some ideas. But it was starting to look more and more like I was done. I was still very involved with MMA, on a lot of levels. I still had my schools. I was still selling training videos. And I had become an on-air commentator for Showtime. For several months, I had been appearing ringside, working with Mauro Ranallo, Gus Johnson, and Al Bernstein. I had gone to St. Louis with them to call a fight right after getting beaten by Nick Diaz. This was my new job. I was good at it and I really enjoyed it. I was able to bring some inside MMA expertise to the fans.

I saw a very bright future for my sport. I was working with Scott Coker to grow the Strikeforce brand. I was working with Showtime to grow our TV presence. I traveled to New York and went to the state capitol to speak to legislators there about making MMA a sanctioned sport in the state of New York. My wife and I started making plans to actually move to New York. We thought we could plant ourselves there and use the energy of that amazing city to build our brand, and build our sport, into the international event we knew it could be.

After a while, I saw that it meant I was going to have to retire. I couldn't keep fighting and be a representative of the sport. It was too hard. My body was too damaged. The training was brutal, and I didn't think I could continue to operate at the level that the fans had come to expect and that I had come to demand. If I couldn't be the best—*my* best—then I didn't want to continue.

I took advantage of my good Showtime relationship to turn my retirement into an event. On the night of June 26, 2010, I was in San Jose ready to work ringside calling the Fedor Emelianenko versus Fabricio Werdum fight. I had on my dark suit and a cool green tie. The lights went down, and the Showtime folks showed a video about my history with MMA, starting with my Pancrase titles in Japan.

When the lights came back up, I was standing inside the cage with a microphone in my hand. Surrounded by the fans and the people who loved me—even my son had come out to be there—I made my announcement.

"When I was twenty-two years old, my brother gave me two important things—he gave me an ass-whupping, and he gave me my love of mixed martial arts. Since that time, I've traveled the world, teaching mixed martial arts, preaching mixed martial arts, and dragging my poor family with me from country to country and city to city. I'm thirty-seven years old now, and my time has come. The stars like Gilbert Melendez and Cristiane Cyborg, they are the future, and I am the past. Tonight I announce my retirement. And I just want to say, it has been an honor to bleed for you, to break my bones for you, and to entertain you. And before I leave I would like to bow for you one more time. Thank you!"

I handed someone the microphone. I looked at Amy. I bowed four times, once to each corner of the arena.

I was done.

15

FIGHT NO MORE

I was now fully engaged in my new role as a regular commentator on Showtime. My partners were Mauro Ranallo and Gus Johnson. Mauro is a senior sports announcer with decades of experience in calling combative sports and everything else. He was the voice, alongside Bas Rutten, of the pay-per-view series *Pride Fighting Championship*, held in Japan. He hosted multiple television shows and has been in radio for over twenty-five years. He is also a huge wrestling and fighting fan and called my fights with Renzo, Baroni, Le, and Diaz. Gus started his career calling play-by-play in the NBA for the Minnesota Timberwolves. He went on to call Big East basketball and college hockey, and then boxing for Showtime and MMA for CBS.

What I brought to the game was the inside stuff, and maybe a fan base. I could see things in the cage that these guys couldn't, or I could see it faster or earlier than they could. And I think MMA fans felt my presence gave the commentary a little more legitimacy. It made it a little more real. When I said a guy was out of gas, or a punch rang someone's bell, they knew that I knew what I was talking about.

I thought the Showtime gig was a great opportunity for me to present my idea of where the sport could go. It was a way for me to put a positive face on MMA. For a long time I had been concerned about the sport. I had seen the increasing dominance of the UFC, and the increasing media presence of its figurehead, Dana White. They were making great headway. I didn't want to take anything away from them, but their way was not my way. Their way was sort of like boxing with no gloves. It felt like legitimized street fighting. The story they told continued to be "Two men go into the ring. Only one will survive." It seemed kind of barbaric, and kind of ugly. It wasn't martial arts, and it wasn't the martial way, and I didn't think, in the long run, it was the story that was best for our sport.

That's why I had said no to Dana and the UFC back in the beginning, when they were just getting started. I didn't trust him, and I didn't believe he would make it. That's why I was trying to build the relationship with Strikeforce and Showtime. I wanted to be involved in telling *that* story—which was the story of the fighter, of the warrior, of the mixed martial artist who really *was* an artist, who had trained and was trying to live a life of Bushido, the moral code of the samurai that stressed frugality, loyalty, martial arts mastery, and honor unto death (honor, respect, and discipline). All my efforts were driven by that dream.

I got an opportunity to carry the dream into the electronic game world. In 2010 I was contacted by the people at EA Sports, the electronic game giant. They had done really well with computer-simulated versions of everything from football to basketball to golf to soccer to hockey. Now they were getting into MMA, and they wanted me to come talk to them about being a character in their game. Of course I said yes. I loved the idea of being a character in a video game for Xbox or PlayStation. I loved being able to fight again with Bas Rutten in cyberspace. I think they even set it up so I could fight Ken Shamrock, in virtual reality, if not in actual reality.

After I announced my retirement, I started thinking about the future in different ways. If I wasn't going to be fighting, I wasn't going to be training. If I wasn't going to be training, I didn't necessarily have to be in San Jose. I started thinking about where I wanted to live, where I could make myself most useful. I decided to move to New York.

There were a lot of things behind the decision, but the main one was that I felt I could best serve the sport and my dream for the sport by moving to the information capital of the world. New York is the image center of America. It's where the message gets packaged and delivered. It's also the place where MMA is still not a sanctioned sport. I decided to plant my flag there and begin the campaign to make the case for MMA as a legal sport in the state.

Pretty soon I was driving around Manhattan with real estate agents. Amy and I looked at apartments and houses. We looked at schools and preschools. We put our house in San Jose on the market. I made an appearance at the New York state capitol, in front of a crowd of state senators and representatives. I told them why MMA needed to be a sanctioned sport in their state, the way it was in neighboring New Jersey.

I also made some speeches about bullying. I discovered I had a lot to say about that. As I was making the transition from MMA fighter to MMA spokesperson, a lot of people asked me questions about the future of the sport. A lot of them had questions for me about the UFC because it was the dominant brand in my sport. I've never been one to mince my words. I told the truth. I said I thought the UFC was not the best future for my sport. I said I thought Dana White and the kinds of fighters he represented, and the kind of fighting he stood for, were not the best image for the future of MMA. I didn't get too personal about it, but I said I thought the whole down-and-dirty MMA image was the wrong one. I didn't see how we could sell the world a sport if the image was of a foul-mouthed, trash-talking, super-tattooed street fighter who dated porn stars and had run-ins with the law over drugs and alcohol. I wasn't talking about Dana White or any one specific fighter. I was just talking about the UFC image and what I thought was wrong with it.

Dana White went a little nuts on me. He called me "a liar and a two-faced chump." He said I was "an irrelevant idiot." He said I was "the biggest two-faced jerk-off" he'd ever met in his life.

I've been around guys like Dana White my whole life. I understand guys like him. They're mostly small, scared guys who huff and puff and try to make themselves look big by pushing around someone weaker. I was retired and no longer any kind of threat to him, so he felt he could say this kind of stuff without having any consequences.

And that's when it hit me. I realized I was being bullied. I understood bullying in a whole new way, like I'd never understood it before. I've always been a tough guy and a fighter. For a long time, I was kind of a big guy. So I didn't get pushed around that much. I didn't understand what that felt like—to be the little guy being pushed around, and not having any way to stand up or fight back. Now I felt that. I understood what it felt like to be dominated and defenseless.

I didn't like it. So I decided to do something about it. I went online and started reading about bullying. I found out there were various organizations, all around the country, working on parts of the bullying question. There were experts on the psychological aspect. There were experts on bullying in schools. But there was no national face to the issue. I decided to begin a national dialogue on the question of bullying. Within a week or so, I had met with several people, online or over the phone. We had agreed to create a national campaign for the anti-bullying idea.

I got busy really fast. I launched a charity golf tournament. I started an organization called StandTogether. I started fund-raising and consciousness-raising. I went on the Jimmy Fallon show to talk about the problem and the solution to the problem. I went down to Los Angeles and spent a few days shooting a video series opposite the great fighter and future Strikeforce female champion Miesha "Takedown" Tate, showing women some basic rape-prevention tactics for protecting themselves from an attack.

I got really into it. I had no idea this problem was so serious. I discovered it was a national epidemic. I had spent my life fighting with people who were able to defend themselves, in an arena where the fight is stopped as soon as one guy *can't* defend himself. MMA was the fastest-growing sport in America. But bullying seemed to be the fastest-growing problem.

I saw a great opportunity. In MMA gyms all around the country we had an army of twelve-year-old kids looking to us, to their MMA teachers, to show them how to act and how to live and what to do with their lives. As their teachers, we have an obligation to educate them properly. We are the chosen warriors, the ones who get to spread the message. We believe in the way, the martial code, and we have chosen our path. That doesn't involve threatening people. I saw that we could use our leadership role to fix this thing. We could use it to help take away the shame of being bullied and to let people know that there is no excuse for abusing another human being—physically, mentally, sexually, or psychologically.

The psychological part was important. Until the Dana White incidents, I hadn't really experienced cyber-bullying. But now I saw the viciousness and unaccountability of bullying via texting, the Internet, or in social media. I talked with parents whose children had harmed themselves, or even killed themselves, because of bullying things that people had written about them and posted online.

I had spent years teaching kids how to fight and protect themselves. But this was different. I needed to find a way to teach kids how to fight on the Internet. I needed to find a way to teach them to have confidence, and to know that words in cyberspace are forever, and they do hurt people, especially if you remain quiet or alone.

It was personal for me, too. I was the father of a little girl. I knew how to teach her to defend herself physically. I needed to learn how to teach her to defend herself against this new kind of bullying. Obviously my MMA experience was the way in. MMA had saved my life. I saw this opportunity to share that in a new way.

The funny thing, the really ironic thing, is that I myself had personally taught Dana White how to fight. I had taught him, or tried to teach him, the rudiments of MMA and the way of the martial artist. It was in the very early days of the UFC. I had known Dana for a few years, back when he was a nobody in our sport. He was running a kickboxing studio and teaching a kickboxing class. Then he became Tito Ortiz's new manager. I knew Tito, of course, so I started seeing him and Dana here and there. Out of the blue, Dana White got these guys named Frank and Lorenzo Fertitta into the business. They were Las Vegas guys who owned the Station Casino company. They had gotten interested in MMA and had formed a company called Zuffa to explore opportunities in the fighting world. They had hired Dana White to be president of their sports operations.

Suddenly Dana White was the head of an MMA company. But he didn't know anything about MMA, so he did two things. He tried to get me to sign as a UFC fighter. When I wouldn't do that, he tried to hire me to teach him how to fight. I had just become a free agent in September 1999, after the Tito fight. I had retired from fighting. I was living in Los Angeles and doing my thing. They desperately wanted me to fight for the UFC. But I wasn't feeling it—I saw what they were doing. I didn't think it was wrong, exactly, but I didn't see it for myself. But I did agree to work as a commentator. They signed me to a three-show contract. Then they hired me to move to Las Vegas for two weeks to train them in how to fight, MMA style. I was going to be the personal instructor for Dana White. So for the next thirteen days, it was just Dana and me. I taught him all the basic moves.

After that, I guess he thought if he asked me again I'd come fight for the UFC. But every time he asked, I said no. I just didn't share their vision. They had a plan. They had a direction. I didn't think it was right for me, or for my sport. So, respectfully, I always said no.

Now it had come to this. A guy who I had trained in my sport was calling me out in public, on TV, on the Internet, calling me horrible names and telling ugly lies about me and my character. I gave a couple of interviews. I tried to clear up the question of whether I was a two-faced liar and a chump. I said his comments about me were ridiculous and insulting and that I was sad to see them associated with my sport. I pointed out that I had never attacked Dana White or the UFC, that I had never insulted them, or assaulted them, or been angry with them—but that in return for my being honest about going my own way, I had been attacked and ridiculed and bullied and had my character assaulted in public.

In reply, I said, "MMA breeds confidence, builds character, and creates strong, diverse communities whose foundation is honor, respect, and discipline. Dana White, I refuse to be bullied by you. Further, I respect a man who truthfully stands up and fights for his family with honor. So any time you want to become a real man, and not a bully, you let me know. I would be happy to oblige you with a personal introduction to Shamrock MMA."

I pointed out that Dana White's behavior was a perfect example of why I thought he was a terrible representative of our sport. I said that it was a great example of what happened when corporate interests began to dictate martial arts. I didn't point out that in my opinion, Dana White had already been given the litmus test as a martial artist and he had failed terribly. (He really put it on a female grappler who came to help with his wrestling, overpowering her and grinding her into the mat. That's not something you do in my class.)

On March 12, 2011, I was completely blown over to learn that Zuffa, the parent company of the UFC, had made a deal to purchase Strikeforce. The MMA world was rocked by this news. It was a huge deal, a huge story, and it took me completely by surprise. I had gotten up early that day with my daughter. It was just a normal weekday morning—except my cell phone had been going crazy with texts. When I finally had time to check them, there were all these messages—text messages, Tweets, e-mails—from guys asking me if it was true about Zuffa. People thought I would know if something was going down. But I was completely blindsided. Scott Coker was my contact at Showtime. But he had gone underground about a week before. This wasn't unusual. We had talked once a week, at least once a week, for years. But it wasn't unusual for me not to hear from him when he was busy with something else.

Then I finally found a video of Dana White online, announcing the acquisition. It appeared that Silicon Valley Sports, which owned the controlling 51 percent interest in Strikeforce, had sold out. No one consulted me, or asked my opinion, or warned me. That's big business. It wasn't their job to warn me. It wasn't Scott Coker's job to warn me. It was their job to maximize profit.

I was shocked, but I wasn't surprised. I hadn't seen this coming, but I knew something had to change. The financial partners were strained. The company had spent a lot of money expanding the brand, competing with the UFC, trying to open the New York market, trying to grow the sport. Silicon Valley Sports is an old-fashioned, traditional sports company. They were tired of writing the checks and not seeing the returns.

I made some calls. I told my wife. She was pretty freaked out. Everybody was freaked out. I put in a call to Scott. I spoke to some of the Strikeforce team. It was a small group, and we were all very close. Everyone was shocked. No one was popping any champagne corks.

When I didn't hear back from Scott, I sent an e-mail asking what was up. An hour later, I sent him another e-mail, thanking him for being my promoter and my friend. I felt horrible. There was no reason or explanation given. It came without warning. It felt like someone had died in a car accident, and you didn't want to ask questions about what happened, or who was at fault. It was just . . . over.

When I finally talked to Scott, I asked him, "What do we tell the press?" I had been the public face and the brand spokesman for Strikeforce. I had a long and friendly relationship with many of the MMA journalists, and I was getting pounded by their texts and e-mails. I had to tell them something. Scott sent me an e-mail explanation about how the Silicon Valley Sports guys had wanted out of the MMA business, and that they had no place else to go except Zuffa. They needed Strikeforce. Strikeforce needed Zuffa. We're all going to be one happy family now as the sport moves on to its next great level.

I couldn't sell that. These reporters were friends of mine. They're smart. They knew what was going on. Their articles already said, "Good-bye, Strikeforce. Good-bye, Frank." It was the end of two brands.

I did my job. I tried to put a nice face on it. But I had a lot of weird feelings about it. Scott and I were very close friends. I was the spokesman for our brand. It was a real kick in the nuts *not* to know we were being sold. It would've been nice if he had shared it with me.

It would have made it easier for me to think about my future, for one thing. The news about the sale threw that wide open. I was getting ready to move to New York. My house was on the market. My wife and I had been looking at houses in Manhattan. We had visited schools for our daughter. We were committed. Now it looked like all of that was going to change, too. I had a contract with Strikeforce. Strikeforce had its arrangements with Showtime.

But Strikeforce was going to be owned by the UFC, and the UFC was run by Dana White. And it was clear to everyone what Dana White thought of Frank Shamrock.

In the first interviews, Dana White insisted that everyone's contracts would be honored, and that the new ownership of Strikeforce wouldn't change anything. Strikeforce fighters would continue to fight for Strikeforce. Strikeforce officers would continue to work for Strikeforce. In the short term, that made sense. Long term, it didn't. I wasn't sure whether my role had changed, or how it had changed. A good business mind told me to prepare a good exit strategy. But I felt unsure, and being unsure is a bad business strategy.

There didn't seem to be a future for me with the UFC, and I wasn't sure I wanted one. For a long time, they continued to look like the same old thing. They were gathering steam. They kept getting bigger. They had great fighters. They had become the dominant force in the industry. They had achieved their goal in buying Strikeforce. They had created a sport, but it was now going to be known as UFC. One of the first rule changes to Strikeforce was to add elbows and make the rules the same in both leagues. I was originally the person who convinced Coker to remove the elbows from the Strikeforce to cut down on the blood and cuts. But the UFC was now MMA. I didn't think the way they'd done it was appropriate and fair. They used their power to stop other people's growth and to stop the sport itself from growing. They took the sport of MMA and made it into *their* sport.

They did that in ways that weren't cool. My own experience shows this. They were angry at me for not agreeing to fight for them when I was a free agent. They retaliated by taking away my history. My championships and my records disappeared. I'm not in the UFC Hall of Fame. If you study the history of MMA as told by the UFC, I don't exist. That's how they repaid me for not sharing their vision.

But I didn't share it then and I don't share it now. By the time the UFC came along, I had already seen a couple of versions of MMA. There was the Japanese execution of martial arts, in the version that was Pancrase. There was the first UFC, run by Bob Meyrowitz. He founded the UFC and sold it to Zuffa in 2001. Now I had seen a decade of UFC under Zuffa and Dana White.

I did the math. With Zuffa's UFC, you've got Dana White, a boxing fan with no martial arts experience, backed by financial people from the casino business, who are very schooled in the management of sports and boxing. If you combine those two things, you don't get MMA. You get white-collar boxing. That didn't make sense to me. It was going to be a business about making money off fighters. It was not going to be about talent and the artists. It was just going to be another way of making money.

They were 100 percent sure their vision was the right one. I was 100 percent sure their vision wasn't the right one. I saw a sport steeped in martial arts history and culture, and athletes who respected the fighting art and their bodies. They wanted to own the sport. I'm fine with that. But I'm not fine with them erasing my history from their sport. If they do that, it's not a sport anymore. It's just a business. I understand that, too—but I don't want any part of it.

Was I wrong? Yes—kind of. I misjudged them. I didn't share their vision, and I thought they would crash and burn. I had seen other big companies come and go. Look at the Extreme Fighting Championship. It was a big, rich, well-organized company. Look at the Full Contact Fighting Federation. Some big money guys had come and gone.

Dana had seen inside the world of MMA when it was sexy and interesting but immature. He had the right guys, with lots of money. Lorenzo knew the fight commission. They had the right connections, and the right qualifications and the right network. They were casino operators, which is a service business with huge overhead and huge payroll. I knew they could run a big business.

And they did. I may not like how they got from point *A* to point *B*, but they got there. They have moved the sport forward. They have made it a global sport. Their MMA model is now the only model. They control the marketplace.

But did I make a mistake? No. Not for me. I have no regrets about leaving the UFC or resisting the offers to rejoin the UFC. All I have to do to know that is look at my brother. He went with them and fought for them, until they cut him. They brought him back for a trilogy of fights with Tito Ortiz that revived the UFC on pay-per-view, which many said saved the company from early bankruptcy. They made millions off him. He fought some more, and then they cut him again. So he sued them in court and lost and had to pay them back, $172,000 in attorney bills. Now he's done, and he has had no control over anything that happened during most of his career. He has no promotional rights. He can't use the photographs or the video footage of any of that and say, "Here, this is who I am, and what I did." Dana White controls that, not Ken Shamrock. It's his life, but someone else owns it.

Back in 1999, I was just beginning to understand my brand, my personal brand, and what it could be worth. I saw an opportunity to create something with lifelong value. I saw the future. I knew I was going to be a world champion fighter. I wanted that to be my job, and my career, and my brand. And I wanted to be able to make money off that, and control the images associated with my name, after I stopped fighting. There was no way I could have done that as part of Dana White's UFC.

This is my *life*. This is my job. This is my journey. I love MMA. It's my church. It's not just where I go on Sunday. It's where I have gone every day of my adult life. I have lived and breathed mixed martial arts, and the martial artist way, right down to my marrow.

But suddenly, as the spring of 2011 turned to summer, I began to think that my future as a martial artist might not include MMA. For the first time in almost twenty years, I was not sure what was coming. I was not sure what I was going to do. I had been a guy with a one-year plan, a five-year plan, and a ten-year plan. Now I was a guy with no plan at all.

16

COMING TO TERMS

I tend to be a little obsessive, and I'm very highly focused. Strikeforce had been my life. For the past five years, it was almost all I had done. I put all my energies into developing the brand. I shut down or stepped away from my other businesses. I believed in the Strikeforce dream. When it died, I was left feeling high and dry. I felt completely screwed. So I started drinking. I thought, "Well, the last fifteen years of my life is just . . . gone. I might was well whoop it up."

The brakes came off. Where I used to have a drink in the evening to chill out, or smoke a little weed at night to relax, now I started almost first thing in the morning. I had nothing better to do. There was no training. There was no media work. There was just nothing.

So I started drinking, every day, and earlier in the day. I'd get Nicolette up for school. I'd get her fed and dressed. And then I was done with my day. I had no other responsibilities except sit and worry about my future. I had nothing else going on. There was no reason not to smoke a joint and have a cocktail.

I had really gotten into drinking rum. It's the nectar of the gods. It gave me such a warm and cozy feeling. Rum and Coke became my brunch. I'd have a drink or two, maybe do a little shopping, maybe smoke a little pot, and then come home and have a nap. And then get up and have some more rum.

The drinking got serious for me really quickly. I had always been purpose-based. I had always struggled so hard to survive, to get ahead, to excel. Drinking and drugging didn't go with that. When I was training for a fight, I'd quit everything for three months before the fight. Even when I wasn't training, I stayed focused, didn't go too crazy. And even after I retired, my drinking was minimal. Over the last couple of years, I'd have a drink every night—but just a little one. I'd have a beer, or a little wine. Maybe a glass of rum. But rarely to excess.

Now, with Strikeforce gone, the struggle was over. There was nothing to fight for or against. I really quickly hit a very low place. There was no reason *not* to drink. There was nothing to be sober for.

Pretty soon I was drinking every day, and drinking hard every night. I started seeing fewer people and doing fewer things. I became antisocial. I'd have my morning drinks and lunchtime drinks. I'd run an errand. I'd smoke a joint. I'd sober up by late afternoon, when I'd go pick my daughter up from school. When she was home safe I'd start it up again. Looking back, my behavior was not surprising. I had been using and abusing drugs and alcohol since I was a boy. I had gone through periods when it really dominated my life. So I guess it wasn't all that weird that I fell so hard.

Amy was *not* happy about it. She saw what was happening, and she was pretty vocal about it. She worried. She kept telling me I was in a terrible mood. She wanted to talk about it. She wanted me to do something about it. She kept telling me I was an alcoholic and that I needed help.

I didn't hide the drinking from her. I didn't see any reason to. I didn't think I was an alcoholic. I still had my job as a commentator. I didn't drink on the job. I still had money in the bank. I wasn't doing anything bad. I was just upset. I felt like my baby had died. I was grieving. I felt like my only problem, in fact, was *her*—and her telling me all the time that I was an alcoholic. I told her she was crazy, that she should quit bugging me about my drinking. When she asked me what was bothering me, I said, "You. The thing that bugs me most in my life, right now, is you bothering me about the drinking."

When she wouldn't shut up about it, I said, "You know what the problem is? You're crazy. You need to see a psychiatrist. You should make an appointment and go see someone, because you're nuts and you're making *me* nuts." I was seriously not worried about the drinking. I felt angry inside. I felt sort of cut off from everything. The drinking seemed to help. But Amy did what I told her to do. She saw the psychiatrist. She came home and told me about it. The doctor had said to her, "Your husband is an alcoholic. He has to stop drinking. If he can't, you should take your daughter and get out." So she came home and told me that. She said, "He told me that if you keep drinking, I have to take Nicolette and leave you."

Nothing was going to cut me off from my daughter. Nothing can get between me and my daughter. I would die before I would let that happen. So I said I would quit, and I meant it. But then I got up the next day, and all I wanted to do, all I wanted to do more than anything in the world, was have a drink. So I took Nicolette to school and came home and had a drink.

For a month, Amy and I fought. I stayed drunk and she stayed mad. She kept saying, "I'm serious. You're an alcoholic and I'm going to leave." I thought she was being ridiculous, and I told her that. I told her she was crazy. But then something happened that made me think she might be right. We had a plan to look at houses in Los Angeles. I wanted to be near the ocean, near my friend Henry, near the TV and movie businesses. Amy and I were going to L.A. to check out some real estate.

Then we found out Amy was pregnant. Then she had a miscarriage while we were in L.A. We flew back to San Jose right away. She saw a doctor and got taken care of, but she was pretty beat up. The doctor put her on bed rest, so she asked me if I would please pick up Nic after school and bring her home.

I had agreed to do a charity golf tournament the next day. I got Nic up and took her to school, and then I was going off to play golf. I started drinking around eleven in the morning. The tournament went all right. I drank all day. I had a good time, Tweeting and texting like crazy. Then I looked at the clock, and it was 5:30. I was really drunk. Wasted. I knew there was something I was supposed to be doing, but I couldn't really remember what it was. And my phone had died, so there wasn't anyone to call and ask, "Hey, am I supposed to be somewhere?"

Then I remembered I was supposed to pick up my daughter. At the school. At 4:30. I drove over there. It was 6:00 when I arrived. The place was dark. The doors were locked. I started pounding on things and yelling. There was nobody around. I figured the only person who could have picked Nic up, other than Amy or me, was our friend Cheri. So I got back in the car and drove to her house, all drunk and out of my mind with fear, and anger, and shame. I had never driven drunk or high with my little girl before and now I couldn't even remember where she was. I was freaking out.

She was there. Amy had called Cheri and asked her to pick Nic up. She was in the bath. Everything was fine. So I relaxed. I asked Cheri, "Can I just lie down on your sofa for, like, fifteen minutes? I'm *really* tired. Then I'll take Nic home." Cheri said that was fine. So I lay down and went to sleep. When I woke up, it was around midnight. The house was dark and Nic wasn't there. I asked Cheri what was going on. She said, "We took her home." So I drove home, too. The house was dark and everything quiet, so I went to bed on the couch.

The next morning, I got up to start the day like always. Amy came downstairs, and she seemed really, really mad at me. I couldn't figure it out. Had something bad happened? She asked me if I remembered what had happened the day before. I said, "Yeah, I had that golf thing." She asked, "Do you remember what happened with your daughter?" I said, "No, what happened?" Then it came crashing back. I suddenly remembered—the golf tournament, all the drinks, getting drunk, forgetting Nicolette, driving to the school, driving to Cheri's house, falling asleep . . . .

And I saw that Amy was right. I *was* an alcoholic. I had to be. I had to be an alcoholic or totally out of my mind. Because I would never, never, never leave my daughter unprotected like that unless I was very crazy or very sick. So I must be sick. I told Amy I was sorry. I told her I understood I was an alcoholic. I apologized over and over again. I said I would take care of it.

I had been around twelve-step programs almost my whole life. Being in group homes, I was taken to meetings. When I got into trouble with the law, sometimes going to meetings was part of the punishment or the probation. And being the smart, self-educated man that I am, I had read quite a few books about alcoholism and drug abuse. So I knew I wasn't the guy with the problem. I never drove my daughter around while I was drunk. I never killed anyone driving drunk, or lost my job, or anything like that. So in my mind, I wasn't an alcoholic.

But I knew something very serious was wrong with me to make me leave my daughter like that. So I knew what to do. I got into my car to leave. I'd been doing that every day for a while—just getting in the car to leave, so I could go drink or get high or whatever without my wife bugging me. That day I did the same thing, with the intention of going to some kind of twelve-step meeting. I drove somewhere and parked and thought about things. I started crying and kept crying for about thirty minutes—thinking about what I'd done, what I'd done to my wife, what I'd done to my daughter.

Then I went rummaging in the glove compartment for a tissue or something. I found a joint. I decided to smoke that and go to my first twelve-step meeting.

I found a meeting about ten miles from my house. I walked in, totally baked and really nervous. I was really high, and really hungover. I didn't think I would get very much out of the meeting. But I got something. I had been to so many meetings over the years, and I'd listened to all these people tell their stories. I might sympathize, but I didn't identify. I would think, *I'm not that guy.* Well, now I saw myself, and I realized, I *am* that guy.

I didn't go home after the meeting. I puttered around and avoided Amy. That night I went back to the house and told her I was sorry, again, and said I was going to get sober. I meant it.

I didn't have a drink that night. The next day, I got up and went to another meeting. I didn't drink. I went to another meeting. I went to seventy meetings, seventy days in a row. That became my day. I'd get up, get Nic ready, take her to school, go to a meeting, putter around, then pick Nic up again and bring her home. That was my sober life. I didn't drink, but for the first two weeks, it was really hard not to. And smoke. I missed the weed. Since I'd retired, I had been a daily weed smoker. I had been an every-other-day weed smoker for years—since I was a kid. I only quit when I was training for a fight, because I was always subject to drug testing. With big fights, they test a little closer. I *never* wanted to fail a drug test, which seemed like the stupidest reason in the world not to win a fight. So I was really careful about that. But otherwise I smoked. It made me feel calm. I missed it.

I started meeting men in the meetings. They'd give me their phone numbers and tell me I could call them if I felt like taking a drink. They were very friendly and supportive, but I never felt comfortable in the meetings. I've always felt a little weird in groups. I've always felt apart from things. I'd listen to these guys talk, and I couldn't believe how bad off they were. Amy would ask, "How was the meeting?" and I'd say, "Great, but you can't believe what happened to this one guy." I couldn't identify. It seemed like I was always the youngest guy in the room. And I was the guy who had suffered the least. These guys had lost *everything*. They had just been destroyed. Well, I drove to the meeting in a BMW. I had money in the bank. I wasn't in trouble with the law. My wife still let me come home. I couldn't believe I was a "real" alcoholic, if that's what it was to be a real alcoholic.

That's how I felt for the first ninety days. Then I went to a new meeting. It was a very young group. I met all these people who were just starting out. Some of them were being brought in from group homes, just like I had been when I was a kid. There were all these young guys wearing the institutional blue pants and white shirts. And I thought, "That was *me.*" I recognized myself in them. And that's when I got it. That's when I understood my alcoholism as a sickness, as a disease. I understood the progressive nature of it. I saw these guys at the beginning of their disease, and these other guys at the end of their disease, and I understood I was just another alcoholic somewhere in the middle. Not different, just at a different stage.

After that, things got easier. I felt much more like we were all on the same page. I felt more relaxed in the meetings. I felt more comfortable. After a while, it seemed more comfortable to be in a meeting than to be *not* in a meeting.

I had trouble getting people outside the meetings to understand that things had changed for me. I was at an event and everyone was drinking shots. They kept offering me shots, and I kept saying no, thank you. They got drunker and drunker. One guy finally asked me why I wasn't drinking. So I told him, "I'm an alcoholic. I can't drink." He said, "No problem! Let me get you a beer!"

There have been times when I wanted a drink, or when I remembered how I used to drink. I get to feeling down emotionally, or feel
like things are just too complicated, and I start finding my mind sort
of . . . going there. When I see that happening, I say the Serenity
Prayer and it passes.

I still get nervous about the future. It's so undetermined. I had
all these plans and strategies in place, and then they were gone.
But I've turned those things over to a higher power. I've surren-
dered. The other night I was at an event watching Nick Diaz kick
B. J. Penn's ass. I was watching a guy I'd trained get beaten by a guy
who'd beaten me. I was watching two generations of MMA fighters,
both of whom I'd helped educate and form, doing their thing.

And all night long people came up to me, saying, "Mr. Shamrock,
I've always wanted to meet you," or "Mr. Shamrock, I want to thank
you for all you've done for the sport." In the past, I would only have
thought, "Why is this guy bugging me?" or "Why is this guy inter-
rupting my moment?" This night, though, all I could think was that
these are real men coming up to me, speaking from their hearts
and saying something really, really cool. I wouldn't have had the
courage to say that kind of thing to a man I respected that much. I
thought, this is pretty cool, to be the guy they're saying that about.
I felt like I had earned their respect.

17

THE MARTIAL WAY

My introduction to martial arts was my introduction to life. It was my first exposure to the concept of a moral code. It was my first exposure to the ideas of honor, respect, and discipline, which to me are the three ideals of the martial way.

I didn't choose it. It happened to me. I became a martial artist because I had to survive in the fighting world. I was training with Ken in the Lion's Den and getting hurt, so I needed to grow and change. I was learning about fighting, but I needed something bigger than that. I found it in Japan, when I was first exposed to true martial artists.

I remember the very first moment of my consciousness about this. I had arrived in Japan along with another Lion's Den guy, Jason DeLucia. We were being introduced to people. One man called me "Shamrock-san" and bowed very deeply. So, being a smartass, I bowed back and made fun of him. Jason hit me and said, "Don't do that! Never do that! He was showing you respect! You can't make fun of him."

This was a whole new idea for me. I had been trained in the *reverse* of that. I had been trained in juvenile hall, and in jail and prison. I had been trained in gyms, with all the Lion's Den guys. There was no respect. There was no honor. There was no discipline. Guys came to the gym dirty and sweaty. They brought their girlfriends and wives. No one bowed. No one trained. They just showed up and started beating on each other. In Japan I saw a new way. Over time, this new way developed into an idea. I based the idea on the concept of Bushido—the warrior's way.

I learned that everyone has a warrior's way. Everyone has a warrior's mission. It's a life mission. Whatever you choose for yourself or whatever you think your life is about, you must go on that mission. You have to do battle and you have to fight along the way, whether it's a fight for your health, or your life, or the life of your business, or your marriage, or whatever. And you must fight fairly and honestly and stay true to the three ideals of honor, respect, and discipline.

This became the basis for my whole life. I learned it from the people I met in the martial arts community and developed it, over time, through my exposure to them. Every time I met with them, I saw that the martial arts people were different from the fight people. I'd go to this gym to train, or I'd go to that gym to teach, and I'd see fight people who wanted to challenge me to show off. No one showed any respect. No one seemed to have any discipline. Then I'd be asked to come teach at a tae kwon do school, or a karate school, and I'd have a completely different experience. They wore clean uniforms. They were quiet and respectful. They bowed. They were orderly and disciplined.

I observed and absorbed that. It became the basis for the martial way as it pertains to how I live my life. This is how I *learned* to live my life. I saw the application to everything I did, and I applied it to every action.

I learned that if I run my business life with honor, respect, and discipline, I enjoy success. I learned that from doing it the wrong way and getting the wrong results. I learned that if I screwed a guy over in business, I would meet him again and he would try to screw me, or that my reputation would be damaged and *that* would screw me. Either way, some negativity would result from the negativity I had put out. And the opposite was true. Something positive always results from something positive I put out.

I learned the application in my personal life, too. I had not been parented well, or coached well. As a child, I was taught by being punished. As a fight student, I was taught by getting beat up. In both cases, I learned the lesson without getting any information. I knew I had done something wrong because I got punished for it. But I didn't know what I had done wrong, and I didn't know how not to do it because I had not been taught. I had not been exposed to honor, respect, or discipline.

So when I became a teacher and a parent, I tried to do it the other way. I saw that bad parenting gives you bad children—who in turn may grow up to be bad parents. Bad teaching gives you bad students—who may go on to be bad teachers. I tried to develop a method of teaching and parenting so that the information I had got transmitted in a way that could be retained and in a way that helped create a good child and a good student.

These are the tools I learned and developed to live my life. They work in my business life and in my marriage. I try to bring honor, respect, and discipline into every part of my life. I also developed a system for teaching and learning that seems to work in every part of my life. I developed it from years of writing and thinking about fighting and the martial way. I was a good student of fighting. Part of my training, starting from my first weeks at the Lion's Den, was trying to write down exactly what I was doing and exactly what results I got. I used to have whole notebooks full of information about this move, or this hold, or this diet, or this exercise regimen. Over the years, I developed a system for thinking about things, for studying things, through the writing I was doing. That's how I came up with the idea of plus, minus, and equal. This is my formula for success.

What it means is that, in order to be successful in any part of my life, I need a plus, a minus, and an equal. I need someone who is my plus, who can teach me. I need someone who is my minus, who I can teach. I need someone who is my equal, so I can test myself.

In the gym, that means I need a trainer who can teach me things I don't know. He's my plus. I need a student, or a group of students, so I can pass along what I'm learning and learn it better in the process. They are my minus. And I need a sparring partner, a fighting buddy, so I can test and perfect what I'm learning. That's my equal.

I do this in my work life, too. When I started commentating fights for Showtime, I had a mentor—Al Bernstein. He's been commentating for thirty-five years. He knows everything. He's my plus. Then I had a partner—Mauro Ranallo. He's been a television guy for a long time, knows a lot about sports but not as much about MMA. He's my equal. Then there was the new guy—Pat Miletich. He's been around MMA for years as a fighter and a trainer, but he was new to commentating. So he's my minus. I was learning from Al, developing what I was learning with Mauro, and teaching what I was learning to Pat.

If you can control those three pieces, you can master anything, and you can control the information better than anyone. This system comes from the martial way, and it's how I approach everything in my life.

It's been especially important for me to find mentors in life. But mostly I didn't pick them. I didn't choose to meet Bob Shamrock. I didn't choose to work with Ken Shamrock. I didn't choose to study with Masakatsu Funaki. Somehow I pulled them into my life and was able to learn from them.

It's also been important for me to be a mentor. Teaching is a big part of learning. Passing on the knowledge is an important part of mastering it. I've learned the hard way what happens when I ignore these ideals and when I don't follow the martial way in some part of my life. When I follow these things, everything good comes to me. When I stop, or I take away the minus or the plus, it all falls apart.

For example, I got involved many years ago with the American Kickboxing Academy. I originally worked with two partners. One was Bob Cook, a student. He was my best student. He was so devoted. He was working as a tree faller. He'd work eight hours a day, then drive three hours to train with me—then train for two hours and drive three hours home. I called him Crazy Bob Cook. My other partner was Javier Mendez, an amazing kickboxing champion who started teaching and training me and later became my business partner. Together we became the first really well-rounded MMA school in the country, and we started Team AKA, one of the most successful fight teams in the country.

Javier was my mentor, my plus. Bob was my student, my minus. I was learning from Javier and I was teaching Bob. But I forgot my own system. I had retired from fighting and moved to Los Angeles. I stopped communicating with my partners. I stopped connecting with them and telling them things and asking them things. So I had removed my plus and my minus. And I kept taking meetings and creating media. I assumed out of ego and trust that my partners wouldn't doubt or question anything I said or did. But Javier came and told me they weren't comfortable with the way things were going. He said that he needed to be above me in our business, whatever that meant. I freaked out and clammed up. A couple of phone calls would have made the difference, I think, and would have repaired the damage. But I didn't make the phone calls. The American Kickboxing Academy became the biggest fight school in the United States. They have trained dozens of champions. The team is still run by Javier and Bob, and I don't have anything to do with it.

What happened? I asked Maurice Smith, my trainer and partner, what had gone wrong. He said, "You messed it up." He was right. I didn't see that until it was over, and it was too late, but I had a valuable asset and I lost it because I forgot my own system.

I have tried never to make that mistake again. I try to remember to use it in all my relationships, even in my marriage. I think it makes me a grounded, honest, communicative person, which makes it possible for me to be a good partner to my wife, and a good husband. Because I am loving, and communicative, it's easy for her to tell me what she needs from me, and it makes it easy for me to give it to her. When I have difficulties in my relationship, I go to my mentor, to my plus, or to one of my equals. I ask them to help me. I ask them to give me their opinion and their experience. I don't try to figure it out on my own.

When I have an issue with someone who's more like my minus, I just try to share what I know. Years ago I trained a guy I called Shoulders. He was sort of a genetic freak. He had these massive arms and shoulders—beyond anything I'd ever seen. It was natural; he wasn't training or lifting to get that way. He was just built huge. He was a country boy from Canada who played a lot of hockey and got interested in MMA. He joined my gym and got really involved. He practically lived in the gym. He trained *hard*. He would train until he dropped. But he couldn't fight. He had some sort of mental block that was stopping him. So he just trained and trained and trained until he was all broken down.

After many months of this, he finally wore himself out. He was really down and really struggling. His knees were wrecked. So I asked him to help me coach. I was going on the road for some International Fight League event and I asked him to come along. We were sitting at dinner, having a few drinks, and I asked him to tell me what was going on. Finally he told me. He said that his father and mother had forced him to live in a shed his whole life, and have sex with them both. They kept him in this shed, worked him like a mule, and made him have sex.

I couldn't believe anyone could live like that, or that anyone would be able to talk about it. But he laid it all out. I thought *my* journey had been tough. But this was beyond anything I'd ever heard. It was hard for him to tell the story, but he told it. When he was done, he said, "Mr. Shamrock, that's my problem. I don't know how to function. I can't fight. My mother and father took my manhood away from me." I told him, "I don't know what to say about that, but here is what happened to me." I told him *my* story. I told him what had happened in my life and how I'd gotten past it. And I said, "Your mom and dad didn't take *anything* from you. No one can take away your manhood. You *are* a man. That's what we're doing here. That's what MMA is all about. We're becoming men." Soon after that he went back home to Canada and had his knee fixed. He got married, and today he has a fight team of his own.

I have had an amazing life. I have had an amazing career. In the beginning I was scared all the time. I didn't know what I was doing. I got by on athleticism and desire. I never doubted myself. I got nervous because I *wasn't* nervous. That stressed me out. But living through the stress, fighting when I was scared, fighting when I *wasn't* scared, has made me a survivor. I could never have become the man I am today without going through the things that happened to me. I could never have become the man I am, or the man I am trying to be, without fighting.

Fighting has been my way of life. Fighting has been my discipline. Fighting is art. When it's done right, it's beautiful. There is nothing more beautiful than the painted canvas of just totally kicking someone's ass.

I have fought some huge fights. I have fought some fights no one thought I could win. I won them because I brought everything I had to the fight. I didn't leave anything at home. When I fought, I was fighting all the way. I was absolutely willing to die if that's what it was going to take to win. It's hard to fight a man who's willing to die. It took me my whole fighting career, and everything that happened in my life before that, to make me into that guy. It took a lifetime of abuse, neglect, mistreatment, violence, and incarceration before I learned to fight back, to respect myself, and to take care of myself. It took another lifetime to learn the principles of honor, respect, and discipline.

In some ways, the hardest part of that is the discipline. It's the part that's easiest to skip. Training is harder than fighting. Fighting is easy! It's exciting and you get the adrenaline high. Nothing hurts when you're fighting. You don't feel stuff. You might do some damage to yourself, but only one piece of your brain registers it—not as pain but as information. It's as if one part of your brain knows something is going to hurt later. It doesn't actually feel the pain at the time.

That's not true with training. Training can hurt. Training, a lot of the time, is just uncomfortable. But discipline is all about doing the thing that's uncomfortable. It's about doing the things you don't want to do. We're all programmed the other way. We spend all our lives trying to *avoid* discomfort. Discipline is all about learning the opposite lesson. In the fight life, this can be really extreme. The fight life is so isolating, and so lonely. When you're really in it, all you do is train. If you want to be the best, you get rid of all the other things. Parties and birthdays and personal relationships are no longer important. Training is everything. Creating and maintaining your physical machine is everything. This is historically part of the martial way. The old samurai did nothing but train and figure out ways to kill people better. They didn't even take wives. It was too much of a distraction from their training. That takes amazing discipline. To be successful in any area—in business, in sports, in a relationship, in any endeavor—you have to understand that it's OK to be uncomfortable. It's OK to be in pain. Discipline is about knowing that you have to suck it up and humble yourself and do the right thing, which is usually the hard thing. That might be the hardest lesson of all—to do the hard thing when it's the right thing.

But that's how I live my life today. The first thing I think of, when I wake up in the morning, is how can I be better? How can I be a better person, a better father, a better husband, a better man in my community? That all has its roots in fighting and the principles of honor, respect, and discipline. I used to spend hours studying how I could throw a better left hook. Now it starts with the world around me. How can I be a better person? How can I be better at taking care of myself, my family, and my community?

I'm not sure what's next. I'm not sure where I'm going, or where the world around me is going. But right here, right now, it's all come full circle. My daughter Nicolette just took her very first martial arts class. And I just started training again—in a friend's garage, just like in the beginning. I'm going to start teaching again, too. Just like in the beginning.

My world looks fantastic to me. I'm excited about it. The last few months don't look like the end of something, or the beginning of something. It just looks like what *is*. I'm excited about it. I'm nervous about it. But I'm that way about everything. I'm *always* excited and nervous. I have everything I've ever wanted. I've done everything I ever wanted to do. I accomplished what I set out to do. I've been the best fighter in the world. I set two world records. I did things no one else had ever done. But the timing could have been better; I did it all in a sport that no one was watching at the time. Now MMA is the biggest sport in the world. But when I was doing it, our sport was viewed by its smallest audience ever when it was kicked off cable. I still believe MMA is the next level of entertainment in martial arts and combat sports. It's only going to get bigger. Whether I have a hand in that, I don't know.

But I know that my journey as a martial artist will continue, and my experience as a fighter and a martial artist has prepared me for anything that lies ahead. I'm looking forward to whatever is next. I have no fear. I am a warrior.

ACKNOWLEDGMENTS

Many people, knowingly and unknowingly, have made this book possible, and I acknowledge their contributions with deepest appreciation and gratitude.

First and foremost, I would like to thank my wife, Amy, daughter, Nicolette, and son, Frankie, for giving up so many evenings and dinners while these words were hammered out.

My deepest gratitude to Henry Holmes, mentor, super lawyer, and newly adopted father, for seeing a future that I could only dream of and for having the desire and experience to help achieve it.

I am eternally grateful to Charles Fleming. Thank you for your faith in my story and your willingness to walk into the cage with me. Without your brotherhood, patience, diligence, and writing skills, this book would have never been completed.

A special thank you to my editor, Yuval Taylor at Chicago Review Press, for the endless help with editing and shaping these words for human consumption.

I would like to express my greatest gratitude to my adoptive father, Bob Shamrock, for taking me into his group home and teaching me a love for athletics and a respect for myself.

To my partner, Scott Coker, thank you for being my fight promoter in the martial arts, for being honest, and for trusting my vision of MMA.

Thank you to Ken Shamrock, my adopted brother and first teacher of martial arts, without whom I would never have had the courage to fight.

With the utmost gratitude, I pay respect to my trainer, Maurice Smith, for treating me like a brother when no one else would and for showing me unconditional love.

I would also like to thank Lorenzo Fertitta, Bob Meyrowitz, Kelly Kahl, Javier Mendez, Mickey Rourke, Chuck Norris, Al Sehorn, Ernie Reyes, my doctor team—Dr. Carlon Colker, Dr. Mike and Matt Janzen, Dr. David Vik, Dr. Miles Guyton—and Mrs. Tucker, my third-grade teacher, who sent me books and homework while I was in juvenile hall. I would also like to thank my students in martial arts, who taught me so much about life, and all the fighters I have trained who taught me so much about people.

Finally, I would like to thank the fans who have walked alongside me on this journey. Your letters of support and encouragement have always been the secret source of inspiration and energy that have kept me going.

INDEX